T0316825

CAMBRIDGE LIBRARY COLLECTION

Books of enduring scholarly value

British and Irish History, Nineteenth Century

This series comprises contemporary or near-contemporary accounts of the political, economic and social history of the British Isles during the nineteenth century. It includes material on international diplomacy and trade, labour relations and the women's movement, developments in education and social welfare, religious emancipation, the justice system, and special events including the Great Exhibition of 1851.

Life of Sir John Lubbock, Lord Avebury

The achievements of the polymath Sir John Lubbock (1834–1913) spanned banking, politics, science and philanthropy. First published in 1914, this two-volume biography by Horace G. Hutchinson (1859–1932) traces Lubbock's extraordinary life and career. Hutchinson, who knew his subject in later years, paints a highly favourable portrait of Lubbock's varied accomplishments. Notably, Lubbock became a partner of his father's bank at twenty-two, a Member of Parliament in 1870, and in 1900 received the title of Baron Avebury. Tutored in natural history by Charles Darwin in his youth, he remained fascinated by evolutionary theory: it influenced his archaeological and anthropological work, including *Pre-Historic Times as Illustrated by Ancient Remains* (1865) and *The Origin of Civilisation and the Primitive Condition of Man* (1870), both reissued in the Cambridge Library Collection. Volume 1 covers Lubbock's early childhood and private education, his introduction to banking, and Darwin's influence on his passion for science.

Cambridge University Press has long been a pioneer in the reissuing of out-of-print titles from its own backlist, producing digital reprints of books that are still sought after by scholars and students but could not be reprinted economically using traditional technology. The Cambridge Library Collection extends this activity to a wider range of books which are still of importance to researchers and professionals, either for the source material they contain, or as landmarks in the history of their academic discipline.

Drawing from the world-renowned collections in the Cambridge University Library and other partner libraries, and guided by the advice of experts in each subject area, Cambridge University Press is using state-of-the-art scanning machines in its own Printing House to capture the content of each book selected for inclusion. The files are processed to give a consistently clear, crisp image, and the books finished to the high quality standard for which the Press is recognised around the world. The latest print-on-demand technology ensures that the books will remain available indefinitely, and that orders for single or multiple copies can quickly be supplied.

The Cambridge Library Collection brings back to life books of enduring scholarly value (including out-of-copyright works originally issued by other publishers) across a wide range of disciplines in the humanities and social sciences and in science and technology.

Life of Sir John Lubbock, Lord Avebury

VOLUME 1

HORACE G. HUTCHINSON

CAMBRIDGE
UNIVERSITY PRESS

University Printing House, Cambridge, CB2 8BS, United Kingdom

Cambridge University Press is part of the University of Cambridge.
It furthers the University's mission by disseminating knowledge in the pursuit of
education, learning and research at the highest international levels of excellence.

www.cambridge.org
Information on this title: www.cambridge.org/9781108076456

© in this compilation Cambridge University Press 2014

This edition first published 1914
This digitally printed version 2014

ISBN 978-1-108-07645-6 Paperback

LIFE OF SIR JOHN LUBBOCK

LORD AVEBURY

MACMILLAN AND CO., Limited
LONDON · BOMBAY · CALCUTTA
MELBOURNE

THE MACMILLAN COMPANY
NEW YORK · BOSTON · CHICAGO
DALLAS · SAN FRANCISCO

THE MACMILLAN CO. OF CANADA, Ltd.
TORONTO

Geo. Richmond del.t 1867.

Sir John Lubbock
from a drawing by George Richmond R.A. 1867

Emery Walker Ph. sc.

LIFE OF
SIR JOHN LUBBOCK

LORD AVEBURY

P.C. ; For. Sec. R.A. ; F.R.S. ; German Order of Merit ;
Corr. Memb. French Acad. ; Comm. Legion of Honour ; Trustee British Museum ;
D.C.L. (Oxon.), LL.D. (Cantab., Dubl., Edin., and St. Andrews), M.D. (Würzb.),
V.P.L.S., F.G.S., F.Z.S., F.S.A. ; Assoc. Acad. Roy. des Sci. Brux. ;
Hon. Mem. R. Irish Acad., Amer. Ethnol. Soc., Anthrop. Soc. Wash. (U.S.),
Brux., Firenze, Anthrop. Verein Graz, Soc. Entom. de France,
Soc. Géol. de la Suisse, and Soc. Helvét. des Sci. Nat. ;
Mem. Amer. Phil. Soc. Philad., and Soc. d'Ethn. de Paris ;
Corresp. Mem. Soc. des Sci. Nat. de Cherb., Berl. Gesell. für Anthrop.,
Soc. Romana di Antrop., Soc. d'Emul. d'Abbeville, Soc. Cient. Argentina,
Soc. de Géog. de Lisb., Acad. Nat. Sci. Philad., Numis. and Ant. Soc. Philad.,
Amer. Entom. Soc. ; For. Assoc. Mem. Soc. d'Anthrop. de Paris ;
For. Mem. Amer. Antiq. Soc. ; For. Mem. Soc. Española de Hist. Nat. ;
For. Mem. Roy. Soc. of Sci. Upsala ; Hon. Mem. New Zealand Inst. ;
For. Mem. Soc. de Biol. Paris.

BY

HORACE G. HUTCHINSON

IN TWO VOLUMES

VOL. I

MACMILLAN AND CO., LIMITED
ST. MARTIN'S STREET, LONDON

1914

CONTENTS

CHAPTER VI

BUSINESS AND SCIENCE

CHAPTER VII

SCIENCE AND MARRIAGE

CHAPTER VIII

" THE ORIGIN OF SPECIES "

CHAPTER IX

SCIENCE, AND THOUGHTS OF PARLIAMENT

CHAPTER X

FIRST STANDING FOR PARLIAMENT

CHAPTER XI

SCIENCE AND ARCHAEOLOGY

CHAPTER XII

MEMBER OF PARLIAMENT

CHAPTER XIII

" ST. LUBBOCK'S DAY "

CHAPTER XIV

SCIENCE AND POLITICS

CHAPTER XV

VARIOUS CORRESPONDENCE

CHAPTER XVI

MEMBER FOR LONDON UNIVERSITY

CHAPTER XVII

THE DEATH OF DARWIN

CHAPTER XVIII

SECOND MARRIAGE

CHAPTER XIX

MR. GLADSTONE'S HOME RULE BILL

CHAPTER XX

" THE PLEASURES OF LIFE "

CHAPTER XXI

" NATIONALITIES " AND POLITICS

CHAPTER XXII

INSTITUTION OF LONDON COUNTY COUNCIL

CHAPTER XXIII

CHAIRMANSHIP OF LONDON COUNTY COUNCIL

CHAPTER XXIV

VARIOUS ACTIVITIES

CHAPTER XXV

GIVES UP CHAIRMANSHIP OF L.C.C.

INTRODUCTION

I AM grateful that it does not fall on me to assign to Lord Avebury his exact place in any list of latter-day saints or heroes, to apportion him the precise measure of his niche in Fame's temple. Had I to make the attempt it would certainly be too difficult for me, and I think it is a difficulty that any who will endeavour to estimate his qualities by the comparative method will quickly appreciate. It is found at once that there is no common measure to apply to him and to other men. His mind was very singular, very individual in its quality, and his variety of achievement makes it well-nigh impossible to say that he should take rank in advance of this, or behind that other, distinguished man. Sir Algernon West, whose fag Lord Avebury was at Eton, informed me that he was attending a meeting at which Lord Avebury, in the later years of his life, should have been present, but was prevented by illness. Mr. Asquith, who took the chair in his stead, and who is gifted with a faculty for finding the happy phrase, referred to Lord Avebury, while making apology for his absence, as " one of the most remarkable men of our time," and it is an appreciation which the very peculiar qualities of his intellect

renders singularly appropriate. Vivid witness
to the value of his work in the world was aptly
given by another who knew him well, and spoke
of his life as " one of the most useful that was
ever lived." Assuredly that is not praise too
high. This, at all events, I may say, that though
I claim the privilege of knowing him, with some
intimacy, in his later years, it is only while
studying the correspondence connected with the
scientific work to which he devoted himself
before he went into Parliament, that I quite
realised the very high estimation in which he was
held, as a scientist, by such men as Sir Charles
Lyell, the great Darwin, Tyndall, Huxley, and
so on. These, and the like giants received him,
and estimated him, as one of their own select,
yet great company. It is an appreciation which
disposes, for ever, of that ill-considered criticism,
suggested by his extraordinarily varied talent,
that " bankers considered him a great scientist
and men of science a great banker." The testimony of the following pages will be poorly
presented indeed if it does not suffice to dis-
abuse the reader of any impression of the kind
which this sorry epigram may have suggested.
It might be thought that any evidence from
within the bank at 15 Lombard Street is suspect
of partiality ; but at least that is not to be said
of more public business in which he was concerned. Sir Charles Fremantle, at one time
Master of the Mint, and later associated with
Lord Avebury as Vice-Chairman of the Council
of Foreign Bondholders, of which Lord Avebury
himself was long, and for two distinct periods,

Chairman, has assured me that for keen business acumen and wisdom he never met his chairman's equal. Notably he was a great pacifier. From the chair of a stormy meeting his influence spread as oil on the waves, and his dexterous steering and fine vision for a possible haven that would be welcome to all, has averted many a shipwreck.

As I have remarked elsewhere, Lord Avebury was not of those who reveal the inner self intimately in their letters. On the other hand, his correspondence includes a large number of letters on very various subjects, from writers in all parts of the globe. At home he was, of necessity, in touch with the distinguished men of the day in almost all the pursuits which are of import to humanity, and in consequence the interest of the letters which he received is singularly wide and varied. It has been a great difficulty to decide what, where so much seemed worth reproducing, to discard, but I am tolerably confident, at least, of the interest attaching to that which I have been able to retain, and my thanks are due to the writers, and to the legal representatives of the deceased writers, of those letters, to the trustees of Mr. Gladstone, of Mr. Herbert Spencer, and many more, for their kind permission to reproduce them. In the case of some foreign correspondents it has proved impossible, in spite of all reasonable enquiry, to discover their addresses or their living representatives, and for the insertion, without permission, of their letters, I have to make apology and to ask pardon. My debt to Lady Avebury and to other members of the family, and more particularly to the method and care in the arrangement of the papers of the late Lord Avebury himself, is beyond telling. It is right that I should mention, too, the kind help of some of his old friends, such as Sir Algernon West, Sir Charles Fremantle, Mr. Philip Norman, and Mr. Tedder, the Librarian of the Athenæum Club. Above all I am indebted to Mr. Arthur Elliot for the care with which he has been good enough to go through the proof sheets and for many valuable suggestions.

It is not for me to impose upon the reader my own view, either of the intellectual or the moral character of the subject of this biography. My aim must be to make his qualities apparent from a perusal of the pages which carry the record of his achievements, and of the value in which they were held by those associated in them. In all confidence the reader may be left to form his judgment. It occurred to me as a curious coincidence, that on the very day on which I was invited to write Lord Avebury's life, I was reading the definition of a " gentleman " according to the " Note-books " of Samuel Butler. " If we were asked," the writer says, " what is the most essential charactε 'stic that underlies this word, the word itself will guide us to gentleness, to absence of such things as brow-beating, overbearing manners and fuss, and generally to consideration for other people." I have known no other man by whom this characteristic was so fully expressed as by the late Lord Avebury.

SKETCH PEDIGREE SHOWING THE DESCENT OF JOHN LUBBOCK,

FIRST BARON AVEBURY

N.B.—THE NUMBERS REFER TO THE PAGES OF *NOTES ON THE HISTORY AND GENEALOGY OF THE FAMILY OF LUBBOCK.*

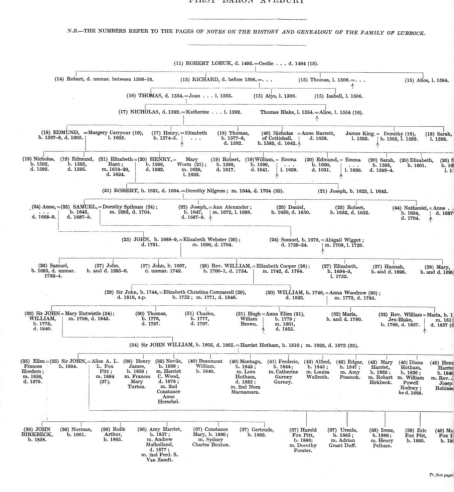

To face page

The material originally positioned here is too large for reproduction in this reissue. A PDF can be downloaded from the web address given on page iv of this book, by clicking on 'Resources Available'.

CHAPTER I

THE LUBBOCK FAMILY

THE following are Lord Avebury's own notes, relative to the family origin :

The name Lubbock, spelt De Lubyck, first appears on a Close Roll of 12 & 14 Edwd. II. ; but this spelling was an exception. The family appear from time immemorial to have formed a small clan in one district. " Although," says Mr. Birkbeck in his history of the family, " the name of Lubbock is to be found at an early period in many Norfolk parishes, they appear to have been chiefly settled in a group of parishes a few miles from Cromer, viz. Hanworth, Calthorpe, Wickmere, Alby, Thurgarton and Aldborough." [1]

Mr. Birkbeck seems to think that the Lubbocks were of Saxon origin, but this is more than doubtful. The name is of great interest. By far the greater number of our family names are either Celtic or Teutonic. Lubbock is one of the few exceptions. The authorities of the British Museum looked into the matter and came to the conclusion that no Teutonic or Celtic

---

[1] Robert Birkbeck, *Notes on the History and Genealogy of the Family Lubbock.*

derivation of the name could be suggested, as it seems to be one of the few remnants of some aboriginal or at any rate pre-Celtic language.

Evidently the Lubbocks have been settled in Norfolk from time immemorial. They are numerous in that county and especially in the parishes round North Walsham and Lamas, to which Lubbocks elsewhere can generally trace their origin. The derivation of the name is practically unknown. It points to emigration from Lubeck, but this is uncertain, nor does it carry us much further. The name has probably come down from some prehistoric language. Its earliest known occurrence in Britain is in the case of John Lubbock of Hanworth in 1378–1379.

The Lubbocks often appear in the records of the Norwich Law Courts, but Mr. Birkbeck in his privately printed book on the family history mentions that he did not find a single Lubbock name in the Assize Rolls.

The family of Lord Avebury trace their descent from Robert Lobuk of North Walsham, who died in 1493.

The earliest family portrait is that of John Lubbock, born in 1668.

Lubbock's business, according to *London Bankers* by F. G. Hilton Price, was started at 11 Mansion House Street, February 5, 1772, by Sir Wm. Lemon, Buller, Furley, Lubbock & Co. In 1835 it was Sir John William Lubbock, Forster & Co. In 1860 it amalgamated with Robarts, Curtis & Co. Lubbock's old house in Mansion House Street was part of Sir Martin

Bower's bequest to the Goldsmiths' Company, and was leased from them.

Robarts, Curtis, Were, Hornyold & Berwick were established in 1792 at 35 Cornhill. Sir William Curtis was Lord Mayor in 1795. In 1797 they moved to 15 Lombard Street, the present site of the bank. It occupies the site of three old houses—Nos. 15, 16, and 17. The two last were Lloyd's Coffee-house, which originated with a coffee-house keeper named Edward Lloyd, who in September 1696 started *Lloyd's News*. The house was at the west corner of Abchurch Lane.

The father of the first Lord Avebury, Sir John William, third baronet, came by inheritance into the command of the business and banking-house, but at heart was more devoted to the sciences of astronomy and mathematics. He published little, an illustrated book of the stars in the various quarters of the heavens, and of the planets at the different seasons, being his best-known work in connection with astronomy. His *Theory of Probabilities* has perhaps been the foundation of more " systems," whether of a gambling or less speculative nature, than is often realised, and the Royal Society awarded him one of its medals for his work on the Tides. For some years he was Treasurer of the Royal Society, and in this office came into touch with many men of science both of this and other countries. The Duke of Sussex was the nominal head of the Royal Society at the time, and Sir John Lubbock's position of Treasurer made him the practical and acting head.

The family appears to have been distributed, for some seven hundred and more years, in the parishes above named and others between Norwich and Cromer, and although the small East Anglian property of Lamas, in East Anglia, is still a family possession, the grandfather of the first Lord Avebury found the inconvenience, for business purposes, of a residence so far from the metropolis, and took up his abode in or near London. He lived for a while at High Elms, the family's present place in Kent, but, finding that again scarcely convenient enough for his business engagements, removed to Mitcham, where he rented a house on the river Wandle. From Mitcham he used to drive up to the City in a four-in-hand, and Lord Avebury used to relate that he always sat in the parlour in top-boots. His son, who had married a Miss Hotham, took a house in Eaton Place—No. 29—where was born on April 30, 1834, John Lubbock, the future first Lord Avebury.

CHAPTER II

(AGE (?) 8)

THERE is a note in Lord Avebury's hand, stating:
" The first two things I can remember are
sitting at a window in front of some red cloth
drapery, to see the Queen's Coronation from
the Royal Exchange rooms in Pall Mall—and
a large insect under a glass."

In view of some later developments we may
perhaps admire the loyalty which places the
Royal Lady, in this brief catalogue, before his
interest in the insect.

He was the eldest of a large family of eleven,
and how exceptionally fortunate they all were
in their parents will be understood by those who
realise the much greater distance and reserve
that used to be maintained at that time between
father and mother and children, in comparison
with the friendliness which commonly exists
between those thus related now. No doubt
we should pronounce the father austere towards
his children, if he were judged by the standards
of the present day, but in a brief manuscript
account of Sir John William Lubbock, by an

unidentified hand, it is written that "he was a most kind and devoted husband and father, and made his children, eleven in number, his constant companions, teaching them in the early morning, before starting for the City, and playing with them on his return. He never allowed his children's questions to go unanswered, and delighted in watching the development of their minds. He was much struck by a question of his eldest child, the present Sir John Lubbock, then about four years old, who sat on the rug watching some paper burning in the fire: 'Where do burnt things go to?'" Doubtless all that his children did was of interest to him, but there is abundant evidence that his authority was very strictly enforced.

I will ask the reader to note this query of Lord Avebury's because we shall find, at a later period, this faculty of asking himself (and others) questions as to the "why" of the common phenomena which surround us very finely developed. And we shall see, too, that it was a faculty which led him to highly interesting conclusions.

In the same year, 1838, when he was just turned four, there is the following note about him in his mother's diary: "His great delight is in Insects. Butterflies, Caterpillars or Beetles are great treasures, and he is watching a large spider outside my window most anxiously."

During his earliest years he, in company with his father and mother, used to spend many weeks at the house of his grandfather and grandmother at Mitcham Grove, and in the then pellucid waters of the Wandle the naturalist that was to be found new wonders every day for his entertainment. In the autumn his parents generally took a house at Brighton, his father not devoting himself very regularly to business, but giving the best of his time and attention to his mathematical studies.

Daguerre, in France, had recently completed that invention for the taking of daguerreotypes by which his name is remembered. The sight of those primitive photographic records affords more amusement than admiration to-day, but they were wonders in their time, and Lord Avebury used to recall how the French inventor sent the first of his machines that ever came to England to Sir John Lubbock. It arrived at Mitcham, and at the age of four or five Lord Avebury assisted at, or, as he suggests, impeded, the taking of the first picture ever recorded by the sun in England. That picture may be looked on as the parent, or at least the eldest collateral, of every photograph since taken in this country.

The grandfather died in 1840, and the Mitcham Grove house was given up, Lord Avebury's parents taking up their residence at High Elms, which was entirely rebuilt.

It must have been very shortly before this removal that Lady Lubbock, his mother, began to keep a systematic record of the sayings and doings of her children, and, perhaps with a little allowance to be made for a mother's natural partiality, this record may be accepted as a valuable indication of their characteristics and capacities. Six of the children mentioned in the preceding "pedigree" were at that time living, and the age of John, the eldest, is entered as $7\frac{1}{4}$. The following brief character-sketch is appended to his name : " A *very sensible* Boy, with an over-sensitive and timid disposition, and requiring great care in his education and management, and more like what I conceive I was at his age than any child I ever saw (I ought not, however, to call myself ' *very* sensitive ')."

The mother whose nature is thus, with charming unconsciousness, revealed, did not realise that in this modest disclaimer, within the brackets, she is affording yet further testimony to the essential likeness between herself and this eldest child, for of his many remarkable characteristics the self-depreciating modesty which these words discover was one of the most striking.

His intelligent mind soon began to prompt him to ask some of those theological questions which parents find so much difficulty in answering. " We were talking," Lady Lubbock writes, " about resisting the Devil, and what that meant, and John said, ' Mama, do you think it's right in us to hate the Devil ? I don't. I thought we ought to hate no one ? ' I said, ' Very true, dear, but the Devil is the personification of Sin, and we must hate Sin.' ' True, Mama, but the Devil was once an Angel, so I think we ought to wish he may some day grow good again, instead of hating him.' The excessive beauty and originality of this remark struck me more than anything I have ever heard said by a child."

One who knew Lord Avebury very intimately was especially delighted by this observation. "Why," was the comment, "it is what he has been doing all his life, trying to convert devils." In his charity and optimism regarding all human nature it seemed impossible for him to believe it ever so bad that he should despair of its conversion.

It is interesting to observe the character of the theology of the day, in which he was strictly trained, the more interesting in view of the brave stand that he was to make in later days for liberality of view, in connection with the storms which beat about the heads of Bishop Colenso, Charles Darwin and others, whose thought was in advance of their time. We find his mother recording of him that " John said to Manie [the governess], ' I have been thinking of a new plan, Manie, which I mean to go upon. I find I am not near so good a boy as my sisters are good girls, and I am going to try a different plan : of a morning before they are up I find they always read in their prayer book. Now I read Bingley's *Natural History*. But for the future I mean to read in my bed every morning the 149th Psalm to remind me God sees us at all times, and the 3rd of Revelations to remind me of the day of Judgment ; and then don't you think, Manie, I shall have more strength to be a good boy ? ' "

CHAPTER III

PRIVATE SCHOOL (1842–1845)

(AGE 8-11)

WHEN he was eight years old he was sent to Mr. Waring's private school at Abingdon Abbey. Apparently it was an excellent school, but Lady Lubbock notes that " Sir John is rather alarmed at the very aristocratic set of school-fellows little John will have. The boys that will be there when he goes are three Scotts, Duke of Buccleuch's sons; three Legges, Lord Dartmouth's sons; Lord Chesterfield's son; Newdigate, poor Lady Barbara Newdigate's son; Bathurst, my friend Mrs. Bathurst's only son; Lord Dunglass; Peel, a nephew of Sir Robert's; Lascelles, etc., etc."

It is evident, however, in spite of the boy's sensitive nature, that he very quickly fell into his place, and found content in this House of youthful Lords. One of his first letters from school—those letters to which a mother looks forward so anxiously to know how the child is faring in that strange new world—is full of happy augury and worthy of quotation for the hint that it gives of a fine quality of mind which

was to be of no little use to him through life,
" My dear Papa, I hope you are all quite well. We
have a half holiday every Thursday. We have
a good many jolly cricket matches. . . . I like
school very much and Mr. Waring says I shall
get on very well. Good-bye, my dear papa.
Believe me ever your affectionate John Lubbock.

" I am a favourit with most of the boys
because I do not care aboute being laughed."

Is not that an invaluable quality which he
discloses in this postscript ?   And is it not rather
singular that at the age of eight years he should
be thus able to recognise its value ?   Throughout life he was tolerably indifferent to " being
laughed," and it became a source to him of
strength and popularity; but that he should
appreciate it at that time as a secret of such
popularity seems to show uncommon acumen.

I do not quite know what sympathy he could
have won from his father, a most devoted mathematician, for a request which he makes amusingly
in another letter, written from Mr. Waring's :
" My dear Papa. I have a great deal to say.
If you write to Mr. Waring about the Algebra,
please ask him only to give it me to do when I
have plenty of time, and not to make it a regular
lesson." We need not follow out at length the
" great deal that he has to say," merely noting
the implied distaste for algebra as indicating a
dislike to mathematics which was always something of a sorrow to the paternal lover of the
exact sciences. A later passage in the same
letter may be quoted as showing the real bent
of his mind : " Dunglass has brought me some

Scotch pebbles. They are quite beautiful. They will be very nice for my collection. And Lady Home " (mother of Lord Dunglass) " sent me a particular favourite of hers. Was it not kind ? " There are in course of this letter, which covers four sides—you may be sure it was written on a Sunday !—two distinct wails of home-sickness from the little boy, plucky though he was. " I do miss you all so much. I do not know what to do at all, and in short am very unjolly." He evidently found this last word aptly descriptive of his feelings, for we have it again on the next page : " Now I know you will think me rather odd, but if I think too much of the pleasure of home it makes me rather unjolly."

There is a hint here again of a mental perception above the childish. He has realised that the only way of tolerable happiness in his present state is to banish from mind the thought of that which he has temporarily lost. It is a profound truth.

Another letter, the last to be quoted from his private school, gives further indication of the future man that he was to be : " A pair of robins seeking a place to build their nest fixed on the sleeve of a coat at the gardens of Hirsel. Was not that curious ? I thought you would like it. The bird hatched the eggs and fledged the young without caring for the multitudes who came to see her house. We had a charity sermon to-day. Mr. Waring preached. I thought it a very beautiful sermon."

He worked hard at this private school, and gave every satisfaction to his master. " I had a letter," writes Lady Lubbock, "from Mrs. Entwistle the other day which made me very happy: she had been at Abingdon and saw dear John looking well and happy, and says that Mr. and Mrs. Waring spoke of him in the highest terms and said he was 'not only a very clever boy but one of the most diligent and painstaking they had in their school.' Of course this account of our darling Boy made my dear Sir John and me *very happy*."

A little later, just before his leaving home for his first term at Eton, his mother writes: " I grieve over parting with him very sadly. He is so *very dear* and such a delightful companion, so talented, so affectionate, so entirely original, entering into everything so delightfully, quite beyond his years ; and I really could not have supposed he was hardly 11, but could well fancy him a clever boy of 16. Then again his love of reading and his very retentive memory give him a great deal of information, and his taste for Natural History makes him an acute observer."

Not an impartial estimate, doubtless, but there seems no reason to question its essential justice. The only anxiety that he caused his parents up to this time was on the score of health. As a boy he was always delicate, and constantly suffered from digestive troubles often acute, and perhaps not very well diagnosed. At all events it is evident that after a complete change of treatment, which was not tried however until he was sixteen or seventeen years of age, his health immediately improved and no trace of the delicacy remained.

But in the meanwhile he suffered severely
at intervals, and doubtless the physical suffering
had its natural effect on his nervous system,
for those who knew him in his childish days
state that in spite of his charm and unusual
talents he had a temper which he found it very
difficult to control, and which was a cause of
much trouble to him, up to the age of twelve.
It is perhaps this hard mental schooling which
enabled him to emerge from those psychic
struggles with a control almost more perfect
and a serenity almost more complete than I
ever remember to have seen possessed by any
other human being.

Lord Avebury's own comment, in his later
years, on the system of education at his private
school is that "Mr. Waring was kind, conscien-
tious and painstaking; but the education given
was not, I think, what Mr. Waring himself
would have preferred. It was an excellent preparation for the profession of schoolmaster, but
not, I think, for life."

CHAPTER IV

ETON (1845–1848)

(AGE 11-14)

IT was just before the future Lord Avebury, then seven years of age, went to the private school at Abingdon Abbey that there occurred the event which perhaps more than any other was destined to influence his life. It is noted, by Lord Avebury himself, in the following words : " My father came home one evening in 1841, quite excited, and said he had a great piece of news for me. He made us guess what it was, and I suggested that he was going to give me a pony. ' Oh,' he said, ' it is much better than that. Mr. Darwin is coming to live at Down.' I confess I was much disappointed, though I came afterwards to see how right he was."

For the moment we may pass that by, with the levity of the little boy himself, to whom the pony would no doubt have been the source of much keener immediate entertainment. Down, it may be noted, is a village about a mile from High Elms, and what the example and the encouragement of the great naturalist meant to him will be revealed in its due place. For

15

the present we have him at the point of leaving
his private school and about to enter the larger
world of Eton.

The following is an account penned by himself of his impression of the life and the course
of education at Eton. It will be seen that in
spite of his criticism, or perhaps as a testimony
to its justice, the preparation given him at Mr.
Waring's, aided by his own uncommon talents
and diligence, enabled him to take a very good
position on entering the big school.

When I was eleven I went to Eton, and was placed
in the " remove," *i.e.* as high as a boy could be placed.
This was rather unfortunate for me as I was in the same
division with boys four or five years older than I was,
and with whom I had no chance of competing. The
division was a very large one containing over 100 boys,
and was consequently divided into two. My place
was generally somewhere between the 20th and 25th.

At that time the whole education consisted of Latin
and Greek with one lesson a week in Geography —
confined mainly to Italy, Greece and Asia Minor. We
had each week to write out a description of some country,
but the master in whose division I was when I first went
to Eton attached so little importance to Geography
that he never once looked at my productions, which I
fear became under the circumstances more and more
perfunctory.

Neither Arithmetic, Modern Languages, Science, nor
Drawing were regarded as essential portions of Education,
and they did not enter into the School course. Arithmetic, French, and German had indeed just been
started, but they were treated as extras—like Fencing
or Dancing. They were only taken if the Parents
especially wished it and then in play time.

My father did not think they were well taught, and
the result was that I never did a sum or had a lesson in
any modern language the whole time I was at Eton,
nor indeed if I had stayed till I was Captain of the
Oppidans should I have done so. The excuse for the

neglect of Science and modern languages is the great importance of a Classical Education. This I do cordially admit, though it does not seem to me a reason for the course adopted. But unfortunately the result of the system is to defeat the very object which it is intended to secure. So far from giving a Classical Education, the result is to give nine boys out of ten a profound dislike of classical literature.

It seems extraordinary that any one should consider that this was a satisfactory education. Nevertheless while condemning the system I gratefully recognise that most of the Eton masters did their best to carry it out effectively. Moreover it was at that time the general type of English Public Schools. The moral tone was good, and our health fairly looked after. Talleyrand is reported to have said in the first half of the last century that our English schools are the best in the world, adding, however, "mais ils sont abominables!" I was between 3 and 4 years at Eton, and went through all the school examinations, reaching what was then known as the Upper Upper Fifth. For a small boy I was fairly good at cricket and fives, but hockey was my favourite game, and I even reached the school " seven," of which I was very proud.

At that time Eton boys, especially if they were quick at writing verses and learning by heart, had much more leisure than they have now. I devoted a good deal of mine to Natural History and Geology, in spite of the remonstrances of my Tutor (Mr. Birch), who thought that my leisure might have been better occupied on the Classics. On one occasion we were given " the Bee " as a subject for a theme. I took some pains with it, and my tutor sent for me and asked me confidentially whether it was all true. From what he said I inferred that they rather suspected I was quizzing them, and doubted whether to commend or to flog me. Happily for me they accepted my assurances, indeed both my tutor and Mr. Carter, to whom I was " up " in school for over a year, very wisely went on the principle of believing what we said, the result of which was that we considered it would be mean and unfair not to treat them in the same spirit.

Possibly the above criticism will enable us

the better to understand the second of the two
following letters from his tutor, which seem to
suggest characteristics that we know from
other sources to have been absolutely foreign
to his mental nature. This is the first of the
two, written immediately on the boy's entry
into the school.

ETON COLL., *Wednesday.*

MY DEAR SIR JOHN—I am happy to tell you that
your son has passed a good examination and is placed
in the Lower Remove. He seems to have settled very
comfortably into Eton ways, and I hope that his career
may prove an honourable one. Perhaps you will have
the kindness to let me know whether you wish him to be
a Private Pupil or not.—I remain, my dear Sir John,
yours faithfully,   H. M. BIRCH.

Both the above brief note and the following,
which is by the same hand, are without the
date of the year, but it is apparent that the
second is written after the tutor had gained time
to become acquainted, as he supposed, with his
pupil's character.

ETON, *December 7.*

MY DEAR SIR JOHN—Your boy returns to you safely
landed in the Fifth Form and with a very tolerable
place in his Remove, but I am disappointed that he does
not improve in his composition prose and verse more
than he does. I think that his natural quickness leads
him to put down what comes uppermost without
analysing his thought, and in consequence of that he is
exceedingly inaccurate. However, I hope that time
and pains will remedy these defects. In his conduct and
dealing with me he is most amiable and pleasant and is
just the same natural boy that he was when he first came
to Eton, but I want to make him a sounder scholar.
I quite agree with you as to the impropriety of his
dabbling into other languages before he has acquired
more knowledge of the ancient ones, but I think that it
is worth consideration whether he had not better com-

mence mathematics soon.—I remain, my dear Sir John,
yrs. most faithfully,   H. M. BIRCH.

It is rather amusing, by the light of later
events, to read this censure of the " exceeding
inaccuracy " of one who was to prove himself
a very model of all that is most accurate and
exact. It seems that in spite of the counsel
given in the above letter he did succeed in his
desire to " dabble " in other studies outside the
statutory course of the classics, for we find this
later note : " He stayed three years at Eton,
leaving in 1848, when he was in Upper Upper
Fifth. At that time, excepting half an hour of
geography, the boys did nothing but Greek and
Latin, not even Arithmetic. Against the advice
of his tutor, he read some Natural History and
Geology and did (considering that he was much
younger than most of the boys in his division)
fairly well with the School's work. Still, the
system did not suit him, not that he disliked
Latin and Greek, but he yearned for other
things also."

Lord Avebury used to tell an amusing little
story by way of illustrating what the Eton
authorities of the day regarded as a liberal
departure in the direction of a scientific course.
His father had several times expressed the wish
that a little science could be included in his son's
studies, and ultimately, at the beginning of some
holidays, the tutor wrote that at last he had
been able to do as Sir John Lubbock wished,
namely, to introduce " some science " into the
holiday task. Sir John, highly pleased, sent
for " the task," but the only reference to science

that he was able to find was the statement—
of questionable accuracy—among sentences for
translation into Latin prose, that " the Sun and
the Moon are Planets."

" The system did not suit him." No doubt
the nail was hit rightly on the head with that
stroke ; and it is indeed somewhat of a Pro-
crustean system which would fit every boy, no
matter what his mental bent, into the fixed curriculum of the classics. " He yearned for other
things also." That perhaps, combined with his
constitutional delicacy at the time, is the explanation of the attitude of which his tutor com-
plains. But possibly there is more in it than this.
It is stated that he did not " dislike " Latin
and Greek. His tutor hoped to make him " a
sounder scholar," but we may doubt whether
his mind was ever really of the type that is
attuned readily to the niceties of scholarship.
Scholarship is very largely a matter of the form,
and it was never the form and always the substance that made appeal to him. His mode of
expression was always lucid and entirely adequate
to his purposes, but never savouring greatly of
" style." It is the language of a man of very
fine intellect who would appear to have almost
a suspicion of " style " in literature, as a mode
of striving after effect which was absolutely
distasteful to his natural simplicity. It gives
the frequent impression of an almost purposed
rejection of the word that might add force, and
a deliberate preference for the more usual phrase.
Probably it is a quality that has worked in aid
of the immense popularity of his writings.

Almost certainly it is a quality which we should not find had his tutor been successful in the attempt to make of him a finished scholar.

It was not, as it would seem, in any degree because the system, as has been said, did not suit him, that his removal from Eton took place at the early age of fourteen, when he had been there only for the brief space of three years. The exigencies of the ancestral banking business suggested the removal in the first instance, and no doubt the fact that the scholastic course did not seem to be developing his powers along their natural lines caused the idea of that removal to be considered more favourably than might otherwise have been the case alike by himself, by his father, and by his tutor. That these considerations had their natural weight is made clear from some notes in his own hand, relative to his early entry into the business.

CHAPTER V

INTRODUCTION TO BUSINESS (1848–1851)

(AGE 14-17)

THE notes referred to in the previous chapter serve to show, incidentally, how circumstances were combining to make the boy thoughtful and self-reliant beyond his years, in spite of the natural sensibility of his disposition. Though one of so large a family, he was rather isolated from the others, the next two to him in point of age being girls, so that there was between him and his next brother, Henry, a gap which at that time of life is considerable. It was always his fortune, for good or ill, to have his elders as his chief companions, and the delicacy of his constitution probably attracted him the more to their society. The notes run as follows :

In 1848, when I was nearly fifteen, my father's two partners being both in bad health, he had to choose between taking another or bringing me at once into the Bank to assist him. Our firm was then Lubbock, Forster & Co., and we did not join our friends, Robarts, Curtis & Co. till some years later. Having so many children to provide for, he chose the latter alternative and in 1849 I began business. He would not of course under other circumstances have brought me in so early. At the same time he did so with the less reluctance

22

as practically nothing but Latin and Greek and a (very little) geography was taught as part of the regular curriculum, and as at Oxford and Cambridge the same system (with of course Mathematics at Cambridge) was adopted. Soon afterwards my father's partners both died, and he and I, with a worthy old clerk (Mr. Higham), carried on the business, so that my father and I could not be away together. I was at first of course very much at sea, and found the City very lonely. No doubt, however, beginning so early gave me a sort of instinct for business. But though I was thus early brought into harness, I had plenty of holidays. My father kindly taught me Mathematics, which like all Science I found interesting, but for which I had no special gift. My father's mathematical genius was in some respects a disadvantage. He could not see difficulties where I did, and though very patient would often at last say in despair, " Well, if Newton does not make it clear to you, I am afraid I cannot. We must go on." In other respects I made good progress, reading seven or eight hours a day and devouring all sorts of books, but especially those on Biology and Geology. My mother's sympathy and kindness were a great help and comfort. My sisters also were invaluable companions, but my next brothers of course were at school, and I had no boy of my own age to play with. This threw me a good deal on myself. My health also was not very good.

In 1850 I gave my first lecture. It was at Down, on the Wireworm, and was well attended by the villagers. Now I began to realise how right my father was in saying that Mr. Darwin's coming to live at Down was an immense advantage to me. He induced my father to give me a microscope, he let me do drawings for some of his books, and I greatly enjoyed my talks and walks with him. My first scientific original work was on some of his collections, and appeared in the *Natural History Magazine* for January 1853. In 1849 I was elected a member of the Royal Institution, and in 1853 I attended my first meeting of the British Association. In 1854 I was introduced to Sir C. Lyell and Sir Joseph Hooker, in 1855 to Kingsley, Prestwich, and Sir John Evans, and joined the Geological Society. In 1856 I met George Busk, Huxley, and Tyndall, and the following year was elected a member of the Royal Society. It would be impossible for me to express how much of my real education I owe to the advice, the sympathy, and the example of these kind friends.

It was really a wonderful society into which the boy thus found himself admitted, and never was there a boy better able to make good use of these exceptional advantages ; but it is hardly to be said that it was gay. The element of youth was singularly lacking. Yet elsewhere his natural joy of life found more natural outlets. " I was very fond of cricket," he writes, " and for some years acted as secretary to the West Kent Cricket Club. We used to practise at Chislehurst every Saturday. Being then only 15 I was at first allowed many holidays (from the business), my father knowing that I was working hard. But after the death of my father's partners he and I could not be away together. Moreover Sydenham was our nearest station, so that we had to drive over twenty miles every day."

It is worth a moment's pause to realise what it all meant—the boy leaving school at fourteen to go straight into the banking business, and only a year later sharing with his father the responsible position of a working partner—either he or his father bound to be there—as if on his fifteen-years-old shoulders might all the burden be borne on the days when his father, engrossed in the higher mathematics, gave finance a holiday ! And the twenty miles or more of drive ! It is rather a pathetic picture. Perhaps it is no wonder that, with his zeal for acquiring various knowledge, especially his zest for natural history, so fostered by the kind help of Darwin, he adopted a strenuous mode of life, early rising and economising the long hours thus gained to the very best advantage. We shall find this a very notable characteristic of the mature man—the time-saving and the time-stretching faculty. His day was not only several hours longer, throughout his life, than that of most even of the busiest men, but it was also packed with wonderful closeness, and into wonderfully tight compartments. He acquired the power of concentration on the subject of the moment, and developed it to a very uncommon pitch, so that of him it could be very rarely said that while doing one thing he was thinking of another. He could pass from a problem in finance or politics to a question in Natural History without any effort in the passage, and allowing no loose ends of thoughts about the one to intrude on or interfere with the unembarrassed consideration of the other.

His father gave him every encouragement in his Natural History, but always maintained that it stood distinctly on a lower level than Astronomy and Mathematics, being essentially a matter of approximation and estimate, whereas they were exact Sciences. One evening, however, he came back from the City and said that the results of the transit of Venus expedition had been worked out, and that the mean distance of the Earth from the Sun was 92,500,000 miles. He pointed out to his father that they had been brought up to believe it was 95,000,000, and that if the Astronomers and Mathematicians could be wrong by such a little trifle as 2,500,000 miles they could hardly lay claim to *exact* Science.

Undoubtedly the father, Sir J. W. Lubbock, was more than a little of a martinet. His austerity was perhaps nicely balanced by the adoring tenderness of Lady Lubbock for her children. The tendency to order things precisely according to his judgment comes out amusingly in the following extract from Mr. Philip Norman's admirable *Annals of the West Kent Cricket Club*:

Sir John William Lubbock, Bart., the eminent mathematician and astronomer, does not seem to have cared much for cricket in his youth, though his name appears once or twice in the records of practice days at Prince's Plain. During his early married life he lived at Mitcham Grove, in a house (now pulled down) which had previously belonged to the Hoares ; but after succeeding to the baronetcy in 1840, he settled permanently at High Elms, which at the beginning of the century had been a mere farm, bought from the Wells family. There, as his sons began to grow up, he made a delightful cricket ground and organised matches in which for some years he used to take part. Having hardly played at all till he was past 40, he was of necessity a very moderate performer, but he enjoyed the exercise, and his matches gave pleasure to many. I remember playing there when quite a little boy. Sir John, on this occasion, marked the positions of the fields by heaps of daisies from which it was deemed treason to stray. He kept a pony saddled at the cricket ground, and mounted and rode off at a rapid pace when his presence was required elsewhere. One of the things that astonished my young mind was his peculiar mode of wearing his pads, or leg-guards ; they were *inside* his trousers, being strips of india-rubber passed through loops, if I am not mistaken, so that they remained as fixtures for the day. I have since found that Felix recommends something of the sort in his book called *Felix on the Bat*.

A quaint figure was Mr. Robert Sessions, of the New Inn, Farnborough (now rather an old inn), who always umpired for Sir John, and in the course of the game would make comments, naturally favourable, on the under-hand bowling of the father. It was he who, when expostulated with for not calling an obvious wide bowled by one of the next generation, replied in a stage whisper, "Hush! hush! the young gen'lman don't like it."

Sir John was father of eight sons, who were all at Eton and at no other school, and are still happily all living. It may without exaggeration be said of them that each has done something worthy of remembrance, while the head of the family, the present Sir John, will always be famous as one of the most useful men of his generation. All the world knows him as a man of science, a politician, a banker, and philanthropist; but it is now perhaps almost forgotten that though he left Eton too young to secure a place in the eleven, he was in his early days a keen and good cricketer, a left-handed batsman, and a fast, left under-hand bowler. For some time he assisted in the management of the West Kent Club, and several of the scores are entered in his neat handwriting. Long afterwards, when he had almost entirely given up the game, he agreed to play one or two matches for the Lords and Commons. In order to prepare himself he used to get Wells, the Bromley professional, to bowl to him for some weeks regularly in the early morning before he went up to London to business, the result being that he scored well against Harrow and I Zingari.

It was highly characteristic of him to take this studious pains in order to do his best in these two matches. Mr. Norman has a note respecting Wells: "Joseph Wells, who kept the china shop and was professional to the West Kent Cricket Club, was father of H. G. Wells, the successful novelist. He performed a remarkable feat in the Kent v. Sussex match of June 26, 1862, bowling four wickets in four successive balls."

CHAPTER VI

FOR some years the life at High Elms went on in its uneventful but exceedingly strenuous course. Young Lubbock confesses, in his diaries, that he was "lonely," but adds that this was probably of ultimate benefit to him, because it threw him so much on the companionship of books. We may be tolerably sure that even in the drives and train journeys to and fro the City a book of some sort was not long out of his hand. One of his sons told me that on the day that his father first took him into the City, to introduce him to the partners of their business house, Lord Avebury drew a book out of his pocket as soon as they were seated in the "tube," and said, "I think you will find it a good plan always to have a book with you, in your pocket, to read at odd times," and therewith he became at once so absorbed in his reading as to be quite unconscious of his fellow-travellers and their conversation.

He had a mode, as he read, of having in his book a slip of paper, cut to a certain size, on which he jotted down in pencil, passages or references to passages which struck him as he read. These slips being tabulated formed a very easily accessible means of reference to all that he had found of most value in the books that he studied from time to time. It was largely by such modes of economising time and the results of his reading that he was able to achieve the immense total of work which he performed during his life.

Partly the reason of the loneliness, to which he refers, was that he had gone into the City at so early an age that none of his contemporaries were yet there ; but that is a condition which he would find improving as the years went on. Moreover, fully occupied as were his days and hours at home, there was much time in them for social enjoyment, riding, cricket, and so on. He played frequently for the West Kent Club, had an average, one season, of $25\frac{1}{4}$ runs per innings, and for several years found time, in the midst of all his avocations, to act as honorary secretary. His diaries of this date abound with references to dances and parties at this or the other house in the very sociable neighbourhood in which High Elms is situated, and he notes, with rather an amusing freedom of criticism, the merits of various young ladies as dancers and companions.

A dweller near Bromley at that time writes to me of Sir John Lubbock (Lord Avebury's father): " He used, in my young days, to go to and from the railway station in a mail phaeton drawn by a pair of horses, with a post-boy. I

can hear the rattle of it now as it passed my
father's house on the way to Bromley station
to catch the 9.19 train. In front was seated
Lubbock père, with a young Lubbock looking very demure. Behind were other young
Lubbocks playing all sorts of tricks." But it
is to be doubted whether Lord Avebury ever
was one of those naughty young Lubbocks.

He joined the Kent Artillery Militia, and
entered into all the duties that it entailed with
a characteristic thoroughness. Altogether it was
a life which did not lack variety in spite, or by
reason, of its industry. He tells us, in his
diary, the mode in which he planned out his
days—presumably it would be the time scheme
for a day on which he did not go up to the City
for business—and certainly its perusal is enough
to take the breath away of the ordinary idle
mortal who lives as leisurely as he may.

It is on Christmas Day of 1852 that he makes
this entry : " Generally speaking, I spend my
day as follows :—Get up at $\frac{1}{2}$ past six, dress,
say my prayers, read the Psalms and Chapters
and go to Papa with my mathematics, which
takes about ten minutes, before breakfast. From
$8\frac{1}{2}$ till 9, read natural history; 9 to $\frac{1}{2}$ past,
prayers; $\frac{1}{2}$ past 9 to $\frac{1}{2}$ past 11, work with the
microscope; $\frac{1}{2}$ past 11 to 1, read natural history;
1 to $\frac{1}{2}$ past, lunch. I generally go out for an
average of two hours in the afternoon, and do
$\frac{1}{2}$ an hour poetry and $\frac{1}{2}$ an hour political economy;
tea, $\frac{1}{2}$ past 4 to 5 ; till $5\frac{1}{2}$ more science ; $\frac{1}{2}$ hour's
natural history ; 6 to $7\frac{1}{4}$, history ; $7\frac{1}{4}$ to 8,
whist ; 8 to $\frac{1}{2}$ past, history ; $8\frac{1}{2}$ to $9\frac{1}{2}$, mathe-

matics ; 9½ to 10, sermons (if I read them any later they invariably send me to sleep, and as it is I cannot always keep awake) ; 10 to 11¼, German, which is the only thing that keeps me awake ; 11¼ to 12, prayers ; 12, Bed." He writes Bed, in the diary thus, with a big " b," as surely he well may, after a day thus disposed. The nice apportionments of the quarters of hours, as three-quarters of an hour for " whist " (it is not said what happened if the rubber were unfinished), is very characteristic of the exact disposition of his time which resulted in such an immense output of mental activity. He adds : " I do rather over 8½ hours' work a day, but the afternoon part is rather irregular, as I often go out three or even four hours, and sometimes not at all."

By the light of later entries it is clear that these strenuous days had much relaxation in the following years. What has to be recognised with less satisfaction is the frequency of what he writes of as " attacks "—of a gastric nature. Probably he was at this time seriously over-working his young strength, but the natural powers of his constitution, aided by the change of treatment already spoken of, triumphed, and at the end of a long life Lord Avebury was certainly able to look back on a more generous gift of health and energy than is granted to most men.

We may notice the short spells, often of half an hour, into which his different studies were divided. In later years it was always a surprise to me to note how instantly, and without any apparent effort, he could switch off his mind, as it were, from the discussion of some intricate point of finance—say the involved fortunes of the Peruvian bondholders—and discuss such a problem of biology as parthenogenesis—and there can be little doubt that this ability was fostered by the habit that he formed thus early of moving quickly from one subject to another. It was a faculty which he had deliberately trained, for the sake, primarily, of its utility in the banking business, where it was essential that he should be able to turn at once from a topic with which he was occupied and give his attention to a client or to any question which incidentally came up. Doubtless, moreover, it was a just economy of the brain cells, for the change of study from one subject to another provides as good, if not better, a relaxation as leisure. Elsewhere he gives an account of the disposition of his hours of study, showing how predominant was his interest in Natural History, and indicating some points of interest in his education.

" When not at the Bank," he writes, " my time was mostly spent in study, distributed something as follows: Chemistry, 1 hour; German, $\frac{1}{2}$; History, 1; Mathematics, 1; Natural History, 4; Literature, $1\frac{1}{2}$. This year my father was High Sheriff and in February I went with him to the East Kent nomination. Mr. Kirkpatrick was my father's chaplain. In March I went again with my father to Maidstone for the Assizes. Visited Kit's Coty House, which first roused my interest in Archæology. I did some drawings for Mr. Darwin. I was far from well and several times in bed for days together.

" We used to have a good many scientific men at H. E., specially Mathematicians.

" In the May of this year Wheatstone brought in his new Stereoscope and Pseudoscope.

" Dined I think for the first time at Morden College on the 24th June.

" I was working at Crustacea.

" In December went with my father and mother to stay with Whewell. Met Kingsley."

His first published paper was a Monograph in the *Annals and Magazine of Natural History*, for January 1853. It was a description of a new free-swimming species from the Atlantic belonging to the family Calanidæ, and forming the type of a new Genus. The specimens belonged to Mr. Darwin's collection. The paper was illustrated by an excellent plate, and he named the Crustacean *Labidocera Darwinii*. This paper was followed in 1853 and 1854 by three others describing several more new species belonging to the same family, partly from Mr. Darwin's collection, and partly from that of the College of Surgeons.

The plates for these papers were all illustrated by himself, and he also made for Mr. Darwin some of the drawings which appeared in his great work on Barnacles.

In 1853 he attended for the first time a meeting of the British Association held that year at Hull. He stayed with Archdeacon Creyke, who had been one of the original Committee of the Association, and from thence went to stay near Manchester with his great-uncle, Mr. Entwistle. This was a visit destined to have a very considerable influence on his life, for it was there that he first met his future wife, Miss Hordern.

This young lady was an orphan, daughter of the late Reverend Peter Hordern of Chorlton cum Hardy. It seems that she stayed a great deal with her relatives, Mr. and Mrs. Haigh, at Liverpool. The young fellow admits himself to have been greatly impressed even at the first meeting, for he writes later, in his diary: "First saw dear Nelly. I recollect it as if it was yesterday. Uncle William and I were walking in the garden. Aunt Hannah and Nelly came and joined us. I was immensely struck by her, and persuaded my mother to ask her down to High Elms."

In spite of this frank avowal, however, it is apparent that his judgment was by no means so disturbed that he was in any haste to disclose his sentiments, and he shows himself curiously able to take an impartial view of the young lady's character. It seems that he went on from his uncle's at Manchester to stay with the Haighs at Liverpool, where, no doubt, he made the lady's better acquaintance, but his mother responded liberally to his suggestion of inviting her to their home at High Elms, and there he had frequent and prolonged opportunity of knowing her intimately. She was at High Elms in January 1854, when he had one of his periodical attacks of illness, and he records that "Nelly Hordern has been a very kind nurse to me and played chess with me a good deal. She is I think a great favourite here, and deservedly, for she is very dear. She has however hardly enough strength of mind, and is of rather too melancholy a disposition *for me.* With some these would be a great merit, accompanied as they are with a very sweet and pliable disposition and great good feeling." It appears, however, that this strictly critical stage was not of long duration. After this first visit Miss Hordern came frequently to High Elms, and he found himself growing more and more attracted by her.

CHAPTER VII

IN 1854, after going out for his training with
the Kent Artillery Militia at Dover, he went
abroad for the first time, and in Paris made the
acquaintance of some of the leading French men
of science. M. Jules Haime took him to a sitting
of the Institut, and M. Fizeau showed him
experiments, which interested him greatly, at
the Observatory. It was in this year that he
commenced his study of the habits of ants—a
subject to which he devoted so many days and
hours at a later time—and gave his first lecture
on them.

He made the acquaintance of Sir Charles
Lyell, to whom in the spring of 1855 we find a
letter asking the eminent geologist to propose
him as a member of the Geological Society. In
sending a gracious consent to this request Sir
Charles makes reference to an interesting discovery of some remains of a mammoth ox which
Lubbock had found in a gravel pit at Green
Street Green, near High Elms. At the same
time and place he had also found some cherty

36

pebbles, which he inferred must have come from the Weald at a time when the river Cray rose much farther to the south than at present.

Sir Charles Lyell writes :

53 HARLEY STREET,
June 16, 1855.

MY DEAR MR. LUBBOCK—I shall have great pleasure in proposing you as a member of the Geological Society.

I am glad to hear of more fossil bones being found at Green Street Green, for I was sorry not to be able to see the exact bed when with you, owing to the removal of some of the deposit which contained the bones.

Last week I examined with Mr. Prestwich the valleys of the Chalk between Henley on Thames and the escarpment of the chalk which overlooks the Vale of Oxfordshire. They are counterparts of the valleys between you at High Elms and the escarpment at Chevening, &c., having deep beds of angular or sub-angular flints, 14 feet thick or more, in their flattish bottoms. But Prestwich had no example to show me of remains of extinct quadrupeds, and I promised to take him to the Green Street Green cave some afternoon, for he will hardly ever sacrifice a whole day. If we go, after I return from Oxford, where I am to be dubbed D.C.L. next week, I will give you notice and hope you will join us.

Prestwich is inclined to doubt the ferruginous clinkers dug up at High Elms having come from the Wealden and wishes to make them out of tertiary origin, but I wish him to see them. They occur in the Green Street Green pit, tho' not very common.

We are making progress in classifying the gravels of the Thames, but it is a laborious work and very curious in the details.—Believe me, truly yours,

CHAS. LYELL.

In June of this year he and Kingsley were staying with Mr. Riversdale Grenfell at Ray Lodge, Maidenhead, and one morning they started for a long walk before breakfast. In the great gravel pit near the Taplow Station they

were fortunate enough to find a great part of
the skull of a Musk Ox. This species is now
confined to Greenland and Arctic America. No
fossil remains of it had up to that time been
found in Britain, or indeed in Europe ; and the
special interest was the additional evidence of
the Glacial period which was afforded by this
discovery of an Arctic Quadruped. The Mammoth and Woolly-haired Rhinoceros had indeed
been met with, but their presence did not necessarily imply Arctic conditions. Since then the
Reindeer, Glutton, and several other Arctic
species have been determined. Another frag-
ment of the Musk Ox was shortly afterwards
found in the Valley of the Avon, and Lubbock
himself met with a third at Green Street Green
in Kent. The Taplow specimen was described
in the *Geological Journal*, and is referred to in
the following letter from Sir J. Prestwich :

MARK LANE, 10/7/55.

MY DEAR SIR—I am rejoiced to hear of the discovery
of the Musk Ox in the Maidenhead gravel. There are
several other large pits in the valley gravel which may be
worth examining. Could you also enquire whether any
bones were found in the gravel cutting of the Wycombe
railway at the hill (Folly Hill) adjoining Maidenhead.
I enquired but was not quite satisfied with the answer
I obtained, altho' it was in the negative and agreed
with my general views on the subject.

On Saturday last, instead of going to Staines, I went
to Brentwood and Ongar. I shall most probably therefore go to Staines on Saturday next, and in that case
shall require the map which I herewith send. If you let
me have it on Friday evening or Saturday morning
before 12, it will do.

Sir C. Lyell and I went to Grays last week, but shall
have to return there or to Ilford or Erith probably on

Friday or Monday next. We shall not remain long at
the pits, but could show them to you and possibly, if you
could accompany us, might have to leave you there, as
I fear there might not be room in the carriage of Mr.
Meeson, who proposes to take us to some other pits in
the neighbourhood.   The Grays pits are however the
great features, and these I shall be happy to show you
and to join you again there.—Believe me to remain, very
truly yours,   JN. PRESTWICH.

The following letter from Charles Darwin
refers to the same discovery :

Down, *19th July* 1855.

DEAR LUBBOCK — I had a note from Lyell this
morning, in which he says you have found the first
Ovibos moschatus ever discovered fossil in England !

I must congratulate you on such a capital discovery.
Considering the habits of *Ovibos*, and the nature of the
drift-beds, I declare I think it one of the most interesting
discoveries in fossils made for some years. . . . I congratulate you, and may this be the first of many interesting geological observations.—Yours very truly,
                                        CH. DARWIN.

I wish you could have come here on Tuesday.   Adios !

With such encouragement as this from the
great men of science, it is no wonder that his
young enthusiasm was fostered and grew keener
than ever.

In 1856 he wrote a paper in the *Transactions
of the Entomological Society* on some Entomostraca, collected in the Atlantic Ocean by
Dr. Sutherland, and in the following year on
eight new species which he found in the English
Channel during a holiday spent at Weymouth.

Here, for the first time, he met Mr. and Mrs.
Busk, who soon became, and till their death
remained, close and intimate friends.

On the death of Professor Busk (as he later became), in 1886, Sir John wrote to his widow : " I need not say how grieved I am at the sad news, and how I sympathise with you all. Busk's friendship has been one of the great privileges of my life, and to his example and advice I have been deeply indebted. It is an immense thing to have known anyone with such a noble nature, so able, so good and so unselfish. . . . I shall always cherish his memory."

He was, indeed, singularly fortunate in his friends, and had a generous capacity for recognising that great good fortune. A brother of Lord Avebury, one of the nearest to himself in age, assured me that Lord Avebury owed to the great Charles Darwin even a larger debt in the respect of character formation than in the encouragement and direction of his mental gifts.

The reader will hardly fail to perceive the peculiar danger to which his circumstances and abilities laid him open, as a very young man. He was early taken from the discipline and companionship of school, and brought into the society of his elders. His father was something of a martinet, belonging rather to the old-fashioned school of parents, and holding himself much aloof from his children, though giving them all encouragement in their cricket, riding, and so on. They gave him ready and unquestioning obedience, but it is hardly to be thought that there was warm sympathy or real friendship between them. The mother, on the other hand, bestowed on her eldest son a degree of admiration and worship which can seldom be lavished with safety on the young human being. His brothers were considerably younger than himself, and he was continually in the company of persons to whom his growing knowledge of natural science seemed scarcely less than miraculous. It was before the day of " Nature study " and the general encouragement given in schools to such pursuits. From the very first he appears to have had a gift of facile exposition which was to make him an admirable lecturer. But for the moment it is evident that the combination of these qualities and these conditions must have put him in much peril of acquiring that intellectual arrogance which is most easily indicated by the word priggishness.

Intellectual arrogance is the very last crime with which the enemies, if he had enemies, of Lord Avebury could conceivably charge his formed character, and in its formation it is well to be believed that a great part was played by that learned, wise, and good man to whom he went eagerly for instruction. While revering the learning and the wisdom, young Lubbock no doubt unconsciously assimilated the goodness —the fortitude with which pain and illness were borne, the patience with which was endured the scarcely less grievous misconstruction which many persons of the best intentions, but of the most narrow minds, placed on Mr. Darwin's great services to science, and above all the singular humility which deprecated all credit to self for any exceptional mental faculty or achievement. The modesty which was characteristic of Lord Avebury was a very eminent characteristic of his great master in science also. There has been some little discussion about the time of his life at which he really did begin visiting Mr. Darwin. It will be remembered that he was still so much of a child when Mr. Darwin came to Down that when his father bade him guess what good thing had come for him, he guessed " a pony." But the regular visits began when he was no longer, indeed, a school-boy, but of an age when most boys now, and even then, would be at school. In a word, he saw much of Mr. Darwin at the time of his life when a lad is perhaps the most readily and, at the same time, the most permanently in-fluenced, for good or for ill, by an example that makes strong appeal to him.

Science, however, in spite of these " finds," and of the notice into which they helped to bring him, was not engrossing the whole of his attention. Miss Hordern came often, as a guest, to High Elms in 1854 and 1855, and a result of these frequent visits was that on Friday, October 13, there is the laconic entry in his diary : " Wrote to Nelly to ask her to marry me," followed, after the decent interval of a week, by the equally brief, but satisfactory note, on the 20th, " Nelly said she would." He adds, on the 25th : " Everybody seems pleased, and all are as kind as possible. We are to live at first at High Elms."

They were married in April 1856, and went to live, as previously determined, with Sir John and Lady Lubbock at High Elms. There are not many alive now who are able to remember

Lord Avebury's first wife at the time of her marriage, but all who do agree in speaking of her as a bright intelligent girl, of much charm of manner.

Marriage did not long divert the young lover of science from his work.

He wrote a paper in the *Entomologist's Annual* for 1856, " On the Respiration of Insects," and in the same year made several excursions with Kingsley, which he always greatly enjoyed, besides that already mentioned which led to the discovery of the Musk Ox.   In 1857 Kingsley having, with his usual impetuous kindness, undertaken to give a lecture on gravels, applied to him for assistance, and the lecture eventually led to the delightful essay on this subject in the *Prose Idylls*.

The variety of Lubbock's interest and industry was really remarkable.   During all these years he was paying a close attention to the banking business, and initiated some reforms therein, which will be mentioned in the following chapter. Yet in 1858, when the Philological Society contemplated issuing a new dictionary, he was asked to participate and did not refuse, eventually agreeing to read Borrow and Evelyn's *Diary* for the purpose—a very pleasant labour for a man of leisure, but a wonderful undertaking for one of his multifarious interests.

Amongst other letters from Huxley on scientific subjects, written about this date, it may be worth while to quote one as a sample of their correspondence.

JERMYN STREET,
Sept. 15th, 1858.

MY DEAR LUBBOCK—I have been greatly interested
in what you tell me respecting the wide occurrence of
the " vitelligenous " glands in Insects. I was quite
unaware they had been described, but I had not looked
into the matter, particularly as it was only a collateral
point in my paper. Von Siebold so far as I recollect
makes no mention of these glandular bodies, which is the
more misleading as he is particularly well up in Insect
anatomy.

I am very much obliged to you for drawing my
attention to the fact that these bodies have been described
already, and I will put a note about them into my paper.
If you will let me put any of your new facts into it, the
work will be all the more valuable.

I have been making no discoveries. On the contrary,
with a more than Roman virtue and stoicism, I pur-
posely left my microscope behind—knowing very well
that the work I had to do would not be done, if I took it.

I have been very busy working at my " Oceanic
Hydrozoa" and the Croonian Lecture, which was not
written when I delivered it. Both are I am happy to
say nearly finished. I used to work from half past eight
in the morning till two, and then stroll about all the
rest of the day.

I am sorry to say I shall be unable after all to come
to Leeds [where the annual meeting of the British
Association was to be held], the death of a connexion of
mine having upset all my arrangements. It is very
annoying but cannot be helped.—Ever yours very truly,
T. H. HUXLEY.

For some time young Lubbock had been
preparing a paper on the Daphnia, the so-called
Freshwater Flea, though it is really a crustacean,
which was eventually published in the *Philosophical Transactions of the Royal Society*, and
led to his election as an F.R.S. in 1858.

There are letters connected with this paper
from Huxley, and also from Professor Owen,
speaking of it in very high terms, but they are

somewhat too technical to be of interest to others than entomologists. They sufficiently show, however, the reputation that he was already acquiring among contemporary scientists not only for careful and industrious, but also for entirely original work. The following portion of a letter from Charles Darwin refers to the same paper :

DOWN, *Sunday Morning*, 1857.

DEAR LUBBOCK — At the Philosophical Club last Thursday, I overheard Dr. Sharpey speaking to Huxley in such high and warm praise of your paper, and Huxley answering in the same tone that it did me good to hear it.   And I thought I would tell you, for if you still wish to join the Royal Society, I should think (Sharpey being influential in Council and Secretary) there would be no doubt of your admission.   Even if you were not admitted the first year it cannot be thought the least disgraceful. I am not aware, but perhaps you have been already proposed.—Believe me, dear Lubbock, yours sincerely,

C. DARWIN.

CHAPTER VIII

"THE ORIGIN OF SPECIES" (1856–1860)

(AGE 22-26)

IT was a curiously patriarchal establishment to which young Lubbock had brought home his wife. There were the old people, his father and mother, the young *ménage*, and, besides, a large number of his brothers and sisters. The brothers were so far removed from him in years and in mode of thought that he could write of them in his diary comprehensively as "the boys," rather in a paternal than a fraternal manner. Then children were born to the young couple, in the order and at the dates that may be seen by reference to the family pedigree, first a daughter, Amy, later to become Mrs. Mulholland, and now Mrs. Van Zandt, and then John, the present Lord Avebury. Young Lubbock was at this time a slight, good-looking man, of medium height, with a great kindliness and intelligence of expression, and possessed of reserves both of physical and mental power of which his aspect did not give promise. At cricket he was a hard hitter and fast scorer.

His diary notes the hitting of two consecutive fivers on the West Kent ground.

While science was, no doubt, his absorbing hobby, it did not preclude an attention to the bank which enabled him not only to carry on its routine work with success but even to initiate some useful new developments. He suggested to the London Bankers the adoption of the system known as the Country Clearing. Up to this time Bankers in London, receiving for collection from their customers cheques drawn on banks in any other town, sent them by post to the Banks on which they were drawn. These Banks then ordered payment of the amount, in many cases less a commission, to the Banker from whom they were received. It was estimated that on an average every 10 cheques involved four letters, or one letter to every $2\frac{1}{2}$ cheques.

The proposal was that the London Bankers should hold a "clearing" and present to one another all the cheques on the Country Banks for which each London Banker was agent, and that Country Banks should send up all such cheques to London to be dealt with in the same way.

The London Bankers were startled at the novelty of the suggestion, and felt doubtful whether it could be practically worked. They asked young Lubbock to attend a meeting of head clerks and go into the details with them. This he did, and after a long discussion Mr. Kentish of Glyns moved, and Mr. Moules of Robarts' seconded a resolution that the plan should be recommended to the Committee of

Bankers. It was adopted by them, and Lubbock drew up the rules, which have been in operation ever since. They were sent down by each Bank to their Country Correspondents, and met with general approval.

The following letter from Charles Darwin is worthy of quotation, as showing both how highly the famous evolutionist already appreciated the works and gifts of Lubbock, who was still, it is to be remembered, only in his twenty-sixth year, and also as indicating the astonishment, which we must all share, that with such various calls on his time he was able to accomplish so much.

Down, *Feb.* 15, 1860.

My dear Lubbock — Many thanks for *Anthropological Review* returned. Thanks also about buds and ovary. I wish I had remembered your discussion. I have now alluded to it in 2nd Edition. Taking the whole sense of Müller's pages, especially one passage further on, I still think he meant to say that buds and germs were essentially the same, but it is far more doubtful than I supposed. I have been reading your address to Ent. Soc.; and the number of first rate papers to which you refer is quite appalling. How do you find time to search up so much matter? I have nothing else to do, and do not hear of half so many papers. It is very unfair of you! Do you take in the *Zeitschaft fur Wissen. Zoolog.*; if so, can you lend me vol. xvii. p. 1, with Landois' " On Noises of Insects " ?

Also can you lend me Desmarest on " Crustacea,"—a thick pinkish volume, if you have it. I want to look at sexual differences. I have been looking at your papers and figures in March and May, and have been fairly astonished (for I had nearly forgotten) at the wonderful structure of the geniculated antenna of male ; but I wish you had figured both antennae, *i.e.* the pair, in their proper position : I should have liked to have given a copy in a wood cut.

If you ever arrive at any definite conclusion, either wholly or partially for or *against* Pangenesis, I should very much like to hear ; for I settled some time ago, that I should think more of Huxley's and your opinion, from the course of your studies and clearness of mind, than of that of any other man in England. H. Spencer's views, I hear from him, are quite different from mine : he says he shall think over the subject, but apparently he does not yet quite understand what I mean.

There is a rather nice Review of you in last *Athenaeum* and a very unnice one of my book ; I suspect, from two or three little points, by Owen.—Ever yours very truly,

C. DARWIN.

This year (1860) was remarkable in the annals of science for the publication of Darwin's great work on the *Origin of Species*. Writing to Dr. (Sir J.) Hooker on March 3, 1860, he gives the following table of those who went with him in his conclusions : [1]

Geologists.	Zoologists and Palaeontologists.	Physiologists.	Botanists.
Lyell Ramsay Jukes H. D. Rogers	Huxley J. Lubbock L. Jenyns (to large extent) Searles Wood	Carpenter Sir H. Holland (to large extent)	Hooker R. C. Watson Asa Gray (to some extent) Dr. Boott (to large extent) Thwaites

The *Origin of Species* raised a storm of controversy, and even of obloquy, on the head of an author so greatly daring as to disturb the ideas of the creation story in which mankind had hitherto—or at all events until the slightly earlier publication of Lyell's *Geology* — been brought up. Lubbock was, of course, on the

[1] *Life and Letters of Charles Darwin*, vol. ii. p. 293.

side of those who supported Darwin, and his advocacy of the evolutionist cause at the meeting that year of the British Association at Oxford is thus referred to, long afterwards, in *Science and the Human Mind* :

The famous scene between Bishop Wilberforce and Huxley at the Oxford Meeting of the British Association in 1860 has often been described. Wilberforce had obtained a first class in the Oxford Mathematical Schools in his youth, and therefore, being regarded by his University as a master of all branches of natural knowledge, had been selected to uphold the cause of orthodoxy. The Bishop endeavoured to kill the notion of evolution with ridicule and sarcasm—ridicule for Darwin and his labours, sarcasm for Huxley and his courage. It seems strange now to think that a majority of the hearers were probably on the side of the Bishop, and were totally unable, from preconceived ideas, to weigh the value of the facts laid before them on behalf of Darwin's theory, or to appreciate the embryological evidence for evolution on which Sir John Lubbock, now Lord Avebury, insisted.[1]

Shortly after the publication of the *Origin of Species*, Mr. Lowe (the Chancellor of the Exchequer) and Mr. Busk (President of the College of Surgeons) were at High Elms. On Saturday evening Mrs. Lowe was between young Lubbock and Mr. Busk, and the conversation turned on the great book. Mrs. Lowe asked Mr. Busk " just to explain " why one germ should develop into a man and another into a kangaroo. He suggested that she should read the book, so she took it upstairs. Next day she sat in the drawing-room with it, and finished it about 4.30, shutting it up with a clap, and saying : " Well, I don't see much in your Mr. Darwin after all : if I had had his

[1] *Science and the Human Mind*, Whetham, p. 214.

facts I should have come to the same conclusion myself."

At Easter, Lubbock had enjoyed a pleasant and instructive trip in France with Sir J. Prestwich, Sir D. Galton, and Mr. Busk, visiting the venerable M. Boucher de Perthes at Abbeville and going in his company to the gravels of the Somme Valley.

He fully satisfied himself that the implements found in these beds were genuine, and that the men who made them were contemporaneous with the Mammoth and the Woolly-haired Rhinoceros. On the other hand, these species were never found in association with polished celts, such as those contained in the tumuli belonging to the Stone Age.

He proposed, therefore, for the earlier remains the name Palaeolithic, or Earlier Stone Age remains; and for the polished and later stone implements the name Neolithic. These names have been so generally adopted, and are now so familiar, that it may be a surprise to the reader to learn that their origin was so recent.

CHAPTER IX

IN 1861 it is probable that the growing increase in the young family made the spacious accommodation of High Elms scarcely adequate to all the demands on it, and Mr. and Mrs. Lubbock, with their children, migrated to a house in Chislehurst, which they re-named Lamas, after the ancestral place of the family in Norfolk. He had been elected a member of the Royal Society in 1858, at an extraordinarily early age, and this year the Society did him the honour of appointing him to serve on its Council. It is not always remembered how very young he was when he had already made a decided mark and acquired a position of distinction in science.

I think it is also to this year that we have to refer an amusing story connected with the loss —merely temporary—of a small handbag which he carried daily with him to London, when he went up to business. He became interested, during the summer, in the study of a curious parasite *Sphaeruleria Bombi*, of the Humble Bee, and contributed a paper on it to the *Natural History Review*. One day, arriving at Chislehurst Station, he laid down his handbag on a seat for a moment, and when he looked round again the bag was gone ! He complained of his loss to the stationmaster, who was sympathetic but not encouraging, saying that he was afraid the bag had been taken by some evil-disposed person and would never be seen again. " But what," he asked, as by an afterthought, " was in the bag ? "

Lubbock replied : " There was very little— only a paper bag containing a dozen humble bees, and a German scientific treatise."

The stationmaster smiled and said that he thought, that being the case, it was quite possible that he might recover the bag. And sure enough, within a short space there appeared a very venerable, white-bearded and apostolic old gentleman bringing back the bag, and with profuse apologies explaining that he had taken it up in mistake for his own and only just found out the error. Whether he had been stung by one of the bees the story does not narrate.

There is rather a curious rider to this story. These bees, in the paper bag, had been obtained by Lubbock by advertisement. He wanted, if possible, to complete his investigations, and as winter came on did not know where to procure the bees. In reply to his advertisement a man wrote offering him a supply of the bees at one and six apiece. The price was high, but in the cause of science Lubbock did not demur. Only, when he had bought all the bees he required, he

wrote to the man and said : " Now that I have
had the bees, for which I am greatly obliged,
would you kindly tell me, to satisfy my curiosity,
how you are able to procure them at this time
of year." The man wrote back quite courteously,
but quite firmly, saying : " No, since I can sell
the bees at eighteenpence each, I think it pays
me better to go on doing so than to tell anybody
else how to procure them." So this matter of
the humble bees appears to remain a profound
mystery even to this day.

There is a further tragic tale connected with
that same handbag which may as well find its
place here. A little later one of the younger
Lubbock brothers had asked John to bring down
some ferrets from London. He duly procured
the ferrets, which were in a sack, and put
them under the seat in the railway carriage.
Then, according to his habit, he became deeply
engrossed in 'a scientific pamphlet, and quite
unconscious of his surroundings, until he
found his fellow-passengers betraying symptoms
of vivid uneasiness. The wretched ferrets had
gnawed their way out of the sack, and were investigating the trousers and persons generally of
the passengers. With many apologies Lubbock
picked them up and inserted them, after a
prolonged hunt and capture, in the handbag.
The creatures must have been very hungry,
for they began work with devouring some
scientific papers, and then, finding these to
be rather dry eating, betook themselves to
the leather of the bag, which they entirely
destroyed. The finale of the story is the most

tragic of all, for either the bag or the science so disagreed with the ferrets' digestion that all three died on the following day ; so that was the end of the ferrets and of the handbag likewise.

From these tragedies we may turn to less dramatic subjects. In the summer he went a tour in Switzerland with Tyndall and Huxley, and writes the following account of it to Mr. Darwin :

15 LOMBARD STREET,
23rd *August* 186ℨ.

MY DEAR MR. DARWIN—I am very sorry to hear so sad an account of your family, but hope that you are now getting out of your troubles. Atherley called here the other day and gave a flourishing account of William, but leaving him for a fortnight was even more complimentary.

My Swiss tour was most successful ; besides spending a week in the mountains with Tyndall and Huxley, which was capital fun, I visited nearly all the collection of Lake antiquities and saw five of the Pfalbauten themselves. Three of them, those at Nernier, Thonon, and Morges in the Lake of Geneva, I saw from a boat. The water was from 8 to 12 ft. deep, but so clear that I could see quite well the piles and other things at the bottom.

We thought we saw a hatchet, and I undressed and dived for it. After two or three ineffectual attempts we poked at it with a pole, and it turned out to be only a bit of wood.

At Wauwyl the old floor (of the lake) is covered by three or four feet of peat, and the lake has been drained. We spent several hours in digging, and got three hatchets, three or four implements in bone, and a great many bits of pottery and more or less broken bones.

There also the beams forming the floor are preserved in the peat, and one could stand, as it were, on the old floor. I have got a hymenopterous insect which uses its wings to swim with *in the water*. Probably it is looking for a victim on which to lay eggs ; but it strikes me as a most curious adaptation, and one which would interest you much.

I have also a case of dimorphism in Psocris, but have not yet been able to make out much about it.   It had been already suspected by Westwood.

Your case of trimorphism makes one's mental mouth water for more information.

Let me know when you return as I am very anxious for a talk with you.—Yours afftly.,

JOHN LUBBOCK.

Most of Sir John's letters to Darwin, except the very earliest, are signed thus " affectionately," as addressing one who was to him almost a second father.

At Easter he made another excursion in France with Sir J. Evans and Sir J. Prestwich.

In the autumn he joined Huxley and Tyndall in Switzerland, and had the accident on the Jungfrau which is graphically described by Tyndall in *Hours of Exercise in the Alps*.   After leaving them he joined the distinguished Swiss Archaeologist, M. Morlot, with whom he visited most of the Swiss Museums and Lake Dwellings which he described in the *Natural History Review*, and subsequently in *Prehistoric Times*.   The same autumn he wrote a paper on the life history of Lonchoptera, one of the Diptera, which were previously unknown, in the *Transactions of the Entomological Society*.   The larva is very curious.

He also wrote for the *Natural History Review* an elaborate Memoir on the Daphnidae, an article on " The Habits of Insects," and a paper on the " Remains of Man in the Somme Valley " ; and contributed the first part of his work on Thysanura in the *Transactions of the Linnean Society*.

At this time the thinking world was much

agitated by the celebrated volume of *Essays and Reviews*. Considering the moderate and reasonable position taken up by the writers, and that some of the statements most severely condemned were thoroughly well-established scientific truths, the excitement created by the book is an extraordinary evidence how little the then leaders of the theological world knew about the actual world in which they lived. Two of the essayists were suspended by the Court of Arches, but the decision was reversed on appeal. Wilberforce, who had stood as the champion of orthodoxy at the meeting of the British Association against Darwin and Huxley, wrote an article in the *Quarterly* condemning the rationalistic views advanced.

One of the writers was Dr. Jowett, afterwards Master of Balliol; another, Dr. Temple, at that time Head Master of Rugby, later Bishop of London, and finally Archbishop of Canterbury !

The literary and scientific world of London felt that the authors of the book were very unfairly assailed, and a Committee of which Mr. W. Spottiswoode and Mr. Lubbock were secretaries drew up the following address to Dr. Temple as author of the first Essay in the volume.

To the Rev. Dr. Temple

We the undersigned have read with surprise and regret a letter in which the Archbishop of Canterbury and the other English Bishops have severely censured the volume of Articles entitled *Essays and Reviews*.

Without committing ourselves to the conclusions arrived at in the various Essays, we wish to express our sense of the value which is to be attached to enquiries conducted in a spirit so earnest and reverential, and our belief that such enquiries must tend to elicit truth, and to foster a spirit of sound religion.

Feeling as we do that the discoveries in science, and the general progress of thought, have necessitated some modification of the views generally held on theological matters, we welcome these attempts to establish religious teaching on a firmer and broader foundation.

While admitting that each writer in the *Essays and Reviews* is responsible only for the opinions expressed by himself, we address to you, as author of the first article, this expression of our sympathy and our thanks.

The address was very readily and numerously signed by men of science and others, the signatures including those of Charles Darwin, Charles Lyell, Leonard Horner, George Bentham, Thos. Graham; Airy, the Astronomer-Royal; and Busk, President of the College of Surgeons. It is interesting to note, at this critical juncture in the relations between religion and science, the rally of the men of science in support of the more liberal theology which the growth of knowledge led reasonable men to adopt.

In February 1863, for the first time, he gave a Friday evening lecture at the Royal Institution. It was on the ancient Lake Habitations of Switzerland, and is eulogistically described in a letter from Professor Tyndall to Mrs. Lubbock.

28*th February* 1863,
ROYAL INSTITUTION.

MY DEAR MRS. LUBBOCK—No doubt you have been already informed of the success of last night's lecture; but probably your husband will not tell *how* successful it was. The style throughout was clear and straightforward, and the winding-up admirable. I could number on my finger-ends the lectures which have been equally successful during the ten years of my connection with the Royal Institution. Not more than three or four have been equally well received. At the conclusion there was a loud and long-continued outburst of applause; this subsided; but the feelings of those present had not quite discharged themselves, and, like what we call the residual discharge of electricity, a second general rumble occurred. As for me, who, it must not be forgotten, stirred up his mind to the performance, I feel quite bright by the reflected radiance, I am like a little glass bead silvered within and set in the sunshine, complacently radiating from a little reflected sun pictured on my own surface. With this very pretty figure I leave you to muse pleasantly, as of course every wife does, on the solid triumph achieved by my friend your husband.—Believe me, always yours,

JOHN TYNDALL.

This immediate and remarkable success owed something, we may be very sure, to the manner, as well as to the matter, of the discourse. Already he had acquired the great art of lightly handling weighty subjects. Something, too, of his success may be attributed to the extremely youthful aspect of the speaker. Professor Ray Lankester, writing to me after Lord Avebury's death, says of him : " He was a friend of my father's, and I knew him forty-five years ago. He had, when he was thirty, so juvenile an appearance that he was sometimes mistaken for a young undergraduate or even a schoolboy ! In early days he was a great feature at the Red Lion's dinner at the British Association, and used to keep the whole thing alive by his wonderfully humorous speeches. I think his *versatility* as a naturalist (let alone his business capacity) was his most remarkable quality, and in *all* he dealt with his work was up to a high level of excellence. Prehistoric man, ants and other insects, forms of leaves and flowers—he did good and original work in all."

Possibly Lord Avebury's gift of humour has not been appreciated as it ought to be. The above may be accepted as a striking witness to it. We must realise that he had quite an active dislike to wit that was barbed with malice or instinct with cynicism, nor was willing to admit that such maxims as La Rochefoucauld's could be redeemed by all their cleverness. Yet his own humour was occasionally of a gently ironic kind, as in the following passage from the *Pleasures of Life*: "The Medicine man is a Priest, or rather a Sorcerer, more than a Doctor, and his effort is to exorcise the evil spirit. In other countries, where some advance has been made, a charm is written on a board, washed off and drunk. In some cases the medicine is taken, not by the patient, but by the Doctor. Such a system, however, is generally transient; it is naturally discouraged by the Profession, and is indeed incompatible with a large practice."

His activity, especially in science, during 1863 may be judged from the following brief summary :

At Easter he went down to Scotland to visit the Elgin shell-mounds.

He was made President of the Ethnological Society.

He gave several lectures, including his first at the Royal Institution.

He was made Secretary of the London Bankers, August 17.

He contributed to the *Transactions of the*

Linnean Society the first part of an elaborate Memoir on the development of Ephemera.

A paper on two very remarkable swimming (Hymenoptera) insects.

A paper on some Freshwater Entomostraca.

An article on North American Archaeology, and another on the Ancient Shell-mounds of Scotland, for the *Natural History Review*.

In the autumn he went with Mrs. Lubbock and Miss Arbuthnot, afterwards Mrs. Brandreth, to Denmark and Scandinavia. Mrs. Lubbock wrote for Mr. Galton's *Vacation Tourists* an interesting account of their visit to the Danish Shell-mounds.

In Scandinavia they visited Copenhagen, Gothenburg, Stockholm, Upsala (where they were very kindly welcomed and were given mead in a horn on the tumulus of Odin), Christiania, the Dovrefield, Trondhjem, Bergen and the Fillefield. He was amused at a story told by Steenstrup to show that if foreigners were often ignorant of English ways, we also sometimes made mistakes. He said that an Englishman wishing to write to him took the address from a Memoir which happened to be illustrated " with a map and a plate "—in Danish " med en kort og en tavle "; so he addressed his letter :

> J. Steenstrup,
> Prof. Zoologia,
> Med en kort og en tavle,
> Copenhagen.

The following letter of this year's date is interesting as an expression of Sir C. Lyell's views with reference to the probability of the existence of Man in Miocene times. He was also of opinion that the ancestors of the human race at that period would have differed so much that they could hardly be regarded as belonging to the same species.

53 HARLEY STREET,
February 20, 1863.

DEAR LUBBOCK—In reference to p. 399, it strikes me that if there had been some representative of the *family* to which man now belongs, *Satirus sapiens*, in the Miocene period, and he had by transmutation been superseded by *Homo sapiens*, there would have been so much progress and instrument making in the older Pliocene epoch that we should have found fossil ships, etc., in the Subapennine strata. See p. 379 as to what progress or improvement reason in millions of years must lead to.

Please let me have the benefit of errata which you may have seen. I know it is tiresome to write them out, but a great boon to the author.

I have struck out Galton and Prestwich at p. 11, who will be surprised to learn that they were in Denmark.

Max Müller, I am happy to find, has nothing to object to, whether as to facts or opinions, in what I say on languages in ch. xxiii., and he even says that Darwin's theory of " Natural Selection and the struggle for life was wanted to unlock the mysteries of language."

Fortunately Müller is a layman, and therefore need not be expelled the University at the instance of three canons of Christ Church for declaring what he believes to be the truth.—Ever truly yours,   CHAS. LYELL.

J. Lubbock, Esq.

In this same year he was invited on behalf of the Liberal Committee to stand for the City. At that time the Liberals had a large majority, there would probably have been no opposition, and his election would have been certain. To his great regret Sir J. W. Lubbock declined to agree, and he was obliged to communicate this decision to the agent, who assures him, in reply, that as soon as his name was mentioned the universal feeling was that his election would *at that time* have been certain, nor did he doubt that his judgment would have secured the seat as long as he desired to retain it. He expressed the highest respect for Sir John Lubbock's opinion, to which in this case all must needs bow, but deeply regrets losing such an opportunity. If there should be the slightest hope of a change, he begs Mr. Lubbock to let him know.

On November 3 of the following year was started the " X Club " : the only name being the mathematical symbol for an unknown quantity, and the only rule to have none. The members dined together once a month, and the original members were :

> Mr. George Busk,
> Mr. Edward Frankland,
> Mr. Thomas Archer Hirst,
> Sir Joseph Dalton Hooker,
> Professor Thomas Henry Huxley,
> Mr. Lubbock,
> Mr. Herbert Spencer,
> Mr. William Spottiswoode, and
> Professor John Tyndall.

The original number was never added to ; though guests were often invited. Of the nine, 5 received the Royal Medal of the Royal Society ; 3 the Copley ; 1 the Rumford ; 6 were Presidents of the British Association ; 3 Presidents of the Royal Society ; 5 Associates of the Institute of France ; and they also included a

Secretary, Foreign Secretary, and Treasurer of the Royal Society.

Their numbers remained unbroken for nineteen years, until the death of Mr. Spottiswoode in 1883.

The Club has never been formally dissolved, but the last meeting, attended only by Professor Hooker, Mr. Frankland, and Sir J. Lubbock, was in 1893. The Club met 240 times, and for many years the average attendance was 7.

His father had made a racecourse at the top of the Park at High Elms. At first the meetings were almost private, but gradually the numbers coming grew unmanageable. The last was held in 1864, when the papers estimated that 40,000 persons were present, " including the Archbishop of Canterbury, the late Lord Chancellor (Lord Cranworth), Lady Dyke, Mr. and Mrs. Robarts," etc. " On approaching the course through the magnificent grounds the scene became animated in the extreme. Tents and marquees of all descriptions were erected on the hill." " The first race was won by Mr. Harris's Polly ; the second by Mr. Godden's Fion-nu-alla ; the third by Mr. B. W. Lubbock, who rode Queen Mary and handled her in such fine style that he landed her by two clear lengths. . . . The hurdle race was won by Mr. H. Lubbock on Lady Blanche. The pole jump was won by Mr. A. Lubbock, who cleared 8 ft. 6 in. The foot race was also won by Mr. A. Lubbock. This terminated one of the best day's sports in the county of Kent, and in one of the most lovely spots in the county."

It is evident enough from this and other accounts that the house at High Elms, in spite of the mathematical tastes of the father and the various industries of the eldest son, was the scene and centre of much social entertainment. The young scientist found himself in touch with life at very different points.

CHAPTER X

IN 1865 Lubbock was invited by Mr. George
Warde Norman, the distinguished Political
Economist, and Chairman of the West Kent
Liberals, to contest that constituency. As his
father had so recently declined to approve of
his standing for the City he at once refused.
The City was a safe seat, and one peculiarly
suitable to a Banker. West Kent, on the contrary,
was a forlorn hope, the Conservative at the
previous election having had a majority of 2000.
Mr. Norman, however, would not take his refusal,
but applied directly to Sir J. W. Lubbock, who
to the son's great surprise gave a cordial consent. The result was that young Lubbock stood
with Mr. Angerstein against the sitting members,
Lord Holmesdale and Mr. (now Sir W.) Hart
Dyke.

His scientific friends expressed some very
natural regret at his attention being thus, in
part at least, diverted from Science, but as for
the rapid change of view of his father, it is
characteristic of the simple sincerity of the future

Lord Avebury that he does not seem to have made any endeavour to probe beneath the surface in order to perceive its motive. May we not shrewdly guess that it was for the very reason that the hope was a forlorn one, and that there was virtually no chance of his being sent to Parliament as representing West Kent, that his father approved of his candidature, though unwilling that he should stand for the safe seat offered him in the City ? The father may well have thought that the days and hours of this very remarkable son were already sufficiently occupied between his scientific pursuits and his business, without the further detachment of a seat in Parliament. And, on the other hand, he may have reflected that the candidature itself, with the speech - making and canvassing that it involved, might be a very useful training for a young man, for whom he may have foreseen a considerable and eminent public career. The father's consent in the one case and refusal in the other do not really, of necessity, imply any change in his opinion.

The son, however, was but for a few months longer to be subject to the guidance of the father, whether for good or ill, for in June of the same year Sir John, who had been in failing health for some time, passed away. His death, though far from unexpected, was deeply felt by his eldest son. The latter was past thirty years of age, yet we have seen how immediately, and without demur, he had accepted his father's verdict against his standing for Parliament as the City's representative. To judge by the entries in his diary, it does not seem to have occurred to him as possible at any time to doubt the wisdom of his father's advice or to dream of acting in opposition to it.

Very keenly do I regret that in attempting to portray the life and character of the subject of this book, whom I will now, until the date of his elevation to the peerage, refer to as Sir John Lubbock, it has not been possible to make any considerable use of those self-revelations afforded by letters which are often the best of all assistants in the biographer's task. It is hardly to be imagined that a more industrious letter-writer than Sir John has ever lived, and yet in the fullest sense of the term it is not to be said of him that he was a letter-writer at all. The vast number of letters that he wrote were in all cases perfectly clear expositions of the objects for which he took them in hand. Whether it were a problem of science, or intricate matter of business, or a measure that he wished to pass through Parliament—he would deal with one and all of these with an ease and lucidity of expression which were the reflection of the lucidity of his mind.

But when he had said that which he set out to say, he had finished. In none of his letters do we find any outpouring of his thoughts or feelings, any revelation of the innermost self. Such exposure of the holy sanctities of his being would have been impossible to him and quite contrary to the sensitive reserve which was one of his characteristics. Moreover, it is the kind of literature which would have made no appeal to him from another pen. He took an avid interest in human psychology, but his own sensitiveness made him very averse from the unveiling by another of the soul's secrets to make a public spectacle. I cannot imagine him reading with the smallest interest anything in the nature of a " human document." The scarcely seemly outpourings of a Marie Bashkirtseff would have left him not only cold, but very strongly repelled. He would have failed to understand how any human creature could so throw back the veil from before secrets of the soul that should be hidden. They would have appeared to him far too sacred for such publication.

Very much more freely does he reveal himself in his early diaries, which were designed for the perusal of no other eye than his own. But it has not seemed to me that it would be right to make more than the most sparing use of documents so clearly intended to be private. There is one phrase which is very frequent in them, and which is worth noting because it is so expressive of the simple modesty of his nature. Again and again we find it recorded, after reference to a meeting or a conversation with some one whom he had met in society or elsewhere, that he or she, as the case might be, " was very kind." He makes the remark with an unconsciousness, which is very charming, that his own unfailing and wonderful kindness could not but elicit a response of like sort from all with whom he came in contact. He might fairly, one would suppose, have expected at least that reward—that as he was ever kind and courteous to others so

they should be to him. But on the contrary
he appears to have accepted their responsive
courtesy as an act of pure goodness and charity
on their part. And so it was, to the very
end of this long and full life, his gratitude for
the simplest services rendered, even for the
ordinary politeness of social intercourse, was
curiously touching.

No doubt the death of his father, and his
accession to the baronetcy, and to the head
place in the banking-house, made a considerable
material difference in the position of the new
Sir John Lubbock. In the course of the year
he and Lady Lubbock moved from their house,
Lamas, at Chislehurst, and came to take up
their residence at High Elms. The traditional
patriarchal character of the house was maintained. His mother moved down to rooms at
the farm in the Park, close by, and some of the
younger brothers continued to live at High
Elms itself. There was strong fraternal attach-
ment between them all. In spite of the extreme
gentleness of his manner and character, Sir
John Lubbock had a firmness of will, and a
pertinacity in attaining his ends, which made
him perfectly competent to be the head of this
curiously associated family party.

It is using no idle phrase to say that Sir John,
after his father's death, stood in a quasi-paternal
position towards the younger of his brothers.
The following letter from one of them will bear
witness both to this position and to the willingness with which it was conceded and recognised.
It is the letter of a schoolboy, with a schoolboy's

ambitions, but it is the letter of a thoroughly
healthy-minded schoolboy ; nor is it to be said
that the ambitions have fallen far out of their
right perspective :

Eton College, Sunday.

My dear John—I write to you now to inform you
how earnestly I desire to stay at Eton until next summer.
I will explain my views to you candidly and the reasons
which induce me to make this request. To be Captain
of the Eleven and President of Pop are almost the
highest aim of anyone's life at Eton, and as by staying
at Eton I should attain to these distinctions, I naturally
hope for another year at this place. I believe before
going into business I should want French, and so in
the holidays I could pick it up very well, and I would
give anything up for another year at Eton. If I was to
leave now, this idea would always weigh heavily on my
mind : " If I had stayed another summer I should have
been Captain of the Eleven." My mother spoke to me
about staying at Eton, if I wished, and here everyone
of my friends, and also hopers of the welfare of cricket,
have asked me to stay at Eton. I would give up everything in the holidays for the fulfilment of my wishes.
Of course you know of our defeat, sustained on account
of the superiority of the Harrow Eleven, and I really
wish to stay at Eton, and by the greatest energy at
everything to put a stop to the repetition of these
defeats. I cannot see that another year at Eton would
make much difference in my progression in any business,
and as I so earnestly wish to stay, I hope you will see my
views and acquiesce with my desires. By staying at
Eton I would most strictly make myself subservient to
any wishes of yours.—Ever your affect. brother.

One cannot but be glad to learn that after a
little more correspondence the request was agreed
to, the boy fulfilled his ambitions, and it does
not seem to have been at the cost of any efficiency
in the sterner business of life. But does not the
letter breathe a curious spirit, as written from
brother to brother ? Is it not much more the

letter of a son to a father? We do not often find brothers writing to another that they will be " strictly subservient to any wishes of yours," even though, as in this case, the promised subserviency is held out rather in the way of a bribe for the elder's complacency. The whole tone of the letter bears witness to the paternal attitude of Sir John towards the younger brothers, and their almost filial view of him. It is curious to see how the boy instructs the man, as if forgetting that the latter too had been at Eton, in the enormous value of such distinctions as the Captaincy of the Eleven and the Presidency of " Pop." Among brothers, who were Etonians, these things would commonly go without saying. The younger even suggests a doubt whether the elder as much as knew that Eton had lost to Harrow at "Lord's"; and this, although Sir John, as we have seen, was himself a keen cricketer.

It is an illuminating letter in the light that it throws on the relations between the brothers. It could hardly have been written except as a consequence of a life at High Elms in which the eldest brother was regarded as rather apart from the rest—a little above the others, may be— but it speaks of an isolation that sounds a little pathetic. At the same time it bears witness to the very serious bent of Sir John's mind, grave beyond his age, although he was always a very social being, and even to the latest years of his life liked to have friends of both sexes and of all ages about him.

His father had lived long enough to have

the satisfaction of knowing how ably his son acquitted himself in the new rôle of parliamentary candidate. Every reference to his speeches is couched in the terms of congratulation. It is evident that the line which he struck out for himself in his first venture in public speaking, as distinguished from lecturing, was that which he adopted throughout his career. He spoke simply, lucidly, with a conviction that carried his audience with him, and without any rhetorical arts. His father wrote to him, in regard to his first speech at Maidstone, the following brief note, which has a sad interest in that it is the last he ever penned :

HIGH ELMS, FARNBOROUGH, KENT,
Wednesday 26th, 1865.

DEAR JOHN—I wish to add my tribute of applause. Your excellent speech at Maidstone appears to me to be in the best possible taste and admirably suited to the occasion. Go on and prosper.—I am, dear John, yours most affectionately,   J. W. LUBBOCK.

His ever kind friend, Charles Darwin, had written on the previous day a letter of highest encomium on his address :

DOWN, BECKENHAM, KENT,
February 25, 1865.

MY DEAR LUBBOCK—Although you will be overwhelmed with congratulations, I must write to say how heartily I rejoice over your success. Your speech at Maidstone struck me as quite excellent, and I fully expect to see you a great man in Parliament, as you are in Science. But even in the moment of triumph, I must let one little groan escape me for poor deserted Science. Anyhow, I know that you will always love your first-born child, and not despise her for the sake of gaudy politicks.

I wrote to ask you a question about savages and suicide before I had heard of Maidstone ; otherwise, of course, I would not have troubled you. If, in the course of a few weeks, you can inform me, I should be glad, but the point is not very important for me.

Once again, I do most sincerely congratulate you.— Ever most truly yours,   CH. DARWIN.

From his political opponent, Sir William Hart Dyke, he received a very kindly humorous letter saying that he had been a little surprised at first to hear that there was a chance " of the ' Sensation Drama ' of Lubbock v. Dyke being enacted," but assuring him that neither " during the Performance of the Piece nor after the Curtain dropped " should any ill feeling on Sir William's part enter into the contest.

It was an assurance that was perfectly fulfilled.

John Stuart Mill's is one of the distinguished names that appears on Lubbock's committee in his electoral campaign.

In spite, however, of the fervour with which his speeches were received, and the congratulations accorded them, the " forlorn hope " failed, and he was handsomely defeated. The majority against him, odd as it may now seem, was larger than it would otherwise have been in consequence of the opinions on the Antiquity of Man expressed in his *Prehistoric Times*, which had appeared during the contest. He was urged to keep the book back till after the election, but thought that such a course would be scarcely honourable.

As a curious illustration of the state of popular opinion at the time, it may be mentioned that at Tonbridge, even as late as 1871, a meeting was held to reply to a lecture he had recently

given in that town. The speaker, the Rev.
J. B. M‘Crea, considered that " Science was the
cause, science *is* the cause, of the degeneracy of
man. It was not man's natural tendency and
development that made him scientific. Science
did it. The Bible told us distinctly and plainly
it was not the devil that did it. A great deal
more was laid to the door of the devil than belonged to the devil, although he cannot be made
worse than he is " (*Bromley Tel.*, Dec. 16,
1871).

The reviews of *Prehistoric Times* were very
favourable, and there was a general and cordial
approval of the book by all who were qualified
to judge.

Sir A. W. Franks, Director of the Society of
Antiquaries, and Keeper of the British Antiquities in the British Museum, writes, in acknowledging a copy which had been sent him :

A thousand thanks for your very welcome present.
I congratulate you and the world at large on your book
being out, more especially as I have been telling every
one to wait for your book. It fills a great lacuna in
early Archaeology, and fills it well.

.   .   .   .

If you have a copy to spare for the Antiquaries, it
would, I think, be very acceptable.

The book was soon translated into the principal
European languages. It has gone through six
editions in England, and what is even more
remarkable, three in France.

The *Examiner* praised it as " an able and
original work." The *Athenaeum* said : " It teems
with information on everything that has been
yet discovered, bearing on the early history of

our race, and is written in so clear and agreeable a manner that it is sure both to gratify and instruct every class of reader." Such praise was, of course, the more welcome as coming from so high an authority as Mr. Wallace.

All the complimentary notices that it received would fill a volume as large as itself.

In June of the same year Sir John read a paper before the Statistical Society on the London Clearing System, which was the subject of an elaborate and complimentary review in the *Money Market Review*, the writer describing him as one who " pursued his avocation as Banker not only as a means of money getting, but as a Science."

He gave for the first time some figures showing the relative use of cheques and bills, notes and coin, in our financial transactions.

Taking the last days of 1864, he found that the relative amounts passing through his Bank were :

Clearing Cheques and Bills .	£16,346,000	
Other Cheques and Bills .	5,394,000	
		£21,740,000
Bank of England notes .	£1,137,000	
Country Bank notes . .	139,000	
		1,276,000
Coin	.	79,000
		£23,095,000

In the same paper he described the foundation, and conduct, of the Country Clearing.

He had been invited to take the chair as President of Section D at the British Association meeting at Birmingham, but resigned in consequence of his father's death. He and Lady Lubbock, however, attended the meeting, and on the way down very nearly lost their lives in a railway accident. Just beyond Banbury the axle of the engine broke, and the train, except the last two carriages, ran off the line. " If," said the *Birmingham Daily Post,* " the disaster had happened two minutes earlier the train would have been passing over the Hardwick embankment, and would probably have been thrown from a considerable height into either the Canal or the Cherwell."

The following is his account of the accident given in a letter to his mother. It appears, not unnaturally, to have had a lasting ill effect on the health of Lady Lubbock. At all times a highly-strung and sensitive creature, the shock to her nervous system must have been exceedingly severe ; the more so that in September, only two months later, their son Rolfe was born :

BIRMINGHAM,
Sunday, 10th July 1865.

MY DEAREST MOTHER—You will already have heard from Nelly what a terrible accident we have had, and how narrow an escape.

We were coming down here yesterday by the 3.40 train from Paddington, when, about two miles on this side of Banbury, suddenly we began to bump about, and I felt certain at once that we were off the line. I gave one look out of the window, and from the pace at which we were going, it seemed to me almost impossible that we could escape being killed.

The bumping got worse and worse, we were thrown backwards and forwards in the carriage, and though it seemed rather a long while, the only distinct idea I remember was that in a few minutes more we should probably solve many of those questions which interest us so much.

At last there was one much worse bump, then a dreadful scrunch, and then everything was still, and it seemed from the contrast almost a supernatural quiet.

For a moment I expected the carriage to be crushed by the next, but of course a second was enough to show that this was not going to happen. Then I hardly knew whether I was dead or alive; I felt, however, no pain, but my hands and coat were covered with blood. All this happened, as it were, at once. Nelly had fallen into my arms, and though she assured me that she was all right, still, as I found she was bleeding very much, I could not tell how much she might be hurt, or what effect the shaking might have.

Our carriage was lying on its side, partly in the field, and partly on the hedge. So we had to scramble on to the top, and get down as best we might. One poor fellow was fainting, with a terrible gash on the top of his head, but no one was actually killed.

We got Nelly into a field and tied up her hand and arm. She was very brave, and declared that she was not hurt.

It appeared that while we were going express speed, the driver said 60 miles an hour, one of the wheels of the engine came off. The engine then went off the line and at last broke from the tender and plunged into a field, ploughing up a thick thorn hedge for some distance in its fall. The tender was dragged off the rails by the engine, and after going on a little while it also fell into the field, but fortunately clear both of the engine and the rails. The guard's van was next, it was dragged off the rails by the tender, and ran past it and into the ditch, but did not turn over. We were next to the van, which also pulled us off the line. We ran, however, right clear of the lines and turned over by ourselves. We also dragged the next carriage and so on, but, fortunately, each carriage fell clear of the rest and of the lines.

If this had not been the case, if the carriages had fallen on the line, and run into one another, it would have been far worse. Or if we had been on an embankment, many of us must have been killed. Only the last carriage remained on the lines, and the last but one, in which Annie [Lady Lubbock's maid] was, ran off but did not upset. The sleepers were all broken for about 160 yards.

The arrangements for getting us on to Birmingham were very bad, and it was 11 instead of 7 when we got here.

I am only a little scratched and bruised. Nelly's cuts are deep and bleed much, but nothing is broken. I fear she must be much shaken. . . .

It appears to be from this accident that we have to date a long period of ill-health for Lady Lubbock which only terminated with her death. I had not the privilege of knowing her, but a cousin and life-long friend of the first Lady Lubbock writes of her : " Ellen was an immense help to John in his early scientific days, she acted quite as a secretary, kept his papers in order, looked up references, did all the diagrams for his lectures. She was an exceptionally charming letter - writer, and kept up all the correspondence with his scientific friends. She wrote a beautiful hand and was a clever, brilliant woman, with the kindest heart and the most genial manner, and made all the friends who came to Lamas (and when the elder Sir John died it was all kept up at High Elms) so welcome and happy that every one felt at ease with her. We used to go on Sunday afternoons to Lamas and sit on the long flight of high steps having delightful talks with Tyndall, Hirst, Huxley, Herbert Spencer, and all the rising scientific men of the day."

Another friend writes of her as " a charming and clever woman until her life was clouded by bad health."

Sir John spent an autumn holiday this year in Switzerland with Professor Hirst and Professor Tyndall, being most of the time at Zermatt. On his return he gave a Friday evening lecture at the Royal Institution on the Metamorphosis of

Insects, read a paper on the Bronze Age at the Ethnological Society, and during the course of the year gave lectures at Birmingham, Plymouth and Sevenoaks.

He was appointed to the vacancy caused by his father's death in the Senate of the University of London.

CHAPTER XI

SCIENCE AND ARCHAEOLOGY (1866–1867)

(AGE 32-33)

IT is hardly necessary to tell the reader that the Lubbock family was distinguished among bands of brothers such as the Lytteltons, Studds, Fosters, and so on, for cricketing talent. Alfred, no doubt, was the most eminent of them, but in the year 1866, at which we are now arrived, Edgar was Captain of the Eton Eleven, and Sir John, in his diary, records of him with pride that " in a match against Old Etonians he got the head score and took nine wickets—a most unusual performance." We find Sir John himself playing cricket at a date considerably later than this, but I do not think that he was taking part in this particular match.

It was a busy year with him—a remark which might be made equally of every single year of his long life. He was continually solicited with requests to be on committees, and so on, of various scientific societies, and frequently to act as their president. Such letters as the following, which has an interest of its own, are frequent, and typical of much of this correspondence. It

is from the Honorary Secretary of the Archaeological Institute of Great Britain and Ireland.

SIR—I have been desired by the President and
Council of the Archaeological Institute to bring to your
notice their forthcoming Annual Meeting in London
in July next, under the especial patronage of Her
Majesty.

The proceedings on such occasions have usually been
divided into three heads, under which Archaeological
Science has been ordinarily arranged, viz. : Antiquities,
Architecture, and History. It is, however, the wish of
the Council to sub-divide the section of " Antiquities "
and afford due prominence to those studies relating to
the primæval period which have, especially of late years,
attracted so much attention. It appears to the Council
that the holding of their first great meeting in London,
the chief city of the valley of the Thames, in which so
many objects of a primæval character have been found,
affords a good opportunity for this sub-division. Your
researches in this branch of science have induced the
Council to feel certain that no better inauguration of the
section of " Primæval Antiquities " could occur than by
their being favoured with your presidency of that branch
of their proceedings.

I am desired, therefore, by the President and Council,
to express the hope that you will consent to occupy the
position of President on that occasion.

The other presidents of sections will be :

      Antiquities, S. Birch, Esq.

      Architecture, A. J. N. Beresford Hope.

      History, The very Rev. Dr. Stanley.

Our meeting will be opened under the presidency of
the Marquis Camden, in the Guildhall of the City, on
Tuesday July 10th.

And as his popular fame grew with the years
the number of applications of this kind became
very formidable indeed.

On March 13, with the assistance of his brother
Frederick, he read a paper before the Ethnological Society " On the true assignation of the

Bronze Weapons, etc., found in Northern and Western Europe."

It is evidence of the remarkable progress made of recent years in the study of Archaeology that even at so late a date as that it was a common, if not the prevalent, opinion of Archaeologists that our bronze weapons were Roman.

This view was held by no less distinguished an antiquary than Mr. Thomas Wright, and had recently been strongly urged by him in a learned and interesting memoir. Sir John and his brother showed that bronze weapons were comparatively rare in Italy, that they were seldom found in Northern Europe in association with Roman remains, and that the cases relied on by Mr. Wright were (not through any fault of his) either erroneously reported or at least very doubtful. The most important case mentioned by Mr. Wright was that of two bronze celts described as having been found at Pompeii. In a subsequent visit to Naples Sir John looked them up. They were in the Pompeian collection, but on getting them out of their case he found that they were in their wrong box, and that they were marked as from a tomb in Magna Graecia !

In view of all the later successful development of deep-sea cable laying, a letter from Sir Gabriel Stokes, then Secretary and later President of the Royal Society, is interesting. Sir John had been asked to take part in a company for the laying of a cable from Ireland to America, and knowing that Sir Gabriel (or, as he then was, Professor) Stokes had been consulted on this matter, he wrote to him for advice, eliciting a reply as follows :

LENSFIELD COTTAGE, CAMBRIDGE,
24th March 1866.

MY DEAR LUBBOCK—I only arrived from London this morning, when I found your letter.

I had best explain to you in the first instance my connection with the telegraph matter.

Wheatstone called on me one day at the R.S. and showed me a letter authorising him to appoint a committee consisting of himself, Dr. Miller and me to act as scientific referees in relation to a scheme for establishing telegraphic communication between England and America by the North Atlantic. I had some conversation with him on the subject. He seemed to feel very strongly many advantages which this route offered over the more direct route. With reference to the most obvious objection—the ice—he lent me a pamphlet (not published) containing the opinions of men experienced in Arctic Navigation (such as Sir Leopold M'Clintock) as to the obstacles arising from ice. The formation of the Committee was contingent on the formal establishment of the Company. The scheme is a revival of one started many years ago. I understand from Wheatstone that the formal establishment of the Company depended mainly on the possibility of obtaining certain concessions from the Danish Government, which have now, I believe, been obtained. So I looked on the Company, in my own mind, as virtually established, except as to certain formalities. I was not then aware that the capital had yet to be raised. I should not myself have looked on the raising a capital of £2,000,000, or thereabouts as so light a matter as you City folk seem to regard it. Miller and I both consented to act in case the Company were formed. I am not, however, a shareholder, nor, I believe, is Miller. The promoters urged Wheatstone to let the Committee commence work at experiments, but he declined to act till he got an appointment signed by the directors, not wishing, as he told me, that our names should be mixed up with an undertaking, which, for aught we could be certain at present, might prove only an abortive attempt to raise a company. I feel grateful to him for having acted thus firmly.

The scheme, on the face of it, opining that the ice difficulty is not serious, certainly seems to offer a great advantage in breaking up the route into detachments. It seems a terrible venture to lay 2000 miles at a stretch, when a single flaw would spoil the whole. Supposing the odds 19 to 1 that any given 100 miles would be laid without accident (except such as could be easily repaired), still when you come to 2000 miles the chance of success is only $(\frac{19}{20})$ 20 = .3585, or about 2 to 1 against it. On this account, I think the breaking up into much shorter lengths a very great advantage. The North route has also the advantage of having much less very deep water, in which the risk of laying, from the strain on the cable, is greatest. The cold is favourable to insulation. The rate of signalling can be much greater with a series of shorter lengths (not exceeding 800 miles or so) than in one great length of 2000 miles, when " electrostatic induction " becomes very serious.

There remains the ice. As to this, I don't see what one can do but read the opinions of experienced Arctic voyagers, and use one's common sense. I would have you answer this point for yourself.

I have no doubt Wheatstone would lend you the short pamphlet he lent me.

On the S.W. Coast of Greenland (a little west of the southernmost point), to judge by the accounts, the cable would seem to be well protected by the existence of long fiords with very deep water in the middle, less deep at the two sides, so that any icebergs would ground at the sides, and the cable would lie in the middle. True, there is floe ice 7 feet thick ; but that, Arctic men look on as a trifle. However, you had best read the pamphlet for yourself.

As for myself, I am ready to act as scientific referee if others decide that the scheme shall be tried, but I do not look on myself in any way as a promoter of the undertaking. I have not gone into its merits sufficiently for that, though, as far as I have considered the matter, I think favourably of it.—Believe me, yours very truly,
G. G. STOKES.

Sir John Lubbock, Bart.

In the spring of this year he made an excursion to Vienna with Lady Lubbock and Sir John Evans.

They visited Hallstatt, where they made some excavations, and as the Austrian Government proposed to drop their investigations, he and Sir John Evans arranged with M. Ramsauer, the late Director of the mines, that he should go on with the work on their joint account. This was the origin of the Hallstatt antiquities now at High Elms. The arrangement went on for several years, when the Austrian Government themselves again took the work in hand.

From Vienna Sir John Evans returned to London. Sir John and Lady Lubbock went on to Italy, visiting Florence, Perugia, and Rome, where they saw the Pope bless the people at Easter ; and from Rome they went on to Naples, where he received the news of the great financial panic in London, and immediately returned. He found all quiet again, though there were several more failures.

About the same time he engaged in a friendly discussion with Mr. James Ferguson as to the age of Avebury and Stonehenge, respectively. Mr. Ferguson considered Avebury to be post-Roman, and Stonehenge to be British as late as A.D. 467. Sir John regarded Stonehenge as belonging to the Bronze Age, and Avebury to be the earlier of the two. As regards Avebury Mr. Ferguson based his opinion on the idea that Silbury Hill rested on, and was therefore later than, the Roman Road from Bath to Marlborough. Sir John Lubbock, on the contrary, maintained that after steering straight for Silbury Hill the road ran round it, so that the hill must be older than the road.

The Wiltshire Archaeological Society, naturally taking much interest in the question, appointed a Committee to examine the evidence, and invited Mr. Ferguson and Sir John Lubbock to attend, which they did. The examination took place in October. Two trenches were cut, and evidence was discovered which satisfied Mr. Ferguson that the road diverged, as Sir John had maintained.

It is singular to find him thus early interesting himself in the site of these splendid Druidical monoliths at Avebury, which must have been to Stonehenge, as an old writer says, as a cathedral to a parish church. Later he acquired the hill, with the few remnants of the great stones that the vandalism of the local builders had left, and eventually took his title thence.

His father had left a fine mathematical library at High Elms, and as none of the family were serious students of this science he offered to the Royal Society the choice of such volumes as they might not have in their library. It was an offer the more gratefully accepted on account of the long association of his father with the Society, and of his own more recent relations with it. The rest of the volumes were given to the London Mathematical Society.

In September he and Lady Lubbock attended the British Association meeting at Nottingham. They had lodgings with Mr. and Mrs. Busk, Tyndall and Hirst. He took the Chair at the Red Lion dinner, and at the end of the evening the landlord tendered him 10s., which he said he understood was the subscription, and which he thought it only right he should pay, as he had never enjoyed an entertainment more in his life ! It is to be feared that the Boniface of this noble liberality and appreciative spirit is very nearly extinct.

The " Red Lion " dinners were among the esoteric mysteries of the British Association which did not commonly find their way to the public ear. In a paper of December 1893, there is a passage stating that " the late Professor Tyndall, like Huxley, used to like to relieve his dry scientific studies by indulging in a little unconventional conviviality. They were both members of the Red Lion Club, which was instituted as a protest against dons and donishness in science. With this object the ' Red Lions ' made a point of holding a feast of Spartan simplicity and anarchic constitution, with rites of Pantagruelistic aspect, intermingled with extremely unconventional orations and queer songs by way of counterblast to the official banquets of the British Association."

Mr. Leonard Huxley, in the *Life and Letters of Thomas Henry Huxley* (vol. i. p. 87), writes :

Several letters from 1851 to 1853 help to fill up the outlines of Huxley's life during these three years of struggle. There is a description of the British Association meeting at Ipswich in 1851, with the traditional touch of gaiety to enliven the gravity of its proceedings, and the unconventional jollity of the Red Lion Club (a dining-club of members of the Association), whose palmy days were those under the inspiration of the genial and gifted Forbes. This was the meeting at which Huxley first began his alliance with Tyndall, with whom he travelled down from town, although he does not mention his name in this letter.

Three pages later, in the same volume, there is a quotation from a letter dated July 16, 1851 :

There has been a notice of me in the *Literary Gazette* for last week, much more laudatory than I deserve, from the pen of my friend Forbes. . . .
In the same number is a rich song from the same fertile and versatile pen, which was sung at one of our Red Lion meetings. That is why I want you to look at it, not that you will understand it, because it is full of allusions to occurrences known only in the scientific circles. At Ipswich we had a grand Red Lion meeting ; about forty members were present, and among them some of the most distinguished members of the Association. Some foreigners were invited (the Prince of Casino, Buonaparte's nephew, among others), and were not a little astonished to see the grave professors, whose English solemnity and gravity they had doubtless commented on elsewhere, giving themselves up to all sorts of fun. Among the Red Lions we have a custom (instead of cheering) of waving and wagging one coat-tail (one Lion's tail) when we applaud. This seemed to strike the Prince's fancy amazingly, and when he got up to return thanks for his health being drunk, he told us he was rather out of practice in speaking English, he would return thanks in our fashion, and therefore he gave three mighty waves and wags, to the no small amusement of every one.

It is likely that the newspaper reporter above quoted has touched in his colour just a little too luridly in his " rites of Pantagruelistic aspect." It is possible even that he was no better acquainted than he should be with his Rabelais.

A letter of December 1866 to Lady Lubbock from Mr. Walter Bagehot indicates how novel were the views expressed in *Prehistoric Times.* The following extract will suffice : " I am afraid," he writes, " it will be a very long time before people will give up talking nonsense on *Prehistoric Times*. They have not quite given it up as to present times, and views so new as Sir John's and so entirely contrary to strong traditions will not be thoroughly understood, much less universally accepted, for many years. Argument moves men but very slowly, then there is a great inertia to oppose it."

In 1867 one of his first acts, after appointment as Honorary Secretary to the London Bankers, was to suggest the publication of the Clearing House returns. The Committee agreed to do so, and the following is a copy of the circular which he addressed to all the London Clearing Banks in order to carry out the plan.

LONDON, 7 *Feb*. 1867.

DEAR SIR—The Committee of Bankers at their last meeting passed a resolution that it would be desirable to publish regularly—say once a week—the total amount passing daily through the Clearing House. To effect this, it will only be necessary that the principal Clearing Clerks should enter, on the sheet given to the Inspector, the total of each side of his account, as well as the balance, and that the Country Clearing amount should also be brought in.

The Inspector on duty will then add the amounts together, and thus obtain the total, which, of course, is all that would be of Public interest.

It is not apprehended that any objection will be entertained to the Publication of these daily totals, without which, indeed, our Commercial statistics must always be regarded as deficient, and the Committee therefore hope that the proposal will meet with your approval.

If I do not hear from you to the contrary, I shall conclude that this is the case.—I remain, dear Sir, your very obedient servant,   JOHN LUBBOCK, Hon. Sec.

No difficulty was raised by any Bank, and the publication has been continued ever since.

Mr. Bagehot, who was then brilliantly editing the *Economist*, wrote on the same subject.

My dear Lubbock—I have written to New York for the Reports of the New York Clearing House, and have no doubt I shall get it soon.

I cannot help thinking the publication of the returns of the amounts passing through the Clearing House would be very valuable; . . . both as a guide to the public as to the quantity of business done, and as a *datum* to statistical enquirers in many important problems. I have often heard it lamented that there is nothing later on the subject than Mr. Babbage's antediluvian figures of 1839.

Under date May 27, 1867, he received the following letter from Charles Kingsley, rather belated, in acknowledgment of *Prehistoric Times*:

My dear Lubbock—I have just received, from Macmillan, a copy of your excellent book (*Prehistoric Times*), sent to me on the 20th of May 1865.

This may explain to you why I have never acknowledged it. I had always hoped that you would send me a copy—and was afraid that you had forgotten me. The book must have been in this back shop all the while and I none the wiser. I now thank you heartily. I had, of course, known all about the book by reviews ; but had not had time to read it. I have just been looking into your last chapter, which is excellent and true. I used much the same arguments in 2 lectures at the R.I. last year. But still, I think there is more to be considered, and will some day tell you what I think. I am sure that civilisation does *not* decrease man's inclination to sin—in the true meaning of ἁμαρτία, missing the mark, and falling short of the ideal. Witness the siècle Louis Quatorze, when men did wrong with all their hearts knowing it to be wrong. But the nearer man is to the animals, and the less civilised, and therefore the more the puppet of circumstances, the more your theory (quite true in so far) works, and is a great fact. Cognate with this is the question whether certain races of man are degraded. You think not—(as it seems to me)—I am as certain of it, as we both are that whales are degraded quadrupeds, or Cirrhipods degraded Entomostraca or insects.   I am sure that, side by side with Darwin's true theory of development by natural causes, lies a theory of degradation by the same causes ; which I sketched once in serious jest in the *Water Babies* ; and it will be part of our future work to investigate the methods of Natural Degradation.

But of all this more hereafter.   It was a very great pleasure to meet you again : for I have conceived, for some years past, high hopes of what you will do in Science.   It is a reproach to our House of Commons, that there is not one naturalist, or man of Science in it. And I trust to see you in it some day, to support those claims of common sense and fact, which my once tutor, J. S. Mill, seems for the present to have relegated in favour of the barbarism of Bright.

I was deeply moved at meeting, for the first time, Darwin.   I trembled before him like a boy, and longed to tell him all I felt for him, but dare not, lest he should think me a flatterer extravagant.   But the modesty and simplicity of his genius was charming.   Instead of teaching, he only wanted to learn, instead of talking, to listen, till I found him asking me to write papers which he could as yet hardly write himself—ignorant, in his grand simplicity, of my ignorance, and his own wisdom. And yet of that man Owen said to me—" Darwin is just as good a soul as his grandfather—and just as great a goose."—With kind regards to Lady Lubbock, ever yours sincerely,   C. KINGSLEY.

Kingsley's appreciation of Darwin, expressed in this letter, is of no little interest.   Sir John Lubbock's letters to that great man always express a spirit of something like filial devotion, and there is no question but that those qualities of " modesty and simplicity," which were equally remarkable in Sir John Lubbock as in Darwin himself, were in part the effect in the younger man of the example of the older.

He attended the Dundee meeting of the

British Association, and read a paper " On the Primitive Conditions of Man," which was described by the *Spectator* as " perhaps the most interesting paper of the meeting." On the Sunday he went over to St. Andrews to spend the day with Mr. Robert Chambers, the publisher. Mr. Chambers was a good and ardent golfer, but it is not mentioned that Sir John Lubbock took any interest in the game at that time, though he was to become a keen player in his later life. The extent to which he sacrificed inclination to duty in giving so little time as he did to sport or games has perhaps not been recognised as it should be. In 1902 Mr. Sydney Buxton (now Lord Buxton) published a book of sporting reminiscences and sketches, of which Lord Avebury writes to him :

6 St. James' Square, London, S.W.
5th Nov. 1902.

My dear Sydney—I mean to read your book (*Fishing and Shooting*). Hunting, shooting and fishing interest me only too much. Sometimes I despise myself and at others hope I shall be rewarded for my virtue in giving them up!—Yours affectionately, Avebury.

With regard to the above brief note Lord Buxton observes : " This appears to me to throw a very vivid light on one side of Lord Avebury's character—that of suppression of interest and desire where they would appear likely to interfere with concentration and application elsewhere, in regard to matters to which he wished to apply his mind and energy."

Lord Avebury's life was so full and varied that its story does not readily suggest that any large sacrifice of possible interests and pleasures was

involved in it, but certainly his remarks in this
note to Lord Buxton indicate that he may have
imposed on himself more self-denying ordinances
than we might imagine.

In the same year he was invited by a number
of scientific men to stand for the University of
London. The Committee included Sir George
Airy, the Astronomer Royal; Sir B. Brodie,
Sir D. Brewster, Mr. Busk, Mr. Darwin,
Sir C. Lyell, Professor Max Müller, Sir James
Paget, Sir Andrew Ramsay, Professor Frankland,
President of the Chemical Society; Professor
Graham, Master of the Mint; Sir W. R. Grove,
Sir John Herschel, Professor Hirst, Sir Joseph
Hooker, Professor Huxley, Professor Thorold
Rogers, Professor Sylvester, Professor Tyndall,
Mr. Spottiswoode, Sir W. Thomson (Lord Kelvin),
Professor Sharpey, Mr. Herbert Spencer, Mr. A. R.
Wallace, Mr. Wheatstone, and many others.
Sir W. S. Savory, Dean Farrer, Professor Carey
Foster, Professor Odling, and Dr. P. H. Pye
Smith acted as Secretaries.

He expressly states his appreciation of the
honour of being supported by such a Committee,
comprising all, or nearly all, the most eminent
names in Science—no less than nine Presidents
of the Royal Society. The form of their address
made the honour still more marked.

The University of London, for instance, they
said, " has already rendered the greatest services
both to scientific education in general and
especially to the Profession of Medicine. How
better can it maintain its well-earned reputation
and still further influence the country for good

than by returning as its first member one so well qualified to advocate its own principles ? "

He was not, however, the only candidate. Mr. Lowe and Mr. Bagehot had also strong supporters, both were warm friends of his, and all three being Liberals made any contest all the more distasteful to him. His old friends in West Kent, moreover, were very anxious that he should again fight their battle, and this finally he felt to be his duty.

Later in the year we find him staying with the Grant Duffs at Eden, whence he made a trip, with Mr. Archibald Hamilton, to the Orkneys and Shetlands, returning by " the Parallel Roads of Glenroy." He read a paper on the subject of the " parallel roads " before the Geological Society.

CHAPTER XII

MEMBER OF PARLIAMENT (1868–1870)

(AGE 34–36)

AMONG the correspondence preserved by Sir John Lubbock relating to the year 1868 are two notes, one from Mr. Gladstone and the other from Mr. Disraeli. The former is no more than an invitation to breakfast, but has an interest of its own from the subject of discussion proposed for the breakfast party. A common love of archaeology drew Mr. Gladstone and Sir John together, and the latter notes that they had many a talk in the Division lobbies on this subject. Other guests of the proposed breakfast party were Dr. Percy, the eminent metallurgist; Mr. Layard, etc.; and Mr. Gladstone writes: " I hope to get some further light on the question what was the ' χαλκός ' of Homer." Whether the knotty problem was satisfactorily solved over the tea and toast is not recorded.

χαλκός, the Homeric bronze, if that be the right modern translation of the word, was not so much a commercial as a martial metal, fashioned into the short sword rather than the coin. The letter of Mr. Disraeli touches the question of metal, whether bronze or more precious, as the modern medium of exchange. He writes that " Her Majesty is about to issue a Royal Commission, over which Lord Halifax will preside, to consider the proceedings of the Monetary Conference held in Paris last year, and to report on the adaptability of their suggestions to our own monetary system." Knowing that Sir John had given attention to this subject, Mr. Disraeli asks his consent to a recommendation to the Queen that he should be one of the Commission. Sir John consented, and in due course was elected.

In the same year he was appointed, though a Liberal, by the Conservative Government to act as one of the Public School Commissioners. This Commission was already in being, but a vacancy had been created by the death of one of its members, Sir Edmund Head ; and this vacancy he was called to fill.

In April there was an eruption of Vesuvius, and he started off to see it with Professor Tyndall, Mr. A. Hamilton, and Mr. Robert Birkbeck. They went up twice. Once the mountain was throwing up stones, the second day steam only. He was evidently immensely impressed by it. Fortunately there was a high wind, and they were able to get quite to the edge. Indeed at one place, where the sides were rather sloping, he ventured a little over the edge. Tyndall insisted on roping him, so that they might be able to drag him back if he lost his head !

He returned by way of " Mayence, Dresden,

Berlin, Schwerin, and Hanover, to see the museums."

Later in the same year he was again in Switzerland. As a member of the Public School Commission, it suited his purposes very well to pay a flying visit to the Alps with Dr. Hornby, headmaster of Eton, and Dr. Ridding, head-master of Winchester, so as to have an oppor-tunity of discussing the proceedings of the Commission. He had, however, only nine days to spare for the trip. They went straight to Interlaken, then to Murren, by the Wengern Alp to Grindelwald, then to Trachsellauenan and over the Petersgrat to Ried, from which place he returned by the Lötschen Pass to Kandersteg, and so home by Thun and Bern, where he paid his respects to the skull of his friend Professor Morlot, which had been left to the Bern Museum.

Immediately on his return the West Kent contest began. By mutual arrangement no steps, beyond one preliminary meeting, were taken till the middle of August.

The nomination was on November 19, 1868, on the Vine at Sevenoaks. " Animated, no doubt, by that pure patriotic feeling of which Kentish men are proud, they mustered in hundreds at the nomination, which was held in a cricket-field at Sevenoaks yesterday. The town was made quite gay and bustling by the free exhibi-tion of flags, colours and favours, and by the continuous arrival of well-to-do yeomen in vehicles or on horseback, and by the pouring in of humbler voters on foot. Nearly all wore either the orange and purple rosettes of the Conservatives, or sported the Liberal blue, and all seemed to enter most heartily into the business of the day. Notwithstanding that both the South-Eastern and the Chatham & Dover Companies provided good railway service, the wearers of orange colours stuck to their old traditions, and drove their well-appointed four-in-hands, their pairs, or their traps, up to the Conservative house, and there alighted and fraternised in that 'good old style' which looks so well on paper and sounds so well in speeches." [1]

The election was on the 25th, and the numbers were :

Sir C. Mills	.	.	. 3440
Mr. Talbot	.	.	. 3378
Sir J. Lubbock	.	.	. 3323
Mr. Angerstein	.	.	. 3199

Sir John was beaten, therefore, by the narrow difference of 55 votes out of 10,000 electors. The election was throughout most good-humoured.

He had in preparation a new edition of *Prehistoric Times*, and one of the questions which arose for consideration was the origin of bronze. Professor Wibel, in an elaborate memoir, had suggested that the ores used contained both copper and tin, so that when smelted they gave bronze directly. On this subject he consulted Dr. Percy, the great chemist and high authority on metallurgy—*vide* the extract, above, from Mr. Gladstone's note—and Mr. Vivian, afterwards Lord Swansea, head of one of the greatest

---

[1] *Daily Telegraph*, November 20, 1868.

copper-smelting firms.   They both pronounced
against Professor Wibel's theory.

Mr. Percy wrote that he had paid considerable
attention to the subject of ancient bronze, and
that all the information he had gathered respecting it was directly opposed to Mr. Wibel's view.
He considered that the remarkable uniformity
in the composition of ancient bronze was of
itself sufficient to refute that view.   There was
some variation in the composition, according to
the uses for which the bronze implements were
intended — thus, where greater hardness was
needed, more tin was added—but it was impossible to conceive that anything approximating a
uniformity to the composition of ancient bronze
could have been produced from the smelting
of accidental mixtures of copper and tin ores.
Moreover, in remains of ancient bronze foundries
blocks of copper were found, which were, no
doubt, used in making the alloy by the direct
fusion of the two metals together.

In the same year was started the Metaphysical
Society, and the following letter from Mr. Hutton,
for many years the able editor of the *Spectator*,
describes its genesis.   Sir John was elected its
first President.

THE " SPECTATOR " OFFICE,
1 WELLINGTON STREET, LONDON, W.C.,
1 *July* 1869.

MY DEAR SIR JOHN—I am pledged to a visit to
Brighton on the day you name, and it is one we could
not put off.

It would have been a very great pleasure to me to
have met personally Huxley and Tyndall, whom I have
so long known only by their writings.

With regard to to-day's leader and letter in the
Times on Primogeniture, do you know anything of the

effect of the custom of gavelkind in Kent in altering
either the feelings or habits of the landed class in relation
to Wills ?   It would be a curious point in connection
with the expected discussion.

I cannot tell you how personally grieved I was at the
issue of the West Kent election.

Do you know Mr. Knowles, the architect, a friend of
Tennyson's ?   Tennyson has suggested to him, and he
has been eagerly working out the suggestion, to try and
get up a sort of Royal Society of Psychology and Metaphysics,—to contain men of all theologies and schools,—
in the hope of leading to some fixed science at last.
Manning (the Archbishop), Ward, Roman Catholic
convert, Stanley, Mansel, Martineau, Bagehot, and
many others would start it.   Would you belong to it ?
I hope to do so, and our first meeting would probably
be to discuss whether we should ask the eminent physi-
cists, like Huxley and Tyndall, to join us—which I think
we ought to do.   I hope you would give us your help,
which I was commissioned to ask of you.   It would be
most valuable.—With kind regards to Lady Lubbock,
believe me, my dear Sir John, very truly yours,
                              RICHARD H. HUTTON.

Respecting the original membership of the
Society Sir John has left the following note :

When the Metaphysical Society was started in 1869,
there was some doubt among the promoters whether or
no Huxley and Tyndall should be invited to join.   Mr.
Knowles was commissioned to come and consult me.   I
said at once that to draw the line at the opinions which
they were known to hold would, as it seemed to me,
limit the field of discussion, and there would always be
doubts as to where the forbidden region began ; that I
had understood there was to be perfect freedom, and
that though Huxley's and Tyndall's views might be
objectionable to others of our members, I would answer
for it that there could be nothing in the form of expression
of which any just complaint could be made.

The society consisted of about forty members, and
when we consider that they included Thompson, Archbishop of York ; Ellicott, Bishop of Gloucester and
Bristol ; the Bishop of St. David's, Dean Stanley and

Dean Alford as representatives of the Church of England ;
Cardinal Manning, Father Dalgairns and W. G. Ward
as Roman Catholics ; among statesmen, Gladstone, the
late Duke of Argyll, Lord Sherbrook, Sir M. Grant Duff,
John Morley, Ruskin, as well as Martineau, Tennyson,
Browning, R. H. Hutton, W. Bagehot, Frederick Harrison, Leslie Stephen, Sir J. Stephen, Dr. Carpenter, Sir
W. Gull, W. R. Greg, James Hinton, Shadworth Hodgson,
Lord Arthur Russell, Sir Andrew Clark, Sir Alexander
Grant, Mark Pattison, and W. K. Clifford, it will not be
wondered at that I looked forward to the meetings with
the greatest interest.   I experienced also one of the
greatest surprises of my life.   We all, I suppose, wondered who would be the first President.   No doubt what
happened was that Roman Catholics objected to Anglicans, Anglicans to Roman Catholics, both to Noncon-
formists ; and the different schools of metaphysics also
presented difficulties, so that finally, to my amazement,
I found myself the first President !   The discussions were
perfectly free, but perfectly friendly ; and I quite agree
with Mr. H. Sidgwick, that Huxley was one of the
foremost, keenest, and most interesting debaters, which,
in such a company, is indeed no slight praise.

We dined together, then a paper was read, which had
generally been circulated beforehand, and then it was
freely discussed, the author responding at the close.

One of his warmest supporters during the
contest of 1868 had been Mr. W. Lee, M.P. for
Maidstone. As soon as the fight was over, Mr.
Lee came and proposed to resign his seat in
Sir John's favour, saying that he had been many
years in Parliament, and wished to give a younger
man his turn. Sir John declined absolutely
this generous offer, but on Mr. Lee's pressing it,
said that if he was of the same mind a year afterwards the case would be different. Mr. Lee said
at once that he should return at the end of the
year, and insist on his proposal being accepted.
This he did, and consequently early in 1870 Sir

John stood for Maidstone, his opponent being Mr. Foster White, and after a fair and friendly fight was returned by a majority of 102.

He made his first speech in the House of Commons on April 8, on Military Education, advocating that greater attention should be given to Science. This was partly agreed to at the moment, but it was left for a Committee which sat in 1902 to urge the very changes that he had advocated thirty years before.

A few extracts from this, his first effort in the House, may be given as a specimen of the simple unaffected mode of eloquence by which, in the long course of his political life, he was destined to get very many Acts passed by the Legislature. The report begins as follows :

" Sir John Lubbock, who had given notice to call attention to the Report of the Military Education Commission, especially with relation to the discouragement which it gives to the study of natural and physical science, said, that considering the short time during which he had had a seat in that House, he ought perhaps to apologise for bringing forward a question of so much importance. The Commission was appointed in 1868 to inquire into the state of Military Education, and they had recently made their Report, which he did not intend to criticise in any hostile spirit, because he was fully aware how greatly the country was indebted to them for investigating this most important subject. The Commissioners had recommended that certain changes should be made in the examinations for direct commissions." He proceeded to institute a comparison between the present and the proposed new distribution of marks over the various subjects set in the military examinations, the result of his analysis showing that the new suggestions tended to a decrease, rather than increase, in the value assigned to science. " Of late years," he said, " the big schools had been doing rather more science teaching, but he had the express testimony of the masters of the great public schools at Eton and Winchester that, if the scheme of the Commissioners were carried into effect, it would strongly tend to discourage their promotion of scientific instruction. Like Lord Chatham and Sir Richard Strahan the public schools had been waiting for the Universities, and the Universities had been waiting for the public schools ; both, he was happy to say, were now moving in the right direction, and it would be very unfortunate if Parliament sanctioned the recommendations of the Military Education Commissioners, who desired to take a step backwards." He passed to the course of instruction at Woolwich and at Sandhurst, showing that under the proposed scheme even less attention than at present would be paid to science, and none whatever to chemistry at either establishment. " At Sandhurst there was geology, but there was none at Woolwich. It was strange that the subject should be omitted, seeing that it was of such great importance, and that military men—he need only mention Portlock and Murchison— had laboured in it so successfully. The ' book- worm ' objection did not apply to the science,

for to acquire it a man must do something more
than read books. He would call the attention
of the House to answers given by Major-General
Napier and the Duke of Cambridge on the value
of scientific attainments. Lord de Ros asked
Major-General Napier :

> Is not chemistry becoming of more daily advantage
> and importance, both to the Artillery and to the
> Engineers ? He answered—Yes ; and it is taught at
> Woolwich very successfully. The Duke of Cambridge
> was asked—Perhaps scientific attainments should be
> regarded as one qualification among several ? His
> Royal Highness replied—Most assuredly ; and I should
> like to see them extended as much as possible : but I
> think that a happy combination of both is what we
> should strive at.

As regarded geology, he might call attention
to two or three cases, in order to illustrate its
importance to officers. Portsdown great fort
was built on the summit of a chalk ridge, on
what geologists called an anticlinal axis. The
strata sloped in each direction away from the
summit ; a very deep well had been sunk here ;
but as the rain which fell on the hill drained away
along the line of the strata, this was the worst
possible place for such a purpose. When the
military authorities were building the College
at Sandhurst, they had a quantity of bricks
made in the Blackwater Valley of river alluvium.
These consequently fell to pieces, and others
had to be made. Along our South Coast, groins
were placed to arrest the movement of the
shingle caused by the prevalent winds and tides.
The Military Engineers were ordered to set
groins on the Dover coast, and they slanted

them the wrong way, so helping the shingle on. Some of the forts on our Southern Coast having been built on yielding strata had given way, and though the damage might be repaired, it had caused great expense; and, unfortunately, would probably continue to do so. When our Army went to the Crimea, Sir Roderick Murchison applied to the Government to send out a geologist, but that request was not complied with. An unhealthy position was chosen for our troops in the Crimea from the want of a scientific acquaintance with the geological conformation of the ground. Sir John Burgoyne wrote home to Sir Roderick Murchison to ask whether, if an artesian well were sunk, a supply of water could be obtained for the Army. Sir Roderick replied that it was impossible to answer such a question here without a proper knowledge of the nature of the ground; but that if there had been a geologist on the spot with the Army, he would have been able to answer it. He (Sir John Lubbock) did not allude to these facts with any view of criticising the Royal Engineers. It would be easy to quote similar mistakes on the part of Civil Engineers. He wished, however, to show the importance of geological knowledge in military operations. There could be no doubt, then, that there were cases in which a knowledge of chemistry and geology would be extremely useful to our forces in the field; and, moreover, in addition to these practical advantages, the value of the mental training given by the study of natural science was most important. Then, what was a proper system to adopt? By his

Resolution he only asked that they should leave things in *statu quo* as far as science was concerned ; but he confessed he should be glad to see a large step made in a direction the opposite of that recommended by the Royal Commissioners. No man could be deemed properly educated unless he had some acquaintance with all the great departments of human knowledge. He was not advocating the teaching of a smattering of those different departments of knowledge, but the well-grounding of students in them. . . . He did not wish to discourage classics, and he maintained that, even in this respect, our present system was very unsatisfactory in its results ; indeed, it was impossible to teach them with advantage as long as other things were not taught with them ; for the human mind, like the human body, required a variety in its nourishment. He certainly thought that too much time was devoted to verses. Here were some of the lines set for the boys to turn into Latin :

Thou, midmost of our world, I narrate wonders,
Rulest stars, lest they should wander, laws being broken.

And again :

The fiery steed, his tail in air proudly cocked,
Not without much neighing, traverses glad pastures.

Such lines would be familiar to all hon. Members who had been educated at our public schools ; but no man would ever be made a poet by translating such verses into Latin. After thanking the House for the patience with which it had listened to him, the hon. Baronet concluded by moving his Resolution :

That it is not desirable to diminish the value hitherto attached to natural and physical science and the English language in the examinations for direct commissions and for admission to the military educational institutions, nor to lessen the importance of those subjects in the subsequent course of instruction and examinations."

On May 18 Her Majesty was pleased to issue a Royal Commission to enquire and report on Scientific Instruction and the advancement of Science, under the Presidency of the Duke of Devonshire. Sir John was nominated a member of the Commission, his other colleagues being Lord Lansdowne, Sir A. Kay Shuttleworth, Sir B. Samuelson, Dr. Sharpey, Professor Huxley, Dr. Miller, and Professor (afterwards Sir) G. G. Stokes, with Mr. Lockyer as Secretary. Dr. Miller died in the same year, and Professor H. J. Smith was nominated in his place.

The first Bill of his own introduction was read a third time on July 16 at half-past five in the morning. The object was to deal with absconding debtors. It was found that after the first proceedings in bankruptcy were taken, debtors, especially foreigners, often absconded with all their property, leaving nothing for their creditors, and the object was to secure a summary process by which they could be prevented from leaving the country until they were made bankrupt, and their property was secured.

It was this summer that he played in the two cricket matches for the Houses of Parliament, referred to in Mr. Philip Norman's account in a previous chapter. Against Harrow he got 25 not out, against I Zingari 13. The *Echo*, in reporting the latter match, wrote:

There were neither Princes nor Dukes to represent the Houses of Parliament; but there were plenty of earls, a sprinkling of marquises, and a single baronet, to break the fall between the peers and commoners. That baronet was Sir John Lubbock, who did some capital execution with his left hand, scoring 13 runs. There was some doubt on the part of one or two of the fair visitors as to the possibility of the tall gentleman in the Glengarry being really the same Sir John who had written a book on Prehistoric Man, was an F.R.S., and ought, therefore, to look more of a feeble and careworn student than did this tall and "robust" politician. But, after all, they had only to glance down the card in their hand to recognise several well-known names of men who had been dealing with the Land Bill, and had but recently crushed the Deceased Wife's Sister.[1]

Just about this time, so far as can be discovered, the doctors advised Sir John to let his beard grow, as a protection to his throat, which had begun to show some slight sign of weakness. Perhaps in this new development the cricket reporter might have found an aspect more in keeping with that of the savant which he had seemed to expect.

With his entry into Parliament we see Sir John at length arrived at the position in which he was to carry out the threefold main activities of his wonderfully full life as man of business, man of science, and legislator. Of necessity he was obliged, devoting the attention that he did to social legislation, to give less time to his scientific pursuits, though he still followed them with a thoroughness only possible to a man who had brought to a scientific perfection the economy of time. I have been very glad to be able to include in this volume the several letters already quoted

---

[1] *South Eastern*, July 13, 1870.

from the greatest men in science, showing the credit that they assign to him for absolutely original work. Lord Avebury has paid something of the penalty that fame always exacts from a man of varied pursuits. By those who know nothing, it has been deemed impossible that one so versatile could do really valuable and first-hand work in any one department. How untrue that is in his case has been already shown in these pages, so far as science is concerned, and both as regards his business and his legislation will be proved to be no less untrue in the further course of the volume.

There are two notes in his own hand stating his main objects in desiring a seat in Parliament. He states these objects under three headings. " (1) To promote the study of Science, both in Secondary and Primary schools; (2) To quicken the repayment of the National Debt; and (3) To secure some additional holidays, and to shorten the hours of labour in shops." That is one, the more concise statement. The other, evidently later written, runs as follows : " When I was first invited to become a candidate for Parliament I naturally asked myself what use I could be if I should succeed in obtaining a seat, and I thought that perhaps as there were so few scientific men in the House (Mr. Poulett-Scope being almost the only one) I might be useful on scientific questions ; that my practical experience of business might, in the second place, be of some use ; thirdly, I was very anxious to carry a measure to prevent the then rapid destruction of ancient Monuments, and lastly, to secure some holidays and some shortening of hours for the most hardly-worked classes of the community.

" As a matter of fact, I succeeded beyond my utmost expectations as regards the Bank Holiday Bill, which met with practically no opposition. Again, some years afterwards, I had the happiness of seeing the Ancient Monuments Bill placed upon the Statute Book. The shortening of the hours of labour in shops, which seems to me to be one of the Reforms now most urgently needed, has hitherto made little progress. In 1866, indeed, I was fortunate enough to carry a Bill which provided that no young person under 18 should be worked more than 74 hours in the week, and with the co-operation of the Early Closing Associations, and the similar bodies throughout the kingdom, I believe I am right in saying that now, the tradesmen's associations almost unanimously are in favour of the Early Closing Bill. There is, I think, therefore every hope that ere long it will become law, although as yet the opposition of a few members has prevented us from carrying it beyond the Committee stage, and with the present rules of the House of Commons we are not very sanguine of making further progress until we can induce the Government to take the matter up."

CHAPTER XIII

" ST. LUBBOCK'S DAY " (1871)

(AGE 37)

FEW men, perhaps, have entered Parliament
with views so clearly cut or so well considered
in respect of their aims and projects; to few,
probably, has it been given to go into that high
assembly with such pure and unselfish ideals;
but very certainly it has been the fortune of
a very small minority to carry through so large a
proportion of the legislative proposals which they
have put forward.

At the time of his death one of the great
daily papers wrote of him :

" In Lord Avebury there has been removed
one of the most accomplished of England's
amateur men of science, one of the most prolific
and successful authors of his time, one of the
most earnest of social reformers, and—what is
not perhaps generally known—one of the most
successful law-makers in the recent history of
Parliament."

Comprehensive as this brief appreciation is,
it yet passes by one very important sphere of
his activity—the financial, for he was not only

eminently successful in the ordinary conduct of the banking business which came to him as a heritage, but carried through many reforms and exercised a preponderant influence in such large and important operations as those undertaken by the Council of Foreign Bondholders—to name but one of many instances.   The point, however, to which I would draw attention, and for the sake of which I have given the above quotation, is contained in its final clause and in the absolutely just statement that he was " one of the most successful law makers in the recent history of Parliament."   As the writer says, this is one of the aspects of his very various achievement which has not been realised as it should be.

Partly it is on account of the diversity of his gifts and activities that his success as a passer of laws has not been gauged at its true rate, but also, in perhaps larger measure, because party politics never made a really keen appeal to him.   He was deeply interested in measures which he considered useful for the social economy, but except as it affected the passage of these Bills through Parliament, he was seldom profoundly troubled whether the party to which he lent his adherence, or its political opponents, happened to be in power.   When Mr. Gladstone's Home Rule proposals divided the Liberal Party it became incumbent on him to define his line, but that decision does not invalidate the truth of the above statement.

This singular success as law-maker, as passer of measures through the House, we may ascribe to three special qualities of his mind and character apart from the more general gifts of clear vision and exceptional talent—first, to the high respect in which he was personally held by all who knew him in the House, whether on his own side or in opposition, secondly, to his unwearied industry, and thirdly to his unconquerable optimism. It has always appeared to me singularly appropriate that so much of his attention should have been bestowed on the study of those social insects, the bees and ants, which have been ever accepted as types and models of industry. One who was associated with him in a scheme which he worked through to a triumphant conclusion has spoken to me with amazement of the number of letters that he wrote, of the various avenues through which he made his approaches sure, of the scrupulous care to leave no possible detail untouched, no possible helper uncourted. His campaigns were as complete as any ever planned by Napoleon in regard to the care which he took to leave nothing to chance.

And his optimism gave him the courage, if defeated at one point, at once to shift the direction of his attack, and with a rare dexterity and suppleness begin to move on a new front towards the end which he had proposed, and which his tenacity of purpose would never abandon while there was the most remote possibility of victory.

As for the personal regard in which he was held, that is a point which need not be insisted on or elaborated. It was as inevitable as it was universally accorded. Any personal advantage or self-seeking was so transparently absent from any of the measures which he advocated with

ability and success, that any personal bitterness
on the part of even their keenest opponents was
an impossibility.

In spite of, or conceivably by reason of, his
recent election to Parliament, there are few years
which are marked by such scanty records of his
untiring industry as those at which we have now
arrived. He would seem not to have found the
time to write the record. In 1870 he had published his important work on the *Origin of
Civilisation,* which had a great success. His
British publishers write :—" We have sold 725
copies already (1000 printed), besides the 75
presentation copies !! This is grand ! We have
sent to the printers to ascertain how much they
still have in type, for I think there can be no
doubt of our having soon to reprint."

We may venture to see in this, his second large
book on the early condition of man, an advance
on that earlier volume, *Prehistoric Times.* The
latter had been more closely concerned with facts
and data ; in the new work he indulges far more
freely in deduction and speculation as to primitive
man's initial mastery of the forces of nature and
his experiments in sociology and religion. In
regard to the last Sir John was disposed to give
a very large place to dreams as the source of religious suggestion and conjecture to man in the
first phases of his evolution. " What happens,"
he imagines the savage asking himself, " to the
spirit during sleep ? The body lies lifeless, and
the savage not unnaturally concludes that the
spirit has left it. In this he is confirmed by the
phenomena of dreams, which consequently to

the savage have a reality and an importance which we can scarcely appreciate. During sleep the spirit seems to desert the body ; and as in dreams we visit other localities and even other worlds, living, as it were, a separate and different life, the true phenomena are not unnaturally regarded as the complements of one another. Hence the savage considers the events in his dreams to be as real as these of his waking hours, and hence he likes to feel that he has a spirit which can quit the body. 'Dreams,' says Burton, 'according to the Yorubans (West Africa) and to many of our fetichists, are not an irregular action and partial activity of the brain, but so many revelations brought by the manes of the departed.' So strong was the North American faith in dreams that on one occasion, when an Indian dreamt he was taken captive, he induced his friends to make a mock attack on him, to bind him and treat him as a captive, actually submitting to a considerable amount of torture, in the hope thus to fulfil his dream. The Greenlanders also believe in the reality of dreams, and think that at night they go hunting, visiting, courting, and so on. It is of course obvious that the body takes no part in these nocturnal adventures, and hence it is natural to conclude that they have a spirit which can quit the body."

The effect of the book was to enhance his already very considerable reputation in the scientific world.

In the autumn of 1870 he had attended the meeting of the British Association at Liverpool, where he gave a lecture to the Working Men, and relates that one night in the course of this visit the police had conducted him and Professor Huxley round the poorest parts of Liverpool, and showed them how they carried out their duties of inspection. As far as he and Huxley could judge, the duties were well and conscientiously discharged ; but they could not help regretting the necessity. The laws against overcrowding, for instance, involved the right of entering bedrooms in the dead of the night, and it was easy to see how such functions might be used as an engine of oppression or corruption. So far, however, as they could see from the way the police were everywhere received, there was no reason to suspect anything of the kind.

In the commencement of 1871 he had a high honour paid him, on the suggestion of Professor Huxley, to which he had no option but to assent, that he should be first president of the newly formed Anthropological Institute.

" MY DEAR LUBBOCK," Huxley writes, " The Anthropological Society and the Ethnological Society are defunct, and out of their ashes is to arise a Phœnix— hight the ' Anthropological Institute of Great Britain and Ireland.'

" Putting both together there will be something over five hundred paying members, and a debt of about £1100 to £1200, one third of which (roughly) belongs to the Ethnological, and two-thirds to the Anthropological.

" We have taken the Council of the new body, half from one society and half from the other—and altogether I think that the arrangement is a very fair one.

" When we began to discuss the question of the President it was clear that the Anthropological did not want me (I had been led to suppose they did).

" So I, at once, withdrew my name from any further discussion—and proposed yours. At this there was the greatest satisfaction, and I do earnestly hope you will accept the office.

" I think it is a very much better arrangement than taking the President of either Society for the new body ; and personally, as you know, I am only too glad to be out of it.

" Busk, Evans and myself are nominated Vice-Presidents, so you will not lack support, and as we have retained the Anthropological Director, you really will have no particular trouble.

" If you have no very strong reasons the other way, do accept, as a favour to me.—Ever yours very faithfully,

" T. H. HUXLEY."

To this letter, which seems to have taken him completely by surprise, he replied :

THE ATHENÆUM, 26th January 1871.

MY DEAR HUXLEY—I am taken quite aback by your letter. You know that I would do anything in this matter to please you, but you really ought to be our first President, and I could not take a place which on all accounts is properly yours.

Is the name definitely settled ? If we must swallow Anthropology, I should like " Society " after it better than anything else.

Institute seems to me rather pretentious. However, this is in your hands.—Ever, dear Huxley, yours most sincerely,   JOHN LUBBOCK.

It appeared, however, that his name was the only one on which all concerned could agree, and he felt it, therefore, a duty as well as an honour to accept.

On March 7 he seconded a motion for the reduction of the National Debt, a measure which, as noted, was one of his motives for wishing to enter Parliament. Mr. Lowe, then Chancellor of the Exchequer, complimented him on his speech and promised to do something to support the measure in the Budget. He subsequently urged the same course on several other occasions ; and observes, at a much later date, that in the South African War we felt the great advantage of having reduced our debt in times of peace.

He also spoke on the Budget, on the Endowed Schools, and on Elementary Education, urging that History, Geography, English, and Elementary Science should be included in the curriculum. The suggestion was at that time regarded as revolutionary and almost impossible, but is now to some extent carried out, with great advantage and general approval.

Assuredly Sir John Lubbock wasted no time, after his election to Parliament, in prosecution of those proposals which it was his intention to bring forward should he ever get a seat in that assembly. Most intimately and most universally his name is associated with that measure for obtaining holidays for the bank clerks and shop people which is known by the title of the Bank Holidays' Act. These holidays have been styled St. Lubbock's Days, and probably he is better known to the populace of Great Britain in this connection, than by any other act of his life.

The third reading of the Bill passed on May 15. His Journal shows that it was a very varied day, and indicates how fully his time was occupied.

Beginning with the beginning—an hour on the Army Regulation Bill, then to bed at 1.30. At nine breakfasted at the Athenaeum ; at 10 to the Public School Commission, where we discussed the Eton statutes. Then I went for a short time to the Court of Queen's Bench where the Tichborne case is going on. Sir Roger is a large coarse-looking man. Then to poor Sir John Herschel's funeral. I was one of the Pall-bearers, with the Duke of Devonshire, the Duc de Broglie, Sir E. Sabine, President of the Royal Society ; Sir H. Holland, President of the Royal Institution ; Sir C. Lyell ; Mr. Lassell, President of the Astronomical Society, and the Astronomer Royal. The service was very impressive, all the leading scientific men were there. Then I went to the Science Committee; then to the House of Commons, where we had two divisions on the Westmeath Bill. We dined at Cecil Chaplin's, where we spent the night. The Chaplins themselves were dining out, so we had a pleasant *tête-à-tête*. Then we went to the Queen's Ball, after which I dressed again, and down to the House. Lastly, at two this morning, I got the House to consider the Lords' amendments to the Bank Holiday Bill, though it had only this evening come down from the Lords, and also to adopt them, so that the Bill now only wants the Queen's consent, which we shall no doubt get in time for Whit Monday. The House was very kind, and would no doubt have been counted out, if the Government had not kept a House to get my Bill through.

The following comment, in Sir John's own hand, is interesting both in itself and as a reply to the assertion which has sometimes been made that it was only by an accident in the wording of the draft of the Bill that its provisions were made to apply to any other people than those engaged in banking. His own words show that this was not the case, but that its wide scope was part of his original design. And at the same time he replies to certain criticism levelled at the universal character of the holiday by those who have thought that it would have been better had it been more partial. The explanation of the name given to the Bill is also fully set out :

As regards the Bank Holiday I will only say that I never intended it to apply solely to banks. In fact the Bill expressly provides that nobody shall be compellable

to do anything on a Bank Holiday which he cannot be
compelled to do on Xmas Day or Good Friday. The
term Bank Holiday was used for a technical reason ;
on other holidays, Bills of Exchange are payable the
previous day. On our holidays on the following day.
Now if we had used the expression " General " or
" National," the provision would have been doubtful,
and we therefore chose the special distinguishing term
" Bank Holiday."

The Act, we always hoped and believed, would be
generally adopted, and I have always believed that our
August Bank Holiday would become *the* great National
Holiday.

It is sometimes said that it would be much better if
some establishments had one holiday and some another.
This, I believe, is entirely a mistake.

On the contrary, it is a great advantage that the
holidays are the same for all, because friends and
relations, occupied very often in different establishments,
all get the same day, can make their plans beforehand,
and enjoy their holiday together.

It is remarkable that these holidays were the first
ever instituted by any legislature for the enjoyment and
relaxation of the people.

Every one was surprised that the Bill passed
so easily. Sir D. Salmon, M.P. for Greenwich,
and Chairman of the London and Westminster
Bank, told him that it had not a chance. Mr.
Martin Tucker Smith of Messrs. Smith Payne's
told him that he had spoken to Disraeli about
it, who promised to think it over and consult his
colleagues, but finally said the difficulties were so
great that the Government could not undertake
the task.

The enthusiastic delight with which the populace received the measure which brought them
these hours of liberty, may best be estimated
by a glance at some of the articles in the daily
and other papers of the day. Irrespective of

class or of politics the chorus of approval was full and unanimous. It was the *Daily Telegraph* that first suggested the name of St. Lubbock's Day for the holiday.

" The people," the writer said, " may forget a great many deeds of glory and names of renown ; but they will never forget him who has given them a new and universal day of repose and recreation."

The following vivid account of the first Bank Holiday is given by *The News of the World* :

Blessings upon the head of Sir John Lubbock, who invented a decent excuse for holidays to Englishmen. We never wished for a revival of Saints' days, but we did certainly wish that some great inventive genius could discover a reason why the people should not work all the year round, Sundays, Good Fridays, and Christmas days excepted. Well, Sir John Lubbock was scientific enough to invent Bank Holidays, and hence on Monday thousands of Her Majesty's subjects were able to enjoy themselves. It was a surprise to everybody, for thousands of employers acted in the most generous manner, and waived any little technical objection as to the right. For instance, the Act says that no one shall be called upon to pay any sum or to do any act which he cannot be compelled to do on Sunday or Good Friday. These words admit of a very wide interpretation, and they would seem to include all the Queen's subjects, for no man can be compelled by law to work on Sunday. Be that as it may, the employers acted with great generosity on Monday, and so tens of thousands of people were released from work to make a demand upon the railway companies and the steamboats which surprised stationmasters and river captains. From 8 A.M. the cry at every railway station was, " Still they come ! " and the supply of passengers very far exceeded the supply of accommodation. At the Fenchurch Street Station there was a crowd of hundreds struggling for tickets to Margate and Southend, and it is said that the vessels from Thames Haven only reached Margate jetty at 4 P.M., whilst the railway bills announced the return of the steamers to Thames Haven at 3.30 P.M.

The passengers were packed on decks and paddle-boxes like herrings in a barrel, and so great was the hunger of the crowd on board one of the vessels that the steward declared himself to be " eaten out " in ten minutes after the vessel left Thames Haven. Margate Jetty was simply blocked so far as to be impassable, whilst thousands of the excursionists who came down by rail wandered along the cliffs. How many may have gone down it is impossible to say. The people arrived at Cannon Street and Charing Cross for Ramsgate at 8 A.M., and it was 10 o'clock before the surprised but very active officials of the South Eastern could accommodate all their customers. Seven " specials " were sent from Cannon Street, and probably as many more from Ludgate Hill. It was simply impossible to get to the seaside, for at Fenchurch Street one clerk and one ticket-window only were supplied, and the struggle to get to it promised too probable an attack upon either your ribs or your pockets to enable you to venture. At the river-side the last steamer to Sheerness was crowded to excess, and there were hundreds continuing to arrive, in the hopeless expectation of being carried somewhere by water. Vain expectation ! An ingenious individual suggested a reference to the advertisements of the daily papers, and there was an advertisement in which there seemed to be a hope that you might be conveyed " by certain trains " to Henley - on - Thames and the pleasant neighbourhoods of Windsor and Tap-low. . . . There was a train to Shepperton, near to Weybridge, dear to the lover of the gentle craft. . . . On the river there were here and there to be seen the patient disciples of Isaak Walton, seated in chairs with a rod in their hands, " a worm at one end " and a philosopher of course at the other. There was not a rod nor a punt to be had for love nor money. " Bless you, sir, if I liked I could have had forty jobs to-day," said the eminently skilful puntsman to whom we applied at first. Never was such a day in this quiet region, and so unexpected to the inhabitants. There was no tobacco to be had, and even the public-houses were destitute of an article so essential to the comfort of some people. . . . It is impossible to rate overmuch the blessing of the holiday of the 7th of August, and there were doubtless numerous proposals for the presentation of a testimonial in the form of a silver type of Darwin's ape to Sir John Lubbock, the great author of the holiday. Sir John has shown himself to be an inventor of the highest order, and his great reputation as a man of science has been enhanced by the invention of Bank Holidays. The people did him honour on Monday, for on all sides we heard blessings invoked upon him and his. The reflection ought to be a proud one in the mind of Sir John Lubbock, for he has added—substantially added—to the sum of human happiness, and has carried rays of hope and joy into humble households so great as to rank him high as a public benefactor.

It is a little difficult for us, accustomed as we now are to the crush and congestion of Bank Holiday traffic, to realise the surprise that it created when it was all novel.

Bell's Life said :

A Statute Holiday !   A holiday by Act of Parliament ! Well, if loyalty is to be measured by a nation's submission to legislative behests, this country, and more particularly the Londoners, are steeped to the chin in obedience. Sir John Lubbock, a name memorable in natural history, and one to whom we owe an admirable treatise upon the Fauna, fish and fowl of Norfolk,[1] has never issued a more sterling note across his counter than in this piece of paper which commands, in the name of Her Majesty, as the great cashier of her people's happiness, that they, the Queen's lieges, shall each and severally accept draughts of health and coin of pleasure unlimited in exchange for toil and vitiated air. Thus has a real and unqualified summer holiday blossomed into existence, and it may be said the only one we have, for the other escape days are in spring and winter. This holiday is, indeed, an outer (an out-and-outer), as Christmas Day may be considered a family fire-side festival, and Easter and Whit-Monday are too often shrouded in mists or visited with cold easterly winds to deserve altogether the holy name of holy-day. If, therefore, the merits of this act, as all other acts are

---

[1] A mistake. The treatise in question was by the Reverend H. Lubbock, a distant relation.—H. G. H.

judged, is to rest upon its success, thus far it has proved itself a boon beyond price." [1]

The *Daily News* was no less appreciative on the second birthday of the holiday :

How much such a day of relaxation was needed, its universal acceptance proves. This is only the second year of its establishment, yet all London has prepared to keep it. Business will stand still in the City to-day. The Banks, warehouses, and offices will all be closed and the shops shut. In the West-end and in the chief thoroughfares the principal shops will follow the example of the banks, and so general is the disposition to make holiday that an enterprising pawnbroker thinks it needful to advertise that his establishment will remain open. It is perhaps difficult for the general public to realise what such a holiday means. There are thousands in this great City who are at work all the year round. The shops and warehouses are kept open by relays of attendants. In many of the larger of them the humbler employés may have—like the postmen—a fortnight's holiday in the year ; but to vast multitudes only a day of closing brings a chance of release. We have given publicity of late to scores of appeals from philanthropic persons for help to give groups of school children " a day in the fresh air." This statute holiday gives a day in the fresh summer air—and let us hope in the bright summer sunshine—to tens of thousands of persons who might otherwise altogether miss the sight of the yellow corn-fields or the summer woods.[2]

" All other popularity," said the *Daily Telegraph*, " in arms, arts, song, or statesmanship, was as nothing on Monday last compared with that of Sir John Lubbock. If there had been a question that day of electing some one to any office whatsoever, from the Lord High Admiralty of England to the Archbishopric of Canterbury, and Sir John had only stood for it, the women and children of London, let alone its citizens, would have elected him by acclamation." [3]

---

[1] *Bell's Life*, August 12, 1871.
[2] *Daily News*, August 5, 1872.
[3] *Daily Telegraph*, May 22, 1872.

From Sir Lyon Playfair he received a very appreciative letter, of which the following extract sufficiently explains itself :

I had an enthusiastic deputation to-day (Sunday) of Bankers' Clerks, wishing me to take part in a movement to get up a testimonial to you of " *A Million Shillings* " for your Holiday Act.

I told them of my friendly feeling to you, and counselled them in the first place to show the grateful feelings of Bankers' Employés, before they put you in a position of taking a National Testimonial which might not be agreeable to your feelings, and might be misunderstood.

I was assured by the deputation that the Act " will alter the National Character of England and of English Society," so you have thorough appreciation of your good work.

The testimonial was presented to him at a crowded meeting held in the National Provincial Bank, and presided over by Mr. M'Kewan of the London and County Bank.

It is not given to many men in the world's history to receive blessings so unmixed for an act of legislature. Moreover, he was but thirty-seven years of age and had just entered Parliament.

In the same year he introduced a Bill to provide for the better preservation of Ancient Monuments, and received a moderately encouraging letter from Mr. Lowe, saying that he had consulted the Cabinet and found that there was much sympathy with the objects of the Bill, but that they hardly deemed them to justify assistance from public money. The opinion seemed to be that the strong feeling in favour of the proposal, which exists in the country, would make it easy to form a society (which might be incorporated under the Supplemental Clause of the Limited Liability Act), and that it would be quite regular to give such a society all the powers requisite for the protection of the objects contemplated in the Bill. Mr. Lowe adds that he is sure there is plenty of money to be got from private sources for the purpose proposed, and that he would be happy in his private capacity to give help.

Sir John also brought in a Bill to amend the Endowed Schools Act. This was done with the full knowledge and approval of the Commissioners, as will be seen by a letter, shortly to be quoted, from Lord Hobhouse, who gave him a number of instances showing the necessity for the changes suggested. He rose to move the second reading with the conviction that he had a strong and unanswerable case, but before he had said many sentences a piece of paper was put into his hand with the words :

I must beg as a personal favor that you will not use any of the facts I have given you.   HOBHOUSE.

He himself admits that this took him quite aback, cut the ground from under his feet, and wrecked the Bill. " It appeared," he writes, " that Forster, who was Vice-President of the Council, sent for Hobhouse in the morning to consult him as to what he should say in opposition to the Bill. He told Forster the facts he had given me, and Forster said if they came out he had no answer ; that I ought not to have been told, and that at any cost I must be prevented from using them ! I believe that according to etiquette Hobhouse ought not to have given me information without Forster's knowledge.   However, I had supposed Forster would have supported me.   What I felt most was that Forster in his speech, having deprived me of my facts at the last moment, said that I had not shown any practical grievances which the Bill would remove ! "

The following is Lord Hobhouse's letter, above referred to.

16 DEVONSHIRE PLACE, W.,
January 18, 1871.

MY DEAR SIR JOHN — I send you some remarks on those defects of the Endowed Schools' Act on which you wish to fasten.   I hope you will not feel like Hamet, who prayed for water and had the Tigris turned through his garden.   The subject embraces a long period of history, and endless ramifications of detail, and if one labours to be brief, we become obscure.

I have a very strong feeling, and a very clear opinion, about these matters, and should be delighted if you could succeed.   I suspect, however, that you will not, first, because the sons of Zeruiah are still too strong for us ;   secondly, because many men will say, not unreasonably, that the subject is a very contentious and irritating one, that it was settled on an intelligible basis in 1869 after much discussion, and that we ought at least to see how this works in practice before we alter it.

Forster objects also that a simple repeal of sec. 19 will expose to invasion a purely private endowment never intended to have any national character : such as my friends, the Southertians, if they existed and had a school.   On my principles this would be no objection, but they do not prevail, and the difficulty is one likely to be felt, and should be considered.

It must be remembered, too, that sec. 19 was reckoned as fair at the time.   It is a great advance on the recommendations of the Report ; and *that* its formers thought bold, though it always seemed to me a very timid utterance on these matters.

I am disposed to think that an attack in front must

fail; but that one practical object may be gained (except as regards Cathedrals) by a flank movement ostensibly directed against the Ilminster case, or rather against the principle affirmed in that case.

I quite agree, in principle, with your suggestions as to sec. 14; only sub-sections 3 and 4 are very little harm, and sub-section 1 will not hurt much for some time to come.

Will it not be useful for you to have some conversation with me after you have read and digested (if you can read and digest) my remarks? The best and quietest way of discussing these matters is over our cups, and if you could come quite quietly to dinner with me some day, I shall be glad to see you. If this is inconvenient to you, perhaps you could drop in at the E.S.C. some day when business brings you into that quarter.

I am sorry to have been so long in writing to you, but have been very much occupied, and now I send you a mere rough draft, just as it is written off. I have no copy, so be kind enough to return it, as it will be useful some day for reference. The remarks on Cathedral schools are, so far as I know, new. At least they have never been uttered in public; and I should like to reconsider them carefully before giving utterance to them myself.—Very truly yours, ARTHUR HOBHOUSE.

On July 21 he proposed a motion for introducing History, Geography, and Elementary Science into Elementary Schools. The Whip was issued, signed amongst others by Lord Playfair, Mr. Mundella, W. H. Smith, Thos. Hughes, Sam. Morley, G. Dixon, Russel Gurney, and W. Cowper Temple, but the motion was not carried.

It might hardly seem conceivable that in a year so fully occupied as this with legislative activity, he should yet have time to bestow on his scientific hobbies. Nevertheless, we find him writing a book for Messrs. Macmillan's Nature Series on the Metamorphoses of Insects.

The following letter contains Darwin's comments after the perusal of the proof sheets :

HAREDENE ALBURY, GUILDFORD,
August 12, 1871.

MY DEAR LUBBOCK—You will see where we are, and where we remain for 3 weeks more.

I hope the proof sheets having been sent here will not inconvenience you. I have read them with infinite satisfaction, and the whole discussion strikes me as admirable. I have no books here, and wish much I could see a plate of Campodea. I never reflected much on the difficulty which you indicate, and on which you throw so much light. I have only a few trifling remarks to make. At p. 44 I wish you had enlarged a little on what you have said of the distinction between developmental and adaptive changes ; for I cannot quite remember the point, and others will perhaps be in the same predicament. I think I always saw that the larva and the adult might be separately modified to any extent. Bearing in mind what strange changes of function parts undergo with the intermediate states of use, it seems to me that you speak rather too boldly on the impossibility of a mandibulate insect being converted into a sucking insect ; not that I in the least doubt the value of your explanation. Cirripedes, passing through what I have called a pupal state, *as far as their mouths are concerned,* rather supports what you say at p. 52.

At p. 40 your remarks on the Argus pheasant (tho' I have not the least objection to them) do not seem to me very appropriate as being related to the mental faculties.

If you can spare me these proof sheets when done with, I should be obliged, as I am correcting a new Edition of the Origin when I return home, tho' this subject is too large for me to enter into.

I thank you sincerely for the great interest which your discussion has given me, and with thanks for your congratulations on an event that gives us great satisfaction.—Believe me, yours very sincerely,

CH. DARWIN.

I return by this post the sheets.

He found time, moreover, to look abroad,

where the tragic scenes were being enacted
which followed the German Invasion of France.

Fearing that there would be terrible distress
in Paris as soon as the siege was raised, Cardinal
Manning, Huxley, Knowles (of the *Nineteenth
Century*), and he formed themselves into a
Committee to prepare supplies which might be
sent over at once. Having organised the scheme
and ascertained that it would have moral support in France, they proposed it to the Lord Mayor,
who formed a large Committee, and the result
was most satisfactory. Eventually the City of
Paris sent over M. Leon Say, and at a Mansion
House meeting on October 18 he thanked the
Lord Mayor and the Committee for what they
had done.

In this year also commenced his connection
with Avebury which eventually led to his taking
the name of that marvellously interesting place
for his title.

Avebury was first described by Aubrey,
writing at the end of the seventeenth century,
who said of it : " Avebury doth as much exceed
Stonehenge in grandeur as a Cathedral doth an
ordinary Parish Church." Sir R. Colt Hoare
commences his account of Avebury, in the
monumental *History of Ancient Wiltshire*, in
solemn words : " With awe and diffidence, I
enter the sacred precincts of this once hallowed
sanctuary, the supposed parent of Stonehenge,
the wonder of Britain, and the most ancient,
as well as the most interesting relic which our
island can produce."

Part of the site had already been sold to a

land company, which resold it in small building lots for the erection of cottages. Much correspondence, expressing regret at this vandalism, appeared in the papers, and many suggestions that the land should be purchased by some public body. No steps, however, were taken.

One day Sir John Lubbock received a telegram from Mr. Bryan King, the Rector, whom he knew slightly, saying that if nothing were done the erection of the cottages would begin the following Monday; that the cottagers themselves regretted building on that particular site, and would part with their interest for a sovereign apiece. Could anything be done? He telegraphed at once to Mr. King to give them each their sovereign, and buy the land for him. This was done, and he subsequently bought some more land, including Silbury Hill, and afterwards the West Kennett farm, containing the celebrated West Kennett tumulus and Hackpen.

The following letter on the subject from the Reverend A. C. Smith, Secretary of the Wiltshire Archaeological Society, shows that the county, if not the whole country, acknowledged a debt of gratitude to him for the purchase.

WILTSHIRE ARCHAEOLOGICAL AND NATURAL HISTORY
SOCIETY

YATESBURY RECTORY, CALNE, WILTS,
23rd November 1871.

MY DEAR SIR—As Secretary of the above Society, it is only my duty to offer you our most sincere thanks for the public spirit and liberality you showed in purchasing the land at Avebury, which was imperilled by the threatened profanation of villas, and I do so in the name of the " Wilts Archaeological Society," as well as on my own account.

I cannot at the same time but rejoice that you are the possessor of a portion of the area of Avebury, and if you have a fancy to come down and see your purchase I hope you will let me offer you hospitality here (I am only 3 miles from Avebury). You can have a bed here, and I shall be very happy to see you under my roof, and my carriage can fetch you from Calne whenever you please.

Having said thus much to you as the present owner of a portion of Avebury, the next part of my letter may seem paradoxical; but I must now offer, as my good friend Mr. Sotheron Estcourt urges me, and as I feel I ought—that if you desire not to be burdened with the purchase (now that you have rescued it from the spoiler), the County of Wilts, through the Archaeological Society, will feel bound to relieve you of it; and if you desire me to do so, I would at once proceed to collect the necessary funds, and reimburse you.

I hope you understand that we do not *wish* to do this, but are ready to do it, if you express a wish to that effect. In any case, we feel very grateful to you for the signal service you have rendered us.—Believe me, yours very sincerely,   ALFRED CHARLES SMITH.

The same year he was nominated a Vice-President of the Royal Society.

As has been mentioned already, one object that he had in view when consenting to stand for Parliament was to effect something which might ameliorate the lot of small shopkeepers and shop assistants. With this view he caused a Bill to be drafted on the lines of the Factory Acts, by Mr. Wright, subsequently the eminent judge, and submitted it to his friend Mr. W. Rathbone, then M.P. for Liverpool.

Mr. Rathbone was a large employer of labour in Liverpool, a man of generous and philanthropic sentiments and activities, and a co-adjutor with Sir John in many of his schemes for bettering the lot of the people. His reply, however, though sympathetic, is not very convincing :

GREEN BANK, LIVERPOOL, E.,
29th December 1871.

MY DEAR LUBBOCK—Many thanks for your note of yesterday.

I have really not studied the question sufficiently to know whether such a Bill as you propose, fixing rigidly the number of hours a shop can be kept open, would be desirable. For instance there might be cases in which a relay of hands might be desirable, say in the mining districts. These things are sometimes better regulated by public opinion than by direct enactment. I will, however, make some enquiry among those interested in the question and let you know the result.

I am afraid after the decision about Emanuel Hospital we have not much chance of the Endowed School Bill. Public opinion seems running too much the other way for the moment, but you have much better advisers than I am on the spot, as Hobhouse and others will know better whether we are likely to help or hinder their work by pushing it just at present. Whitbread is as much interested in this question, and might give you valuable information, I fancy.

I wish they would make him Speaker. How splendidly he would keep us in order and how well he would look it.—Yours faithfully, WM. RATHBONE.

Sir John Lubbock, Bart., M.P.

CHAPTER XIV

In the year 1872 came to an end the rather patriarchal mode of life at High Elms, which had still included several of the younger brothers, under the roof of the eldest, as well as his own young and growing family. It was a year further notable in Sir John Lubbock's history as being that in which he commenced his studies in the intelligence of Ants. For that type of all popular ignorance, " the man in the street," the name of Sir John Lubbock is associated, in the first instance, no doubt, with the Bank Holidays, but in the second with the " Ants, Bees, and Wasps," about which he published a very delightful and widely-read volume a little later. The idea of this man of business and of legislature poring over the small and hurrying insects struck the fancy of the people by its apparent paradox. It gave them one idea the more of the extraordinarily varied outlook and interest of this gifted man, who was himself of a remarkably ant-like industry.

Napoleon III., then living at Chislehurst, came to High Elms in the spring to see Sir John's archaeological collections, and expressed keen interest in them.

In notes of this year relative to an expedition that he made to the place from which he ultimately took the title of Avebury, he still writes the name as "Abury." Under date March 29 he has the entry, "Morning service at Marlborough. Thence to Abury and on to Devizes. I have bought a meadow at Abury. The Roman road goes quite straight to the centre of Silbury Hill, which was obviously the point steered for." The entry of the following day is worth quoting too, if only for the sake of the name of the Inn, indicating the presence of the bustard recently on those downs and also the abundance there of the Thick-knee or Norfolk plover : "Devizes to Salisbury in two carriages again, as before. At the Bustard found the headquarters of the hawking club. Grant Duff and I went for an hour with Lascelles and Bass to see the hawks flown. They were after the Thick-kneed Curlew. We found some very soon, and it was most curious to see the hawks come back to the lure."

The two following letters refer to the Vice-Chancellorship of London University, which had fallen vacant, and which he was being pressed by Lord Granville to accept :

May 1872.

MY DEAR LORD GRANVILLE—I feel that there are so many Members of the Senate much better qualified to judge than I am as to the best successor to Sir E. Ryan in the Vice-Chancellorship, that I should not venture to make a suggestion except at your instance, but as you wish me to do so, I beg to say that as far as I can judge, either Dr. Stonar or Mr. Spottiswoode would fill the office with advantage to the University.

As regards your second question, although I am much gratified that you should think of me even for a moment, I cannot but be sensible that I am very unfit for such a post. Having been actively engaged in the City ever since I was fourteen, I have not had the advantage of any University training; and especially as regards Classics and Mathematics I am deficient in qualifications which a Vice-Chancellor ought to possess. You will excuse my troubling you with these details, but if, as I gather from your note, some of my Colleagues have done me the honour to think of me, I cannot but feel that they do so in ignorance of the real state of the case. Had it not been for these considerations I should have asked you to allow me to consult you with reference to the duties of the office before giving a reply, for I should esteem it a very high honour to be put in nomination for the Vice-Chancellorship ; an honour the more gratifying to me in consequence of my father's old connexion with the University.

15th June 1872.

MY DEAR LORD GRANVILLE—I have, as you suggested, seen Dr. Carpenter on the subject of the Vice-Chancellorship of the London University. Though I am much gratified at being thought of for such an appointment, I still feel very strongly the objections which I mentioned to you, and which you kindly promised to reconsider, but in other respects I see no difficulty, and I shall be quite content to leave myself in your hands, should you find that my election would be agreeable to the Senate.

If you wish to see me before Wednesday I will keep any appointment you may make.—Believe me, yours very sincerely,   JOHN LUBBOCK.

The Right Hon. Earl Granville.

Lord Granville overruled his objections, and on the motion of Lord Derby he was unanimously elected Vice-Chancellor, and was afterwards re-elected annually until he resigned the office in 1880, when he became Member of Parliament for the University.

At the request of the Society of Arts he

brought in a Bill (The Patents for Inventions Bill) remodelling the law relating to Patents. The Government also had a Bill on the same subject, and eventually most of the proposals made by the Society of Arts were introduced as clauses into the Government Bill.

In the autumn he went for a trip down the Danube, and so to Constantinople and the Troad. This, which was among the earliest in date of many of its kind which he made almost annually until nearly the end of his life, he has honoured with notice at quite unusual length in his diary. As a rule his travel notes are rather meagre, but those of this particular tour are interesting and detailed enough to be worth quotation at length. I only wish that he had kept more such records, for, as one who knew him well writes, " he must have been an intensely interesting travelling companion."

Mr. Arthur Elliot says, " I met Lubbock, whom I knew before, in the expedition down the Danube. I was travelling with Herschell and two other young barristers, and at Pesth we found Lubbock, the Grant Duffs, W. R. Greg, Miss Wilson, Masurus Pasha (the ambassador to London), his son and daughter, Miss Osborne, daughter of Bernal Osborne, now Lady Blake, and some lively Irish young lady cousins of hers. We had a very lively party all the way to Constantinople."

The account which the diary gives of the expedition runs :

This autumn I have been with the Gregs and Grant-Duffs to Constantinople and Asia Minor. Just before

starting I cut my knee, which I was afraid would stop me.
I had to have it sewn up, and started with a silver wire
in it. I met the others at Augsburg. Down to Linz,
where we were kept some time as an omnibus upset and
poor Greg was a good deal hurt. Then to Vienna and
down the Danube by Varna to Constantinople. The
bazaars very interesting. Then to the Dardanelles and
Hissarlik, staying some days at a little farm of the
Calverts in the Troad. I opened the so-called tumulus
of Hector at Bunarbashi. We went up Mount Ida, a
very long and tiring day. Then to Smyrna, from which
we reached Ephesus and Sardis. At Therapia I made
the acquaintance of Ralph Earle. In the Turkish burial
ground at Constantinople every flat gravestone had a
hole. Could it be to let the soul out ? The Dancing
Dervishes we thought very stupid, though it was odd to
see people with such a curious idea of religion. Midhat
Pasha the Grand Vizier was very civil, and gave us
recommendations to all the governors in Asia Minor.
He was very keen to get a railway from Tripoli to
Bagdad. Therapia we thought delightful. In the
Troad the Calverts were very good to us. We went to
stay at the Calverts' farm—Chiflik. On the way we
visited Hissarlik, but unluckily Schliemann was not
there. We got there first at sunset on our way to the
Chiflik. It was rather a wild scene, and at one point
some runaway camels suddenly joined us !
    In the evening the jackals made very unearthly
noises. We had a guard consisting of a captain and two
or three other soldiers. I always regarded the captain's
gun as a sham, till one day to my great surprise he shot
a partridge. The Balidagh at Bunarbashi certainly
showed little signs of human occupation, though Hahn's
excavations and the walls of the old fort were clear
enough. The live rock, however, constantly came to the
surface. The view from the top was very pretty ; the
Scamander winding below, and occupying only part of
its bed which was fringed with willows.
    Sat. 12 Oct.—Started again to Hissarlik. I picked
up a good quartz hammer. Then to the tumulus
of Achilles, where G. D. and I bathed. Then to the
Sigaean point. The villagers brought in some execrable
wine. In the evening we sat on the terrace. From
the verandah on one side one sees low hills, then

the Balidagh, Priamus' and Hector's tumuli, then on the horizon the point of Tenedos, Ujek Tepe, and then the Sigaean promontory, and the tumulus of Achilles. Grant-Duff and Greg made an excursion to Alexandria Troas while I stayed to finish, if possible, the examination of Hector's tumulus.

Monday, 14.—They were thrashing wheat with a tribula. We rode over to Ineh, and in the evening saw a Turkish wedding. There was an open brazier of blazing wood on a pole about as high as a man's head. Round it danced an army of men in bright dresses. The women did not appear. We slept in the house of an Armenian.

Tuesday, 15.—Rode to Evjilar, lunching at Beiramitch. Pitched our tent close to the Scamander, and after a good supper turned in for the night.

Wednesday, 16.—Up at six, had a good wash in the river, and then started up Ida, which took much longer than we expected, so that we did not reach the top till 3. Got back to Evjilar at 8. Had some coffee and rode on, reaching Beiramitch soon after midnight. Fortunately a beautiful night and almost full moon. From the top we saw Mitelene, Tenedos, Imbros, Samothrace, the Sea of Marmora, and Gulf of Adramyti.

Thursday, 17.—Back to Mr. Whitaker's hospitable house at the Dardanelles. He and the Calverts have been most kind to us.

Oct. 1872

Sat. 19.—Smyrna. In the afternoon to the cistern at Tantalus and the tomb of Tantalus. There are three tumuli near together.

Mon. 21.—To Ephesus. Mr. Wood showed us his excavations on the site of the temple of Diana. We went by the cave of the seven sleepers, the Stadion, the great theatre, the Gymnasion, the small theatre, etc.

Wed. 23. — To Sardis. Camped near the village. I got up in the night and walked about to enjoy the scene, but it was quite cold.

Thursday, 24.—Up early. Temple of Cybele. Then to the Bir Bir Tepe which we reached about 11.30. I counted from the top of the tumulus of Alyattes not less than 60 tumuli. Went into the tumulus, but had no good lights.

Friday, 25.—Started home.   G. D. and I bathed from the steps of the steamer.   He was severely stung by a jelly-fish.

Sat. 26.—Syra.   Saw Delos, Milo, and the fine rock of Antimilo.

Monday, 28.—Woke in sight of Etna.   Beautiful sunrise.   Stromboli astonished us all.   We passed close to it about noon.

Wed. 30.—Marseilles.

Would that all his travel notes had been thus full ; but even these omit a point of interest, that at Constantinople he met Nubar Pasha, who invited him to Egypt, and with whom he maintained most friendly relations throughout his life. Soon after his return he attended the meeting of the British Association at Brighton, where he presided over Section D, and took the Chair at the Red Lion dinner, and to this dinner he took with him a guest of a kind that had never hitherto been received in that learned company.

When in the south of France, in the spring, he had tamed a wasp, which he brought with him to Brighton. It had the honour of a leading article in the *Daily Telegraph*, and of a caricature in *Punch*.

" One," said the *Daily Telegraph*, " of the most curious attendants this year at the gathering of the British Association in Brighton was a little gentleman in brown overcoat, with black and yellow nether garments, wearing a sharp sword poisoned at the tip.   We are inclined to think that, next to Mr. Stanley, this visitor might be called by far the most remarkable and best worth attention among all the assembled notorieties.   It was Sir John Lubbock's pet wasp ;

and the respect which would naturally be paid to any friend of the benevolent savant, who has given London its new holidays, was really due to this insect on its own account." [1]

In answer to an enquiry about some of the recent excavations in Greece and Asia Minor he received the following long and interesting letter from Dr. Schliemann :

ATHENS,
14th November 1872.

My Lord—In answer to your esteemed lines of 27th ult., I beg to state that I published in November and December 1871 the details of my excavations at Troy in 5 Greek, in the Athenian journal, "'Εφημερὶς τῶν Συζητησέων," and in 5 German reports in the Augsburg paper, *Allgemeine Zeitung*. Of my excavations of *this* year I published 9 reports in the "'Εφημερὶς τῶν Συζητησέων," which I send you herewith. I regret not being able to send you also those of last year, because I have no copy of them left. In German I have not published anything this year, because I am going to publish a work on Troy with 4 or 5 plans, 1 map, and with the engravings of more than 1200 Trojan terra-cottas or other antiquities discovered at Ilium.

I thought I could not do better than to extract from my German manuscript, which is going to be printed, a summary account which I send you enclosed. The latter has been written in a great hurry, and I beg you to excuse the blunders it contains, but I am very busy just now, and I could not write it better in the few moments I have at my disposal.

I intend to continue the excavations on the 1st February next with great zeal, and, if it is agreeable to you I shall have great pleasure to write you every week of the result of my exertions. I shall now dig with great vigour to bring to light the ancient Temple of Minerva, to which will no doubt lead me the substruction wall which Mr. Calvert has assuredly pointed out to you, and which seems to cover the ancient slope of the entire

---

[1] *Daily Telegraph*, August 26, 1872.

N.E. corner of the Mount. At the same time I shall prosecute with the greatest energy the excavations East and West of the Great Tower, in order to lay bare a great portion of the ancient walls of circumclusion, which Homer ascribes to Neptune and Apollo.

To the East of the Tower I have great hopes to find in the upper layers the Temple of Apollo, built by Lysimachus, and, 14 or 15 metres below it, the ancient one which is mentioned in the *Iliad*. I am sure that from the modern Apollo Temple derive all those Corinthian columns which you will have noticed in a small excavation, and almost at the surface, at the foot of the south-east corner of the Mount.

The Triglyph Clock, which I found in the ruins of the Lysimachus' Minerva Temple, and of which I send you herewith a copy, proves, of course, that this Temple was of Doric order, and, this being the oldest order of architecture, I have no doubt that I shall find the ancient Minerva Temple to be built in the same style. I am going to present to your British Museum a mould of my metope, which Mr. Newton thinks to be a little earlier than the time of Lysimachus. Professor Κουμανούδης here is of Mr. Newton's opinion, and thinks that masterpiece to have been made between the epoch of Pericles and Alexander the Great.

You have doubtless visited on the islands of Thera and Therassia the ruins of the prehistoric buildings, which the members of the French school here have brought to light there by their excavations and which are covered, on an average, with 68 feet of volcanic ashes. The latter have, as the layers of those islands show, been thrown out by that gigantic central volcano, by the lava of which Thera and Therassia have been formed and which must have disappeared about 1500 years *before* our era, and archaeology therefore ascribes to those ruins an age of about 2000 years before Christ.

The objects found there are conserved here in the French school, and I have examined them yesterday again most carefully in order to discover some resemblance with the Trojan antiquities, but I can assure you there is none whatever. Only one copper saw has been found there, and no other vestige of metal. Of flint saws there are but very few, all bad black flint and badly made ; at Troy nearly all are of white flint and well made. Female faces you see on *none* of the vases, but still many of the latter are made to represent the woman, for they have two breasts and a navel. *Many* Trojan vases, and particularly of those in a *less* depth than 7 metres, have also 2 female breasts and a navel, but no female face, but then the shape of those vases is altogether different from those found in Thera and Therassia. If the Trojan vases have ornaments they have always been carved in the clay when it was still soft, and if the Trojan vases or other terra-cottas are coloured they never present more than one colour, whilst the ornamentation of the Thera and Therassia vase is never carved and always painted by various colours. I have neither found the slightest resemblance in the quality of the terra-cotta. These round pieces of terra-cotta without ornamentation have been found there which resemble a little those volcano and carrousel shaped pieces of Troy, but the quality of the clay is inferior to any I found in Ilium, also a broken piece of an ornamented one was found, but the ornamentation consists merely of points which are stuck in on the sides of the piece, and not on its basis as in Troy. The Thera and Therassia funnels of terra-cotta are of immense size and covered with painted ornaments, while the Trojan funnels from 14 to 3 m. depth are only 6 to 8 cem. long, and unpainted. On the whole it is impossible for me to say which terra-cottas show more civilization, those of the two islands or of Troy, because they are *completely different*. The only resemblance I find between the ruins of Thera and Therassia and those of Troy is the architecture, for, like the Trojan houses on the virgin soil and like the Great Tower and the walls in the N. side of Ilium, all houses and enclosures of the primitive inhabitants of Thera and Therassia consisted of stones joined with clay; but I have seen there no wall thicker than 40 centimetres.

I beg leave to send you herewith also some photographs of a part of the antiquities which I discovered last year at Ilium in a depth of from 5 to 9 metres ; these same objects will appear in my present work in 4to, together with all the curiosities I found this year. If you wish to have a photograph of the most ancient Trojan antiquities, say of those objects found in 16 to 19 m. in depth, I shall be able to satisfy you, for I begin to-morrow to photograph my whole Trojan collection, each layer separately.

I still beg leave to send you herewith a book I wrote four years ago on Troy ; prefaces are never read in Paris, but, pray, do me the favour to read the preface of my book, for it describes my adventurous life.—I am, with profound respect, your Lordship's admirer,

DOCTOR HENRY SCHLIEMANN.

Sir John Lubbock, Bart., London.

Pray, my Lord, send me a copy of your report when it is published.

I regret very much that you did not come to Athens, for I would have been so happy to show you all my Trojan antiquities, and science would have greatly gained by it if you had seen them.

Any advice you may be pleased to give me regarding the excavations at Troy will be followed with gratitude.

Mr. Gladstone's continued interest in the question of the ancient metals is shown in the following note of the same year :

11 CARLTON HOUSE TERRACE, S.W.,
November 22nd, 1872.

DEAR SIR J. LUBBOCK—I hope you will go to see General de Cesnola's collection of Cypriote remains at 61 Great Russell Street. I have often pleaded for the recognition of the Copper Age, which is the Age described by Horace ; and the difficulty is the want of adequate remains. I have been obliged to allow that though there were very remarkable remains in Copper, I could not point to them in quantity.

At General de Cesnola's house, yesterday, I had the pleasure of seeing a Copper knife and small axe (as well as the pain of breaking the knife point in trying whether it was flexible), and of his numerous weapons and instruments in G. Russell Street the General tells me that *one-third* are Copper.—Yours very faithfully,

W. E. GLADSTONE.

Recording a life in which so very much was accomplished as in that of Sir John Lubbock's, and in noting, year by year, the results of his extraordinary power and facility of work, it is difficult to avoid giving the impression of a man going at breathless speed, of one totally absorbed in his many projects and practical and scientific interests, of one who can have had no spare time for indulging the domestic affections and enjoying the domestic life.   Such a picture would be very different indeed from a true one of Sir John.   So far from the impression that he gave being one of breathless haste, as it were of an animated hurricane rushing from one sphere to another of activity, the atmosphere that he bore about him was invariably one of the most serene, unruffled calm.   More than that, it was a calm which seemed as if it could not possibly be ruffled.   His serenity, in peculiarly trying circumstances, more than once struck those who witnessed it as so remarkable that they have been disposed to ask if it must not be a cold nature that could be thus unruffled.   The truth was far otherwise.   Few men have been endowed by nature with sensibilities so keen and so nearly feminine in their delicacy. In all the domestic relations, as son, husband, and parent, he was most tenderly devoted ; and no greater testimony of this affection could be cited than the devotion, the love, and the trust which he inspired in return.   Devotion and love are perhaps not uncommon sentiments on the part of children towards parents : that full trust and confidence, as of equal to equal and of friend to friend, with which Sir John's children repaid him his affection for them, is very much less frequent. The gentleness of his manner had a great charm for all children, and he perfectly understood the

value they attach to being treated and talked to
seriously—not as if they were by nature comic
actors eternally condemned to play the buffoon.
By virtue of this seriousness he found himself
made free of their society and intimacy; and by
inviting them, as if they, equally with himself,
were interested in scientific research, to observe
the jewelled brilliance, as seen through the
microscope, of an apparently dingy beetle's wing,
he would quickly fascinate them with the delights
of those investigations in which he himself delighted. The observations on some of his insect
friends could hardly, with his varied avocations,
have been so complete, had he not been able to
enlist his children and their governess as enthusiastic students and observers with him.

Sir John suffered a very deep grief this year
in the loss of his mother. It is little wonder that
she had been the fondest and most admiring of
mothers to him, and her letters, far too sacred to
transcribe, give fervent expression to her adora-
tion (the word is really not too highly pitched)
for this very remarkable eldest son. We have
seen how she appraised his character at a very
early age, and the passage of the years only
confirmed her in the original high estimate. Sir
John was devoted to her, accepting all her admiration with the simple gratitude that was natural
to him, yet never permitting himself to be misled,
by that inevitably partial appreciation, into any
lack of sense of proportion. He was never, at
any period of life, later than his teens, in even
momentary danger, so far as I have been able
to discover, of being " spoilt," as the common

phrase goes, by the atmosphere of adulation with which he was surrounded. It would have been little wonder, indeed, had his valuation of his own talents been a little distorted. We have seen the estimate in which his contributions to science were already held, at a comparatively early period of his life, by the greatest scientists of the day, and it is a judgment that must for ever silence the cheap cynicism of that criticism which proclaimed him " a great scientist among bankers, a great banker among the scientists." Darwin, Lyell, Tyndall, Huxley, to name only a few, have given their liberal witness to the worth of his original contributions to the natural science of which they were common devotees. The comment of the first-named alone on the *Prehistoric Times* were enough to establish the fame of any man of science.

I cannot resist telling you how excellently well, in my opinion, you have done the very interesting chapter on savage life. Though you have necessarily only compiled the materials, the general result is most original. But I ought to keep the term original for your last chapter, which has struck me as an admirable and profound discussion. It has quite delighted me, for now the public will see what kind of man you are, which I am proud to think I discovered a dozen years ago. I do sincerely wish you all success in your election [to Parliament] and in politics ; but after reading this last chapter you must let me say : oh dear ! oh dear ! oh dear !—Yours affectionately,   CH. DARWIN.

The above was written in June 1865. There is no doubt that *Prehistoric Times* did open the public eye to an appreciation of Sir John, as Darwin predicted, but in the wonderful mass of legislative and other work which he accomplished afterwards, his scientific light became, except to those who, being men of science themselves, really knew the facts, rather hidden under a bushel.

It is amusing to read the school-boyish enthusiasm with which Schliemann, in the spring of the following year, writes to Sir John of his further Trojan discoveries :

TROY, 20*th* *May* 1873.

YOUR EXCELLENCY—Hurrah the Skaeangate, which consists of two separate gates, the one 6 metres 13 centimetres distant from the other ; hurrah the copper bolts with which they were shut ; hurrah the house of Priamos, which is the lower one just N.E. of the gate, for, as your Excellency will see, the upper one was only built when the lower one, as well as the Skaeangate and the paved road, were covered 10 feet high with calcinated rubbish. In the lower house I found an enormous quantity of wonderful antiquities, and amongst them an *owl*-headed Minerva, the protecting divinity of Troy, of terra-cotta 60 centimetres high and with engraved princely ornaments ; another owl-headed Minerva with an immense shield, holding in each arm hoses (ἀγκούς) in form of bottles, and on the back with very long cuehair, which is in the shape of that of the Karyatides in the Acropolis of Athens ; also lots of idols with the image of the γλαυκῶπις. On one of the vases discovered there is an inscription which is, I think, in Phrygian characters, but I am not sure. I have also excavated the tumulus which, according to Homer, was attributed by the gods to Myrina, whilst men thought it to be the tomb of Batiaea.[1]

But now my mission is accomplished ; the topography of Troy I have well ascertained by the 15 deep wells I have sunk, and I shall therefore be off as soon as my engineer gets ready the plans.—I am, your Excellency's faithfully,   H. SCHLIEMANN.

This year he brought in his first Bill for the early closing of shops, a movement with which

[1] *Iliad*, ii. 811.

he kept in close touch all through his later life, but on this first attempt could not get a day for the Bill's second reading. Later in the year he took the Chair at a meeting at Manchester, for the same object. The Bishop of Manchester attended the meeting but, to Sir John's disappointment, was in favour of voluntary closing.

He also introduced for the first time the Ancient Monuments Bill, of which the fortunes were so singular and so long drawn out that they inspired some parliamentary joker to speak of it as the "monumentally ancient bill" before it actually passed a third reading, for before accomplishing this necessary final passage it had gone to a second reading no less than seven times.

In the autumn he made a trip to Egypt, but it does not seem to have resulted in any discoveries of importance. At home he writes that he was very successful in various expeditions in search of flint implements.

In the spring of 1874 Mr. Gladstone dissolved Parliament, and Sir John Lubbock again stood for Maidstone, this time in conjunction with Sir Sydney Waterlow. The Maidstone electors received him with enthusiasm. The *South Eastern Gazette*, the leading Liberal paper, describing the opening meeting at the Corn Exchange, said : "The meeting was one of the largest and most enthusiastic ever held in Maidstone. . . . Sir John Lubbock received a perfect ovation."

This year he passed the Falsification of Accounts Bill. The legal conditions which led to the necessity of its introduction were not a little curious. A clerk of Stuckey's Bank had overpaid his account, and had deceived the auditors by falsifying the books, so that his frauds remained for a considerable time undetected. To every one's surprise it appeared that this was no offence in the eye of the law. This Bill for the first time made it a legal offence, and it has proved very useful, as many clerks who robbed their employers by means of false entries had previously escaped scot-free.

He also contributed two articles to *Nature*, on the relation between insects and flowers, of which Mr. Darwin writes as follows :

DOWN, BECKENHAM, KENT,
September 26th, 1874.

MY DEAR SIR JOHN—I have read your two articles in *Nature* and they seem excellently done ; but my object in writing is to caution you, unless you have good evidence, about C. K. Sprengel's notion of Bees being deceived by a nectar-lip nectary. As far as my memory goes, Orchids are his best case, and I think I have shown that he is here mistaken, and my conclusion has been supported by subsequent observations.

I suppose you do not want more cases of coloured calyx, but our common Polygala is a remarkable case, as the calyx during flowering season is bright-coloured, and *then turns green* whilst it protects the seed-vessel after the flowering season is over.—Yours very sincerely,

CH. DARWIN.

In the autumn he attended the meeting at Belfast of the British Association, and gave one of the lectures. The subject was related to that of the articles in *Nature*. Professor Tyndall was President for the year, and the following extract from a letter of his indicates his estimate of the lecture :

"I think you will be as pleased to hear it from me as from anybody else (there is presumption !) that John's lecture was beautiful, and gave the greatest delight to a large and brilliant assembly."

CHAPTER XV

(AGE 41-45)

APRIL 22 was fixed for the Second Reading of the Ancient Monuments Bill. He seems to have been somewhat surprised to hear that the Conservative Government intended to oppose it. Some of his friends counselled its withdrawal under the circumstances, but he decided to persevere. He counted in the Aye lobby, and was very pleased to find that several Conservative Members were voting with him. When the discussion was about half over, one of them as he passed said to him, " We are having a very good division." Some time afterwards another said, " We are going to hit them very hard," and the last man as he went through told him they had won. This was the first defeat of the Government, and a great triumph, but he could never get a day to carry the Bill any further.

The same afternoon he had another piece of good fortune, for all the other Bills ran through, or were dropped, and he got the Second Reading of a Bill introduced on behalf of the College of Surgeons to amend their statutes.

In June he was in Oxford receiving the honorary degree of D.C.L.

At this date the *World* had already begun to give pen-portraits of distinguished persons, and the following, which appeared on August 4, well and justly indicates the verdict of his contemporaries on Sir John and on the work which he had already accomplished :

Sir John Lubbock is a man of universal mind. His intelligence and his occupations embrace everything that is upon the earth. Firmly persuaded of the superiority of bees, wasps and ants to men and women though he be, he has not disdained to write on the origin of civilisation and the primitive condition of man, as well as on the origin and metamorphoses of insects. More than this, he has even busied himself with men, not only in this condition of aboriginal wildness, but as engaged in the complex operations of modern commerce. He has written treatises on banking and finance, and has simplified, if he has not invented, many of the proceedings of the Clearing House. He has strolled in to Parliament, and has made more than one clever and admirable speech on the incomes of the rich and the education of the poor ; on £. s. d. and on the three R's. If Mr. Layard could be called the member for Nineveh, one might appropriately christen Sir John Lubbock the member for Stonehenge. . . . Sir John Lubbock is, of course officially placed with the Liberals ; but if he can be called a politician at all, which is doubtful, he is absolutely void of political partisanship. Perhaps it is here that we may see most clearly the influence of his scientific studies. He has devoted so much time and intellectual energy to the investigations of scientific problems, and to the impartial sifting of scientific evidence, that he can scarcely be expected to muster much enthusiasm or to pronounce a categorical judgment on the positive merits of the bungling tactics of political rivals. He has come to the conclusion that there are certain truths clearly ascertainable in finance, and that they should be enforced ; he is not less clear that the condition of the people, moral, social, and mental, should be improved. An accomplished financier in theory, he is an intellectual philanthropist in practice ; but to call him a politician would be as appropriate as to style a razor a hand-saw. It follows from this that both in politics and science Sir John Lubbock is tolerance and good breeding personified. He was not at a university, but he was at Eton ; and never was there Etonian yet on whom Eton has more vividly and gracefully left her impress. The true impression is, that Sir John Lubbock, banker, savant, member of Parliament, is a country gentleman to whom science—and science not lightly flirted with, but completely mastered — has been a relaxation and a pursuit, just as classical studies were to a bygone generation of statesmen. The intellectual bent of the age is scientific rather than literary ; and if it is necessary that so it should be, the age could have no more perfect representative than Sir John Lubbock, and the rising generation no model whom it could more aptly study.

Although Sir John Lubbock sat as a Liberal, he always had commanded the respect of opponents in the House. We find him, for instance, in May 1876, speaking on the Customs and Inland Revenue Bill, following Mr. Fawcett. He notes " The Conservatives had been very noisy, so Hartington kindly sent me a note advising me not to let myself be put down, but to move the adjournment if necessary, and he would support it. However, there was no need, as the Conservatives treated me very well."

In this year he introduced and carried the Bankers' Books Evidence Act. Up to this time Bankers could be compelled to produce their books in Court. Many accounts being in the same ledger, it sometimes happened that a customer wished to consult his account, but could not do so as the ledger was in Court. Under this Bill Bankers were permitted to send a signed copy.

He received the thanks of the Bankers' Association for carrying this Act, which has proved a considerable convenience.

He took the Chair at the Salisbury meeting of the Wiltshire Archaeological Society. The principal excursion was to Stonehenge. It had not been intended to have any speech-making, but Mr. Parker, the Oxford Antiquary, took upon himself to make an oration, suggesting that Stonehenge was erected in Saxon times. Upon this the Committee asked Sir John to reply, which he did, speaking from the top of one of the stones. He maintained that it probably belonged to the Bronze Age.

The excursion was a large one, conveyed in some twenty-five carriages, and a gentleman farmer who was harvesting, surprised at seeing so large a cavalcade in an out-of-the-way lane, asked his bailiff who they were. " I reckon, sir," said the man, to whom the word archaeologists was not as familiar as it might have been, " it's them Archangels from Salisbury."

Lord Morley, in his fine *Life of Gladstone*, devotes one of its most charming pages to an account of a " week-end " at High Elms, in February of this year, when Mr. Gladstone was also staying there.

" It was my own good fortune," he writes, " to pass two days with him at this moment at High Elms. Huxley and Playfair were of the party. Mr. Gladstone had with him the printer's proofs of his second pamphlet, and was in full glow against Turkish terrorism and its abettors. This strong obsession could not be concealed, nor was there any reason why it should be ; it made no difference in his ready courtesy and kindness of demeanour, his willingness to enter into other people's topics, his pliant force and alacrity of mind. On the Sunday afternoon Sir John Lubbock, our host, took us all up to the hill-top whence in his quiet Kentish village Darwin was shaking the world. The illustrious pair, born in the same year, had never met before. Mr. Gladstone, as soon as seated, took Darwin's interest in lessons of massacre for granted, and launched forth his thunderbolts with unexhausted zest. His great, wise, simple, and truth-loving listener, then, I think, busy on digestive powers of the drosera in his greenhouse, was intensely delighted. When we broke up, watching Mr. Gladstone's erect alert figure as he walked away, Darwin, shading his eyes with his hand against the evening rays, said to me in unaffected satisfaction, ' What an honour that such a great man should come to visit me ! ' Too absorbed in his own overwhelming conflict with the powers of evil, Mr. Gladstone makes no mention of his afternoon call, and only says of the two days that he found a notable party, and made interesting conversation, and that he ' could not help liking ' one of the company, then a stranger to him. In his absence at church, we were talking of the qualities that send men forward and keep them back. ' I should like to know,' cried Huxley, ' what would keep such a man as that back,' pointing to where Mr. Gladstone had been sitting ; ' why, put him in the middle of the moor, with nothing in the world but his shirt, and you could not prevent him from being anything he liked.' And Huxley was as far as possible from being a Gladstonian."

On April 30, Gladstone gave notice of his celebrated resolutions on the Eastern question. The Liberal front bench, with one or two exceptions, did not approve of them, and not wishing to go so far as to vote against him, asked Sir John to move the " Previous Question," which he agreed to do. Eventually, however, Mr. Gladstone consented to modify his resolutions, and so Sir John was spared a somewhat painful duty.

In March of this year his eldest daughter Amy
had married Mr. Mulholland.   It was fated to be
a tragically brief union.   At Easter he had crossed
to Paris where his friend, M. Jules Simon, had
just retired from the Prime Ministry, and thence
went on an excursion into Switzerland, leaving
Mr. and Mrs. Mulholland in Paris, and on his
return was most deeply shocked to hear of Mr.
Mulholland's quite unexpected death.   This was
on June 3.   There is no need to dwell on the sad
days that followed.   On the 5th he briefly records,
" Brought poor Amy home."

Sir John was interested in enquiring into the
origin, etc., of the £1 notes, and the following is a
reply from Lord Overstone, whom he had consulted on this question :

LOCKINGE HOUSE, WANTAGE,
September 11, 1877.

DEAR SIR JOHN LUBBOCK—I cannot give you a
distinct reply to your question respecting £1 Notes.
Their history from 1820 to 1830 has been a curious one,
but as Huskinson was the guiding authority of the
Government upon questions of currency and as the
whole of the provisions are in his Speeches, I think you
will have the best chance of finding there the information
you want.

The issue of the £1 notes in the first place was discontinued, not prohibited, on three grounds as I have
always understood.

1. The increasing amount of Forgeries which shook
the public confidence in the note ; and the multiplied
Prosecutions which affected the public sentiments —
Forgery being at that time a capital crime.

2. A strong feeling, perhaps not very clearly defined,
that a large substratum of gold spread throughout the
whole community, is the safest basis for the security of
specie payments.

3. The failure of many County Banks to redeem their
£1 note issue had induced a general growing dislike to

£1 notes by whomsoever issued. I have said they were discontinued, not prohibited. Such was undoubtedly the case in 1824.

The extensive failure of note issue in County Banks in the autumn of that year had caused a tremendous demand upon the Bank of England sovereign to enable the solvent County Bankers to pay their £1 notes. By this means all the gold in the Bank of England was drawn out, while notice for further heavy demands the next morning were lodged at the Bank. Under these circumstances it was determined, with the cognisance of Huskinson, on the part of the Government, that the Bank of England on opening that morning should declare its inability to pay Gold on demand any longer.

All this time the Exchange was in our favour. Gold was coming in steadily though slowly, and whilst the demand of the County Banks was sudden and instantaneous, someone, however, bethought him that in the vaults of the Bank of England there was an old bundle of disused £1 notes and that there was no actual law prohibiting the resort to this. They were brought forth, answered the required purpose perfectly, and the threatened evil was obviated.

This seems an almost incredible statement, but I am strictly correct. Truth more incredible than fiction !

Whether in subsequent legislation the issue of £1 notes by the Bank of England has been lately prohibited, I am unable to say. George Norman can probably answer that question and will confirm all I have stated.

I wish I could contribute more useful assistance to your enquiries.—Yours very truly,   OVERSTONE.

On January 24 of the following year he lectured at Glasgow to a very large audience. The principal attraction, as humorously noted by himself, is a singular one : " The *Bailie* had advised every one to go because the last time Sir John was there he drove a pin into his leg and made the Lord Provost draw it out ! "

A little later he was paid the considerable compliment, under the circumstances, of being appointed one of the trustees of the British Museum. These appointments had always been made rather on political lines, the Prime Minister virtually controlling them and inviting an adherent of his own Party. Lord Beaconsfield, however, writes to him that " On my motion you were elected a Trustee of the British Museum," and further speaks of his hope that Sir John would accept this " interesting and important post." Sir John accepted the invitation and fulfilled the duties of the position with the zeal of a man whose heart is in the work.

The same year he passed the Dental Practitioners Act. The Medical Act did not apply to Dentists. Their case differed somewhat from that of other medical men, but this Act applied similar provisions to them, with certain slight modifications.

The Acceptance of Bills Act, which he also passed, was rendered necessary by a decision of the Law Courts that the writing of one's name across a Bill was not an acceptance unless the name was preceded by the word " accepted " or some abbreviation of it. But many English, and the great bulk of Scotch bills merely had the name, and were consequently technically not accepted. He was therefore applied to by the Banking profession to bring the letter of the law into accord with what had always been understood to be its spirit.

The following letter of about the same date from B. de St. Hilaire, who was French Foreign Minister under Thiers, may be cited for the value of its generous tribute to the advantages of British rule in India.

Paris, Rue d'Astorg, 29 bis,
22 Mai 1878.

Très honoré Monsieur — Vous m'excuserez si j'ai tardé si longtemps à vous remercier de votre article sur la politique coloniale de l'Angleterre, et à vous dire tout le plaisir qu'il m'a fait. J'ai eu l'occasion de beaucoup étudier l'Inde soit dans son histoire passée soit dans son état présent ; et j'admire profondément et que l'Angleterre y a fait et surtout ce qu'elle fait aujourd'hui. Elle y a 240 millions de sujets, ou immédiats ou tributaires, et elle s'est chargée de faire leur éducation et leur bonheur en les civilisant. Jamais rien d'aussi grand ni d'aussi beau n'a été tenté parmi les hommes ; et j'ai dit souvent qu'il fallait remonter jusqu'au Sénat romain pour trouver dans l'histoire quelque chose qui ressemble à cette prodigieuse entreprise. L'Angleterre y réussit admirablement ; et jamais l'Inde n'a été aussi calme, aussi prospère, aussi heureuse que sous votre main. Cet esprit de générosité et de grandeur ne s'est montré dans l'administration anglaise que depuis Warren Hastings ; il n'a fait que s'accroître après lui ; et depuis l'insurrection militaire de 1857, il éclate avec une évidence que le monde entier commence à reconnaître.

On n'avait songé d'abord qu'aux profits de la domination, mais ensuite on a compris tous les devoirs qu'elle imposait, comme l'a si bien dit Macaulay dans un de ses Essais ; et à cette heure, votre immense empire est réglé par les principes les plus généreux et les plus nobles. Votre œuvre est si vaste qu'on peut dire qu'elle ne fait que commencer ; et si quelque puissance voisine venait à la troubler, ce serait un affreux malheur pour l'humanité. Mais j'ai la confiance que rien ne vous menace dans votre travail providentiel ; et votre juste et bienfaisante influence ne fera que se développer et s'affermir avec les siècles.

Voilà, très honoré Monsieur, ce que je tenais à vous dire ; et ce que j'ai répété plus d'une fois dans les articles du Journal des Savants.

L'Inde est de beaucoup la plus considérable de vos colonies ; mais les principes que vous suivez envers elle sont ceux aussi que vous appliquez à toutes les autres, y compris l'Irlande, qui n'en est pas encore à avoir pour vous la reconnaisance qu'elle devrait ressentir depuis près d'un demi-siècle.

Agréez, très honoré Monsieur, mes félicitations et mes vœux bien sincères pour le constant succès de votre glorieuse patrie.—Votre dévoué,   B. St. Hilaire.

Je me rappelle au bon souvenir de M. Grant Duff.

He attended the meeting of the British Association held this year at Dublin, and received the honorary degree of LL.D. of the University.

The same spring the Bankers formed themselves into an " Institute," and did him the honour of making him their first President. He gave the opening Address on June 9, choosing as his subject the early history of Coinage and Currency, which, many years afterwards (1902), was published by Murray. He had addressed some enquiry on the subject to Sir H. Rawlinson, and the following, from that distinguished authority, refers to the early financial operations of Babylonia and Assyria :

21 Charles Street, *May 4th*, 1879.

My dear Lubbock—I can give you very little information as to the financial arrangements of Babylon and Assyria. An extensive series of business documents (leases, loans, mortgages, contracts, deeds of sale and barter, etc., etc.) have been found at Nineveh and the books of the banking firm of Egibi and Sons of Babylon extending over a century and a half, from Nebuchadnezzar to Xerxes, have also been brought to England, but these tablets have hitherto been examined mainly for Chronological purposes and not with a view to elicitating any general principles of finance, if indeed any such results could be possibly obtained, which is doubtful—I have looked over some thousands of these tablets myself, but the only clear impression I have derived from their study is that the relative value of

Gold to Silver in those days was 1 to 10, and that the usual rate of interest was 2 or 3 per cent. per month.

You will find translations of some hundreds of these tablets in a work recently published by Oppert and Menant at Paris, and called I think *Documens juridiques, etc.*, and for the Egibi banking accounts you must also consult Boscawen's papers in the 5th and 6th volumes of the *Transactions of the Society of Biblical Archaeology*, and Bagster's *Records of the Past*, generally, but particularly vol. vii. p. 111.

I am sorry not to be able to give you a more satisfactory reply.—Yours sincerely,

H. E. RAWLINSON.

A common interest in labour questions, some decisions that he had given as an arbiter in labour disputes, and a general desire to ameliorate the conditions of the poor had drawn him much together with Cardinal Manning. The following letter from the Cardinal will show that their propositions were by no means only of a large vagueness, but occasionally went very closely into detail.

ARCHBISHOP'S HOUSE, WESTMINSTER, S.W.,
July 4th, 1879.

MY DEAR SIR JOHN LUBBOCK—I cannot find a paper I had on the state of the Butts and Cisterns in the homes of the poor. They are often pestilential. It is not enough to say that they ought to clean them. The water supply can be laid on and ought to be laid on, etc., so as to need no cleansing. There ought to be no Butts. I will try also to send you the Death rate; but I can say with certainty that it is double in the homes of the working men as compared with the upper class.

I think a Public Meeting of *bona fide* working-men who pay water rates, from all parts of London, would be useful. Exeter Hall would cost about £30, and some six of us might answer for it.—Believe me, always yours very truly, H. E., Cardinal Archbishop.

It does not appear, however, that any active

steps were taken as an immediate result of the
Cardinal's suggestion.

In July of the previous year Sir John had
been invited by the Liberal Association to stand
for the City at the next election, in conjunction
with Lord Hartington and Sir W. Laurence.
It was however thought well to let any final
decision stand over. The time was now running
on, and eventually he received a letter from
Lord Granville saying that the City Liberals
were unanimous in believing that if he would
consent to stand he would not only certainly
carry the election himself, but would probably
bring in the others. Lord Granville adds that
he need not say how glad Hartington and he
would be if Sir John would allow himself to be
nominated.

On the receipt of this letter he consulted the
Liberal agents and others who knew the state of
feeling in the City and at Maidstone. The result
was to convince him that while he could not
carry the City, the effect of his leaving Maidstone
would certainly be the loss of the two seats there.
He therefore thought it best that he should stay
where he was.

In this year he brought in a Bill to amend the
law relating to Companies. Lord Aberdare was
disposed to support the measure, but writes to
inform him of the opposition that he must expect
to it :

1 Queen's Gate, S.W.,
July 31*st*, 1879.

My dear Lubbock — I saw the Lord Chancellor
yesterday. He said that he must oppose the further
progress of the Bill. His main ground was that the
Companies' Act was passed after very careful delibera-

tion of the Board of Trade—and that no important change in it ought to be made without equal care. He did not say in so many words, but his language implied, that the Board of Trade had not gone thoroughly into your Bill, and he suggested that, between this and the next meeting of Parliament, the subject should be thoroughly discussed with the Board of Trade, the reasons for the change of law brought before them by substantial instances of inconvenience, and the clauses carefully considered. I gather that he has talked over the matter with Thring—a great authority on the Companies' Act and Commercial Law—and that his own opinion has been strengthened by Thring's opposition to the Bill in its present form.

As a minor criticism, he suggested that the security for a Dividend offered by the " Trustee " clause might operate injuriously on the interests of the Company.

Such being the case, I see nothing but the withdrawal of the Bill. This course would be better than its rejection by a vote of the House.

I shall be at the House at 5 o'clock.—Ever sincerely yours,   ABERDARE.

In consequence of this, Sir John saw the Lord Chancellor (Lord Halsbury) more than once, and eventually convinced him that the Bill effected an improvement in the Law. The Lord-Advocate then took exception to it, but eventually he also withdrew his opposition and the Bill passed both Houses.

For many years Lady Lubbock had been in very indifferent health. It seems doubtful whether her system ever recovered fully from the shock of the terrifying railway accident in which she and Sir John were involved, as previously mentioned, only a short time before the birth of their youngest son. On October 19 she passed away at High Elms, and Sir John was left a widower with six children—three boys, of whom the eldest, the present Lord Avebury, was just of age and had lately gone up to Oxford, and three girls, of whom one, the eldest, as noted, had been married in 1876 to Mr. Mulholland and was now a widow. In 1882 the second daughter, Constance, married Mr. Sydney (now Lord) Buxton, and the third, Gertrude, has remained unmarried, and has always taken a very keen and valuable interest in such social questions as the better organisation of charity in London.

Sir John writes, under date Sunday, Oct. 19 : " In the middle of the night I was called up and found Nelly in a sort of faint from which she never rallied, and she passed away so quietly that we did not know the exact moment. It is a comfort to think that I have been with her constantly during the last month."

He did not go to the City again all the rest of that year.

CHAPTER XVI

(AGE 46-47)

IN the House of Commons he introduced two
Bills this year, one to amend the Companies
Act, which was read a second time on February 9
and passed on February 16 ; and the Ancient
Monuments Bill, which was read a second time
on February 10 and passed on February 24—
neither being opposed. The last had already
been through its second reading no less than
six times in the House of Commons, and had
gone through Committee twice, and now he
thought it was really safe, especially after it
passed its second reading in the House of Lords.
As a matter of fact, however, it did not become
law until 1882. Before Lord Stanhope, who had
taken charge of it in the Upper House, was able
to get it through Committee, Parliament was
dissolved. Regarding it, however, as secure, he
enters a pathetic little note in reference to it
in his diary of date, February 24,—" How pleased
Nelly would have been ! "

It may be observed that Lord Eversley, in
his admirable book, *Commons, Forests, and Foot-
paths*, writes : " I was myself responsible for the

framing of the Ancient Monuments Act of 1882.
It need not be pointed out that Lord Avebury
was the originator of the policy which led to it.
For many previous years he had pressed upon
Parliament a measure dealing with this question.
The main provision of his Bill was that the
Government should be empowered to acquire
by compulsion, not the monuments themselves,
which it was intended to protect, but the owners'
right and power to destroy or injure them.   In
dealing with the question I could not bring
myself to place on the Statute Book a measure
recognising the right of an owner to destroy an
ancient monument.   I could not admit the
existence of any such right of property.   In
place of this I proposed a permissive measure,
one enabling an owner to place his monument
under the protection of the State.   Having
effected this by a very simple deed, the State
was to be charged with the duty of protecting
and preserving it, and neither the owner nor any
other person would thenceforward be permitted
to injure it.   But otherwise the property of the
owner in it was to be unaffected."

The dissolution was on March 15, and Sir
John immediately went down to Maidstone.
His friends confidently expected him to win, but
the seat was lost mainly owing to an unfortunate
and purely local influence.   His colleague, Sir
Sydney Waterlow, thinking to benefit the town,
had bought some slum property and pulled the
wretched houses down, intending to build, as
indeed he shortly afterwards did, better ones
in their places.   The immediate effect, however,

was to create a good deal of inconvenience. The people who had to leave were furious, and the small shopkeepers, who lost customers, almost equally so. They showed their resentment by voting for the Tories, and the majority being in any case narrow, the change was sufficient to bring in the Tory candidates Mr. Ross and Col. Aylmer. There were also rumours of some small bribery and much treating, but it is only fair to say that these were never substantiated.

He was much disappointed at the time, for he had become greatly attached to his constituents, but the result was not an unmixed evil. A few weeks afterwards Mr. Lowe, the sitting member for the University of London, was raised to the Peerage, and Sir John Lubbock's was among the names of those suggested to take his place.

No Tory candidate for the University seat came forward, but four Liberals were suggested— Sir George Jessel, the Master of the Rolls ; Sir Julian Goldsmid, Sir W. Gull, and Sir John Lubbock.

Under these circumstances it was determined to hold a preliminary ballot among all those who had voted for Mr. Lowe in his last contest, and every elector was asked to mark his paper in the order of his preference. On examination the papers were found to be marked thus :

	First Votes.	Second Votes.	Third Votes.	Fourth Votes.
Sir J. Lubbock . . .	769	132	53	39
Sir G. Jessel . . .	192	354	203	125
Sir W. Gull . . .	49	130	201	419
Sir J. Goldsmid . . .	33	241	358	191

The result appears to have come as a great surprise. The other three candidates withdrew. Mr. (later Sir) Michael Foster was his Chairman, Sir G. J. Fitch, Sir F. (afterwards Lord) Herschell, Dr. (afterwards Sir) S. Wilks, and Mr. F. J. Wood were the Vice-Chairmen, and Mr. (afterwards Sir) E. H. Busk, Secretary.

The following circular, signed by more than thirty of the principal graduates, was issued to the Constituency, and resulted in the formation of a Committee of over 800. It includes in a brief statement the principal public acts of Sir John's career up to this date :

DEAR SIR—You will doubtless have seen, from the newspapers, that a vacancy in the representation of our University in Parliament is imminent, owing to the elevation of the Right Honourable Robert Lowe to the Peerage, so that the University has again to select a representative. In these circumstances we venture to call your attention to the exceptionally high qualifications possessed by Sir John Lubbock, who has now for many years past devoted a considerable portion of his time to the service of our University, having for 14 years been member of the Senate, and for nearly eight years Vice-Chancellor. If Sir John Lubbock became the member for our University we should not necessarily lose his services as our Vice-Chancellor, and should, by returning him as our representative in Parliament, confer a benefit upon Parliament and the country at large.

Sir John Lubbock combines in himself eminence in many branches of knowledge and walks of life, and thus may be said to represent, as few (if any) others could, the different faculties which combine to form our University. In addition to the valuable work which he has done, and is doing, for us, we find that Sir John Lubbock has in the City of London made himself a name, not only as one of the greatest among the Bankers of Lombard Street, but also as the introducer of the system

of Country Clearing, by which the benefits of the clearing
house were extended to country bankers.

When the Institute of Bankers, now numbering more
than 2000 members, was formed, Sir John Lubbock
was unanimously chosen President. He also introduced
a method of examination for banker's clerks, conducted
by the City of London College in the same manner as
the examinations instituted by the Government under
the Civil Service Commissioners. He is the Honorary
Secretary of the London Association of Bankers, and
thus represents the London Bankers on questions relating
to Government in Parliament, and whenever there is
any necessity for a medium between Bankers and the
Government. In addition to all these labours he has
contributed many valuable papers to financial literature,
and was a member of the International Coinage Commission appointed by the Government. Sir John
Lubbock's career as a Member of Parliament since he
first entered it as representing the Borough of Maidstone,
in the year 1870, has been marked by a success as
brilliant, and by an industry as unwearied, as his career
in the City. In addition to the usual labour of attending
meetings, the sittings of the House and working upon
Committees, Sir John Lubbock has succeeded in
passing through the House of Commons no less than 11
measures, the characters of which are best indicated by
their titles, namely, (1) Apothecaries' Acts Medical Act
Amendment Bill ; (2) Bank Holiday Bill ; (3) Falsification of Accounts Bill ; (4) The Banker's Book Evidence
Bill ; (5) The College of Surgeons' Medical Act Amendment Bill ; (6) The University of London Medical Act
Amendment Bill ; (7) The Factors' Act Amendment
Bill ; (8) The Bills of Exchange Bill ; (9) The Dental
Practitioners' Bill ; (10) The Companies Act Amendment
Bill ; (11) Ancient Monuments Bill, which last, however,
was thrown out in the House of Lords. He was a
Member of the Permanent Committee of Public Accounts.

He has taken an active part in most debates relating
to financial and educational questions ; and the suggestions which he has so long and so strenuously advocated
respecting the increased recognition of the rudiments of
science in the public elementary schools, have thus far
been accepted by the Government and embodied in the
official Code.

Sir John Lubbock has also served on three important public Commissions; he was a member of the Public School Commission, of the Royal Commission for the Advancement of Science, and of the International Monetary Commission.

In Science Sir John Lubbock is scarcely less distinguished than he is in the Mercantile and Parliamentary spheres of life. His labours have been principally directed to researches into the development, habits and structures of the lower animals, chiefly insects and crustacea, and on the History of Civilisation, as Illustrated by the Habits and Customs of Ancient and Modern Savages. On the first of these subjects he has published an elaborate treatise under the title of the *Monograph of the Thysanura and Collembola*, and more popular works, on *The Origin and Metamorphoses of Insects*, and on *Wild Flowers Considered in Relation to Insects*, and more than 60 Memoirs in the Transactions of the Royal and other Scientific Societies. Some of his Lectures on Botany and Entomology have recently been published in a separate volume, as a companion to one of Educational and Financial Essays.

On the development of civilisation, Sir John Lubbock has written two standard works, *Prehistoric Times, as illustrated by Ancient Remains and the Manners and Customs of Modern Savages*, which has passed through five editions, and *The Origin of Civilisation and the Primitive Condition of Man*, which has passed through three editions, and both of which have been translated into all the principal European languages.

Sir John Lubbock has received numerous distinctions, which show the appreciation in which he is held. Besides being the Vice-Chancellor of our University, he is a Trustee of the British Museum, an Oxford Doctor of Civil Law, a Doctor of Laws of Dublin, a Fellow of the Royal, Linnean, Geographical, Geological, Antiquarian and other Societies. He has been President of the Ethnological Society, of its successor, the Anthropological Institute of Great Britain and Ireland, and of the Entomological Society. He has been Vice-President of the British Association and of the Royal and Linnean Societies; and is Honorary Member of many of the most important foreign Scientific Societies.

It is needless to say that Sir John Lubbock's political career has been that of a consistent Liberal.

If, after consideration of the facts above mentioned, you are willing to support Sir John Lubbock's candidature, we shall feel obliged by your signing the enclosed Post-Card.

The *Times* wrote, respecting the comparative claims of the candidates for the seat :

The eminent graduates, whose names were submitted to the Liberal electors together with that of Sir John Lubbock, will assuredly think it no slight that their Vice-Chancellor should have been preferred to themselves. As a choice had to be made, there seems to be a special fitness in the selection of Sir John Lubbock. There was no member of the late Parliament whose rejection by his former constituents was more universally and deservedly regretted than the late Member for Maidstone, and there is probably no public man who is better entitled to enjoy the unfettered security of a University seat. Sir John Lubbock is as much at home in Lombard Street as he is at Burlington House, and his voice in the House of Commons carries as much weight in matters of commerce and high finance as it does on any of the subjects which come within the wide range of his scientific and literary acquirements. It would certainly have been regarded as unfortunate by all who wish to see the House of Commons truly representative of the mind and culture of the nation, as well as of its practical capacity, if Sir John Lubbock, rejected at Maidstone, had failed to find a seat elsewhere, and it strikes us as singularly appropriate that the University of London should have determined to provide him with a safe haven for the future.

Sir John was elected without a contest on June 2, and held the seat for twenty years, until his elevation to the Peerage in 1900.

In 1881 he was unlucky in the Parliamentary Ballot, and thought it useless to bring in the Ancient Monuments Bill again, and accordingly moved a resolution. The Bill had always been approved by the Liberal front bench, and he took it for granted that his resolution would be supported by the Liberal Government. Indeed the Whips themselves were of that opinion.

It came on about 10.30 on March 11, and just before it was taken Lord R. Grosvenor came to him in much surprise to say that Mr. Gladstone was going to oppose, and suggested that perhaps the resolution had better be withdrawn. Sir John, however, declined to do so, and to his own astonishment, as well as that of others, beat the Government by 79 to 56.

It was curious that he should not have been fully informed of Mr. Gladstone's intentions in the matter. Earlier in the year Mr. and Mrs. Gladstone had been at High Elms—Mr. Gladstone "in great spirits" as Sir John notes. But evidently this opposition did not check in any way their mutual esteem, for he further writes that on April 4 he dined with Sir T. E. May where Gladstone was, and had much friendly talk with him. Gladstone told him that once when he was Chancellor of the Exchequer he found that the Malt Tax had been levied for three years without authority!

He spent the Whitsuntide holidays in the New Forest. His eldest son John was now at Balliol, and he frequently went to Oxford, sometimes accompanied by his two eldest daughters, to stay with Professor Jowett.

On May 24 he was elected President of the Linnean Society.

It does not appear that he took any active

part in the vehement scenes of the year in the
House of Commons. His diary notes : " Wed.,
Feb. 2nd — the long sitting of 42 hours from
Monday afternoon to Wednesday morning at 9,
when the Speaker stopped it. I went down
with Grant Duff to York House." " Thursday,
Feb. 3rd. Great excitement in the House. Davitt
arrested. Dillon disregarded Speaker's ruling
and was suspended, then Parnell. The other
Land Leaguers refused to leave the House and
vote, so they also were all suspended." Notwithstanding which he is able to note that at
the " week - end " party at High Elms were
" The Gladstones, Sir D. C. Marjoribanks, etc.,
etc. *Gladstone in great spirits.*"

The Jubilee meeting of the British Association
occurring this year was, of course, a very great
occasion. It was held at York in August and
September under his Presidency. His presidential address was given on August 31. A
temporary installation of electric light was
attempted, which flickered terribly and was
very trying for the reading of the address.
However he seems to have made himself well
heard, and it was very favourably received,
both by its audience and by the Press.

The *Spectator* said that it was " one of the
most remarkable and interesting which any
President of the British Association has delivered
for many years."

" Wherever Sir John Lubbock appeared,"
says a writer in the *Guardian*, " he was attended
by a dense crowd, which never went away disappointed. Zoology and Botany was the depart-

ment which he chiefly favoured, and on Friday
he gave in it a most interesting account on the
manner in which the seed of a certain grass, the
Stipa, buries itself in the ground."

Probably, however, the encomium which gave
Sir John most satisfaction of all was the following
from him, whom he ever piously regarded as
his father in science, Charles Darwin. We may
all echo one sentence of that great man's letter,
" How on earth you find time is a mystery."

DOWN, BECKENHAM, KENT,
August 2nd, 1881.

MY DEAR LUBBOCK—I have read with pleasure your
Address. You have piled honours high on my head.

I have scribbled such thoughts and remarks, as would
have occurred to me if I had read your Address when
published. I fear that this will be of little or no use to
you, except perhaps, in one or two cases, by leading you
to make further enquiry.

I had put a pamphlet on one side for you, as I think
that you would like some time to read it, and it has
occurred to me that from this excellent *résumé* of Dr.
Adler's work (which, no doubt, you have read) you
might easily make a short abstract for your Address,
for I think that parthenogenesis deserves special notice
in recent scientific work.

I have torn out a page for you to illustrate and
strengthen what you say about inoculation.

My suggestions and criticisms are poor affairs, but they
are the best which I could send.

This Address must have cost you much labour, and I
congratulate you on its virtual completion. How on
earth you find time is a mystery to me.—Yours very
sincerely,   CH. DARWIN.

In the afternoon of the first day of the Association's meeting he had walked to the Cathedral
with Huxley. At the entrance they met Professor
Henry J. Smith, who put up his hands with a look
of mock surprise. " Ah," said Huxley, " you did

not expect to see me here." " Well," said Smith, looking up, " if I had it would have been on a pinnacle."

In the department of Anatomy and Physiology his brother Montagu read a paper of which the *Times* wrote :

The paper of most general interest was probably that by Dr. Montagu Lubbock, on the development of the colour sense. It has been a favourite theory recently, countenanced by the name of Gladstone, that the sense for colour is of comparatively recent development, but the exact researches of Dr. Lubbock do not lend much countenance to the theory, though he himself seems to think that it ought to be true.

Sir John's abilities and achievements were so very remarkable that they have rather cast into the shade the talents, far above the average, of several of his brothers, none of whom, however, showed his extraordinary industry and facility of economising time. Besides the Bank, in which Henry and Beaumont were partners, there was another family business, connected with the West Indies, under the name at first of Cavan & Co., and later of Cavan, Lubbock & Co., into which some of the brothers went on leaving Eton. Sir Nevile,[1] the present Governor of the Royal Exchange Assurance, distinguished himself later as chairman of the West Indian Committee. Frederick was one of the brothers who shared Sir John's interest in scientific pursuits. Edgar, at one time thinking of entering the legal profession, came out head of a long list of candidates in the solicitors' preliminary examination.

[1] Since the above was written, Sir Nevile died quite suddenly on September 12, 1914.

He also obtained the gold medal in the Law School of London University, an honourable trophy which is only given as the reward of exceptional merit. But of all the brothers the one to whom Sir John himself ever gave the credit of being gifted with the most original and powerful intellect was the above - mentioned Montagu, a physician. Most unfortunately he had a very bad carriage accident when he was no more than nineteen years old, which completely shattered his health for a long while.

Early in October Sir John's great friends, the Grant Duffs, sailed from England for Sir Mountstuart to take up his office in Madras, and Sir John felt the loss of their close intimacy very keenly.

A note of his diary on the 13th of the same month may raise a smile, in view of subsequent events : " At the Guildhall to hear Gladstone— a magnificent speech. When he announced that Parnell was to be arrested, every one sprang up and cheered."

A little later, Sir John was at Knowsley meeting the Gladstones, and afterwards returned with them to Hawarden, where he had much talk with Mr. Gladstone about Homer, the senses of animals, etc. " His room," Sir John writes in his diary, " is very comfortable, with detached bookcases all round projecting into the room, with just space enough for any one to get in between."

It was in the course of this year, at Castle Howard, that he first met the lady who was destined to become his second wife, Miss Alice

Fox Pitt, daughter of General Pitt Rivers. The General's interest in archaeology, and his museum at Rushmore would naturally supply a common ground of interest which he and Sir John might share.

His very first meeting with Miss Fox Pitt was characteristic of his unfailing kindliness and thought for other people. The party was a large one, and she, a girl of eighteen, a niece of the house, had come down late for breakfast. It appears that he had not seen her the previous night. She received a sharp scolding from her aunt. Those were days when unpunctuality for breakfast, or perhaps even breakfasting in bed, were not a habit as they now are. The rest of the party rose from the table and left the young girl alone—all except Sir John, who remained to keep her company and to attend to her wants.

Under date November 9, Sir John notes that he was at Woburn for the "week-end," where was Count Bismarck amongst the party, and that the Duke of Bedford quoted a passage of Pomponius Mela on Ireland (*De Situ Orbis,* Liber III., caput 6): "Cultores eius inconditi sunt, et omnium virtutum ignari, pietatis admodum expertes."

On December 1 he read a paper at the Linnean on the Limits in Vision of the Lower Animals, showing that they could see further than we are able to, at the violet end of the spectrum.

It was in 1881, too, that he began his interesting study on the form of leaves. I remember his saying to me, " Has it ever occurred to you to ask yourself why it is that the leaf buds of the beech are elongated and those of the oak are round ? "

I mention this not only for any interest that may belong to the answer of the question in itself, but also as a type of the kind of questions which he was always putting to himself. It appears to me that this faculty of asking himself questions about the familiar facts, which most of us note with our eyes, day after day, but take no note of at all with our reasoning attention, is the very faculty which enabled him to find out so much and to be so interesting in disquisition on very many topics connected with science and natural history. Probably he had acquired it in large measure from his great father in science, Darwin, but assuredly it was of none the less value for that derivation. When I confessed that I had never had the intelligent curiosity to put to myself the question which he suggested, he said : " I think the reason must be that the leaf of the beech is not indented at the edges, therefore when it is rolled up it has to assume the elongated form, if it is not to be torn. The leaf of the oak is deeply indented, in many places, so that it can be rolled up round without a tear."

It was such speculations as these, which every most familiar object suggested to him, that made a country walk with him of greater interest than a like excursion with almost any other man.

He notes that it was on October 18 that he began the study of leaf-forms, and " went to the Museum to look them up." On the same date in the following month he was with the

Evelyns at Wotton—" beautiful old place," as he very truly remarks of it, adding a remarkable note that " John Evelyn's dried plants collected in 1645 are still in very fair preservation." John Evelyn, it is hardly necessary to say, was the author of *Sylva*, and probably the first of Englishmen to make any real study of trees.

Some years before, when in Algiers with the Grant Duffs, Sir John had acquired a house and property called the Campagne des Fleurs, and thither he went on December 15, with his daughters Constance and Gertrude, and his youngest son Rolfe. They had lovely weather. He records that he and Rolfe bathed on Christmas Day. They did not return home until the middle of the following month.

CHAPTER XVII

THE DEATH OF DARWIN (1882)

(AGE 48)

In 1882 Sir John and his children returned from Algiers on January 14. Towards the end of the month he was suffering from gout, an enemy that was by way of making fierce onslaughts from time to time on more than one member of the Lubbock brotherhood. It was only with the greatest pain and difficulty—as his diary narrates—that he was able to get to the Parish Church, on February 3, in order to give away his daughter Constance, who was married on that day to Mr. Sydney Buxton. " She has been a dear good daughter and a great help," Sir John records ; " I hope and believe that she has every prospect of happiness."

It is a prospect that was fully, but only too briefly realised. Her death occurred in 1892.

He mentions that on March 24 he made " an elaborate speech " in favour of Free Trade, and against Mr. Ritchie's " Fair Trade " resolution.

He also brought forward the question of Forestry, and discussed the institution of a School of Forestry, but, on the whole, was strongly in favour of using, for education in this direction, the existing machinery of the Agricultural Colleges.

In conjunction with Mr. Bouverie and others he formed a company to introduce Mr. Edison's system of electric lighting into Great Britain, and several letters on the subject, from the great inventor, are among the correspondence of this year.

There is also a letter of about the same date from the then Princess of Wales, the present Queen Alexandra, expressing her appreciation of Sir John's book, *Ants, Bees, and Wasps*. Here and there in his diary are notes of his meeting one or other members of the Royal Family from time to time, and on nearly all such occasions they seem to have spoken to him with the greatest interest of his experiments with these insects. At this period of his varied career it is indeed evident that the aspect of his multitudinous industry which was impressing itself most vividly on the popular imagination was his study of the intelligence of the hymenopterous insects. For the time being, at all events, it was over-shadowing all that he had done in antiquarian research, in other branches of science, in finance, or in social legislation.

A very sad note indeed is sounded in the diary's entry of Sunday, March 19 : " Arnold Morley for Sunday—went up to Darwin's— the last time I saw him." Very shortly afterwards the great teacher of evolution was seized with his last illness and died on April 20. Sir John writes : " For thirty years he has been very good to me, and a talk with him was as good as sea air."

Immediately on hearing of the sad news Sir John drew up the following memorial to the Dean of Westminster.

HOUSE OF COMMONS, 21 *April* 1882.

VERY REVEREND SIR—We hope you will not think we are taking a liberty if we venture to suggest that it would be acceptable to a very large number of our countrymen of all classes and opinions that our illustrious countryman, Mr. Darwin, should be buried in Westminster Abbey.—We remain, your obedient Servants,

This letter was signed by the following :

John Lubbock, N. J. Maskelyne, A. J. Mundella, G. O. Trevelyan, L. Playfair, C. W. Dilke, D. Wedderburn, A. Russell, H. Davey, B. Armitage, R. B. Martin, F. W. Buxton, E. L. Stanley, H. Broadhurst, J. Barran, J. H. Cheetham, H. Holland, Campbell Bannerman, C. Bruce, R. Fort, J. Cropper, E. Marjoribanks, Kensington, T. Burt, T. Brassey, Fawcett, Herschell, Brand.

It is recorded in Sir Francis Darwin's *Life and Letters of Charles Darwin*, that some of the family would have preferred a quiet interment in the country churchyard at Down, but it seems as if they were led to realise that their father, by reason of his greatness, belonged in some measure to the nation, and that the nation could not feel that proper veneration had been paid him unless his remains were laid among those whom the British people most wish to honour.

The funeral took place on April 26, the pallbearers being the Duke of Devonshire, the Duke of Argyll, Lord Derby, Professor Huxley, Sir J. Hooker, Mr. Lowell, Mr. W. Spottiswoode, Mr. Wallace, and Sir John Lubbock.

Such a friend as Sir John Lubbock had, and lost, in Charles Darwin, is given to few men indeed. We may recall his whimsical disappointment when as a boy his father had said to him, " a very fortunate thing for you has come to Down," and he guessed it might be a " pony," only to be told that it was Mr. Darwin who had come to reside there. How many times he must have remembered that guess and that pang of disappointment as he reflected over all that Darwin's friendship and example had meant to him. That Darwin was his " father in science " he never for a moment disguised, nor the immense debt that he owed him in the way of most profitably directing his scientific energies. Nor is it on the intellectual side alone that the counsel and the example of the great Darwin counted for much with him. He was immensely indebted, too, to the example of his fine and serene character—cheerful, uncomplaining, courageous in the midst of the attacks of ill health, and of enemies who were unable to appreciate his work and who misunderstood its tendency.

This moment, when Sir John was still in the first pain of his loss, seems a fitting one for the consideration of his own attitude towards the whole movement of thought with which the name of Darwin is most prominently connected. It was rather a remarkable attitude. We have seen him taking his active part in support of the freedom of the new thought. We have to remember that it was a moment when the new reading of the geological record by Lyell, followed by the more extended inferences of Darwin, had

forced men of sober judgment to abandon many
of the traditions in which they had been reared.
And such abandonment is never without its pain
and struggle. Often it is accompanied with a
violent inclination towards the opposite extreme
of thought to that from which they have been
evicted. But the majority of men are not of
very sober judgment, and of them the traditions
have a sustained grip. All those thus gripped
fell fiercely on the new doctrines and on their
authors, and, as we have seen, Sir John was a
foremost champion in the ranks of those who
supported the new learning.

Nevertheless we find him, when at home on
the Sundays, sedulously attending the services
at the village church. More than that, I have
been told by one who has the best of all opportunities of knowing, that on no single morning
of his life until death was closing upon him did
he omit to read a chapter of the Bible before
commencing the long day's work. It is to be
remembered, as noticed above, that this was a
moment when the swing of the pendulum of
thought was liable to be very violent. It was
the day of the materialists, who believed that
all the problems which the human mind suggests
to itself were to be solved in terms of matter.
Miracles were defined as " things that do not
happen," the universe, it was said, had been
proved " so full of atoms that there was no room
for spirits."

In the midst of that extreme materialism we
find Sir John, though many of his best friends
were among the extremists, surprisingly moderate

in his attitude. He was ever reticent as to his mental outlook on the great mysteries, but I believe that he had arrived at the conclusion, with which most men of science were to wait the best part of half a century before they came into any agreement, that there was some room, after all, among the atoms for the spirits, that the human intellect did rightly and according to the intention of its Maker in reading as accurately as may be the story which Lyell found in the rocks, and Wallace and Darwin in the whole life history of the globe, but that besides these records there was, as man's special gift, through his evolutionary development, that religious sense or intuition, or whatever term you please to give it, which was of other stuff than to be subject to the test of human reason. That I believe to have been his attitude, though I do not claim to have heard him explicit in regard to it. It was at least the attitude with which his life-long practice appears in strict conformity.

An occurrence infinitely more tragic than the death of Darwin, though of less close personal grief to him, happened later in the same year— the murder, by the assassin's dagger, of Lord Frederick Cavendish in the Phoenix Park at Dublin. It may be remembered that, as later evidence went to show, the murderous assault was probably intended rather for Lord Frederick's companion than for himself, but this was not known at the time, nor, even so, does it mitigate the horror. He was a man universally respected and loved. Sir John has the note in his diary that Lord Frederick had been dining

with them only on the previous Wednesday,
when he had made the remark, which came
to have the aspect of tragic significance, " I do
not envy the man who takes Forster's place."

On Thursday, May 11, Lord Frederick was
buried at Chatsworth, and Sir John attended
the funeral.

One of the consequences touching Sir John,
of Lord Frederick's tragedy, was that the conferring of the degree of LL.D. with which the
Cambridge Senate was proposing to honour him,
was deferred until the following year. Lord
Frederick's father, the old Duke of Devonshire,
was Chancellor, and no degrees were given that
year, out of respect for Lord Frederick's memory.

At the end of May, Sir John went with his
daughter Gertrude and his son Norman for a
short tour in Switzerland, but was in his place
again in the House of Commons by July 6, when
his Bills of Exchange Bill passed its third reading.
He notes that on the 29th of the month he went
" to the Maskelynes at Basset Down to meet
Ruskin. On Monday we drove over to Avebury,
a lovely and delightful day. Ruskin had no
idea there was such a place and was enchanted
with it." This is the earliest occasion on which
we find him using the spelling of the place-name
which has now become familiar through his
taking it for his title—" Avebury." Previously
he had written " Abury." Of this visit Mr.
Ruskin himself writes, in a letter, published in his
collected *Works*, to Mrs. Severn : " Mrs. Maskelyne is such a botanist, and to see Sir John
Lubbock and her hunting together over every

field they could get at without breaking the fences, was quite lovely."

On August 22 he was at Southampton with the Wilberforces for the British Association meeting. He was astonished to find himself in an atmosphere of Spiritualism! Mr. Bishop, the thought-reader, was asked to meet him. It was suggested that Mr. Bishop should try to read the number of a £5 note in Sir John's purse. " He placed his hand over, and sometimes grasped my wrist, writing at the same time on a blackboard. The following day he called and asked if he might give an account of what took place. I did not much like this, and thought it better to put the matter in my own words." Accordingly he wrote Mr. Bishop the following letter :

LONDON, 25 *August* 1882.

DEAR SIR—When I met you at Canon Wilberforce's, I did not expect to be asked for a statement of what took place, but as you wish me to put down what occurred with reference to the £5 note, I will not decline to do so.

I took the note out of my purse, looked at the number, and then replaced it without showing it to any one else. The number was, if I remember right, 95,974. You gave the first number right, and almost at once, then hesitated some minutes, eventually making a three, but at the same time expressing doubt. The remaining numbers you wrote down correctly. I was not conscious of giving any indication which could have guided you, and, whatever the explanation may be, the experiment interested me very much.—I am, yours truly,

JOHN LUBBOCK.

W. I. Bishop, Esq.

P.S.—You subsequently rubbed out the three and made a five, but I do not mention this, because I had in the meantime stated that five was the right number.

A note of October 26 is curious.

Dined at May's.   Gladstone said that on one occasion he had peculiar difficulty in making up his Government. He and Mrs. G. wrote the names and the offices on bits of paper, and spent the whole evening in trying to match them.   At last he gave it up, and they went to bed.   He had a good night, and during his sleep everything had arranged itself satisfactorily in his brain.

About this time he began some experiments, which he did not carry to a very satisfactory conclusion, on the intelligence of the dog.   " Am thinking," he notes, " of trying to apply to a dog the system under which the Deaf and Dumb are taught, and especially that used in Laura Bridgman's case.   I went to the Deaf and Dumb Institute and explained my idea to the master. He said he would like to try it, and I arranged to send him a dog."

I ventured to point out to Sir John, and he fully admitted the force of the objection, that in experimenting as he did on the dog's power of discrimination, he was experimenting with the wrong sense.   A dog's real and ultimate sense of discrimination and identification is olfactory rather than visual — by the nose, not by the eye.

The conclusions, such as they were, at which Sir John did arrive, and the experiments that he tried, are recorded in his book on the *Senses of Animals*.

At the end of the year he made an arrangement with the other partners at the Bank which set him free from the obligation of regular attendance, so that he should have the more time to devote

to science and politics. It was agreed that he
should be at liberty to look in when convenient
to him, and that his advice should always be at
the firm's disposal, but that all the routine work
should be done by the other members.

CHAPTER XVIII

SECOND MARRIAGE (1883–1884)

(AGE 49-50)

A PENALTY that Sir John Lubbock rather naturally had to suffer as the result of taking the Ancient Monuments so specially under his personal care, was that of being approached from all sides with requests that he should use his influence for the protection of this or the other work of historic interest. We hardly need to be assured that he paid most careful attention and gave generous response to all appeals on a subject which touched him so closely. Readers of *Tom Brown's Schooldays* will not have forgotten the time-honoured ceremony of the " Scouring of the White Horse." It is by the author of the great picture of school-boy life that the following letter was addressed to Sir John :

BEDFORD STREET, COVENT GARDEN,
15/1/83.

DEAR LUBBOCK—I forget whether the White Horse was scheduled to your Ancient Monuments Bill. If not, your machinery may possibly be able to reach it ; if yes, pray have it looked to. I was startled and angered 3 weeks since in passing Uffington on the G.W.Ry., to see that it was invisible to any eye except one, like

Emery Walker Ph. sc

High Elms

mine, which knows the exact spot to look for it. I daresay
you are aware that it is an absolutely unique pagan
monument. I gave in for popular purposes (in the little
book I wrote about it) to the popular theory in the vale,
that it is a memorial of Alfred's victory over the Danes
at Ashdown (close by), but there is not the least doubt
that it is at least a century and a half older, being in
shape the animal which went for a horse on the pagan
standard of the West Saxons. There were many, thirteen
at least, in other parts of England, all of which have been
lost, as this seems likely to be in our awakened time !
When I was a boy there was a feeling about it all through
the country side which enforced its cleaning (" scouring "
it was called) every few years, whether Lord Craven did
his duty by it, as ground landlord, or not. But then its
preservation was connected with rough rural sports,
which have disappeared before school boards and the
blue ribbon army, and seem likely to carry the Horse
with them. The late Lord Craven didn't care a straw
for such things, and never had it scraped or touched that
I ever heard of, and now he is dead and his heir only ten
or twelve years old. If your Society (is there one ?)
will intervene I will gladly subscribe towards the
expenses of scraping and stamping the chalk, which is
all that is necessary. While I am about it I may add
that I see a heavy clump of trees grown up round
" Wayland Smith's Cave," an interesting Druidical (or
other) cromlech about a mile from the W. Horse, towards
Ashbury, on the hill-top, and it would be satisfactory
to know whether *this* monument (referred to in W.
Scott's *Woodstock*, and round which hangs a curious
tradition) is still there and in what condition.

I hope the Working Men's College flourishes and does
not tax you too much ? I am just up for a few days to
keep term, not too late to wish you all good in the new
year.—Ever yours,   THO. HUGHES.

You will find this White Horse mentioned in Domes-
day Book.

A frequent and valued correspondent, already
quoted, was the Reverend A. C. Smith of Yatesbury Rectory, Calne, not far from Avebury.
The following letter from him shows how great a

danger at one time threatened the better known and better preserved, though originally far smaller, Druidical temple at Stonehenge.

WILTSHIRE ARCHAEOLOGICAL AND NATURAL HISTORY SOCIETY

YATESBURY RECTORY, CALNE,
Jan. 3, 1883.

DEAR SIR JOHN—I must apologize for troubling you with this letter, when you have so many things to attend to, but I know nobody else to whom I can so effectually state my grievance.

In a note just received from a leading solicitor in Devizes is this ominous tale : " Have you heard of the threatened invasion of Stonehenge by a Railway Engineer ? The London & South Western, under the name of the ' Bristol and London and South-Western Junction Railway Company,' are now energetically promoting a Bill in Parliament for taking a railway from a point in the South-Western Railway near Graveley (marked on the Ordnance Map as ' Hampshire Gap ') by Amesbury, Stonehenge, Shrewton, Chitterne, Westbury, and Radstock to Bristol.

" The engineer proposes to take the line *straight through the Cursus* ! ! "

This is the substance of my correspondent's letter, and I am afraid the thing is true, as he is a good authority, and would not have written to me without being sure of his facts.

But what is to be done ? If anybody can put a spoke in the wheel you can ; but I fear the Ancient Monuments Bill will not include the Cursus ! !—With every good wish for the New Year to you and yours, Believe me, my dear Sir John, yours very sincerely,

A. C. SMITH.

In response to this letter Sir John put down a notice of opposition to the Bill, in consequence of which the promoters invited him to confer with them. This he consented to, and Mr. S. Morley, M.P. for Bristol, attended the conference. After some discussion Mr. Morley said he was afraid they would think him ignorant, but might he ask what the "cursus" was. "Oh, Mr. Morley," burst out the engineer, "they do say it was a British racecourse, but I assure you it is entirely out of repair, and not the slightest use to any one now."

Finally the promoters agreed to divert the line, which really involved no difficulty or expense, and Sir John withdrew his opposition. The Bill, however, was eventually thrown out on other grounds.

Ever since their institution, the charge had been brought against the "St. Lubbock" holidays that they seriously increased the national drunkenness. A curious step was taken in order to test the truth of the statement. It was not initiated by Sir John himself, but by a member of the House of Commons who had been a strong supporter of the Bank Holiday Act. He writes to Sir John that he had been having a warm discussion with a friend on the ethical aspect of the Bank Holidays, one of the disputants (the writer of the letter) holding that they encouraged saving habits, and thus temperance, while the other maintained that thousands of unhappy holiday-makers " would spend Easter Monday in never reaching their destinations, and would crowd the Railway termini in a state of drunkenness."

Desiring to provide himself, as he says, with a missile to hurl at this position, the writer induced Mr. Fenton, manager of the South Eastern Railway, to arrange a special staff to count up all the persons the worse for drink, on the next

Bank Holiday, at the three London termini of his railway. He enclosed a copy of the report, forwarded by the manager, adding that " As the patron saint of these festivals, he is sure Sir John will be glad to know, from so official a source, of the increasing sobriety of the ' cheap tripper,' and will be glad to add to his collection of papers on Bank Holidays so valuable and reliable a bit of evidence."

The said report is contained in the following letter :

SOUTH EASTERN RAILWAY, SUPERINTENDENT'S OFFICE,
LONDON BRIDGE STATION,
April 6th, 1883.

DEAR SIR—Referring to your instructions for observation to be kept on Easter Monday with respect to the sobriety of passengers ; I beg to inform you, that at Charing Cross, throughout the day, there were only three persons noticed to be under the influence of drink, and they walked away without troubling any one.

At Cannon Street, only one person, during the day, was noticed not to be sober.

At London Bridge, there were two persons, from early morning until midnight, noticed to be similarly affected.—Yours truly,   E. J. SEARS.

Miles Fenton, Esq., General Manager.

On April 7 Mr. Gladstone again was at High Elms for the Sunday, and Sir John notes that he told them that of the electors who originally voted for him at Newark, sixteen only remained. It shows how closely he watched his old friends. Mr. Gladstone was much interested in the doings of a puppy with which Sir John was working, trying its intelligence. One of his experiments was to conceal dainties behind a piece of cardboard on which " Food " was written, in large

black letters ; but he did not make much success
of the literary education of the dog.

On May 11 he took a short tour, with Mrs.
Mulholland and Miss Lubbock, round the Italian
Lakes, and immediately after their return he
and Miss Lubbock went to Cambridge, where he
was to receive the LL.D. degree. They stayed
with the Vice-Chancellor, Mr. Porter.

The following day the degrees were conferred,
the other recipients being Gen. Menabrea,
Michaelis, Hubner, M. Arnold, Sir R. Temple,
Watts, Stuart Poole, Gen. Walker, Mr. Goodwin,
Mr. Roscoe, Sir A. Grant, and Sir F. Ouseley.
The Undergraduates received Sir John very
warmly.

On June 22 Mr. Sydney Buxton, Sir John's
son-in-law, was returned for Peterborough by
330 majority.

Mr. Spottiswoode, the President of the Royal
Society, died on June 26 and was buried in Westminster Abbey on the 5th July. Sir John was
one of the pall-bearers, among the others being
the Duke of Northumberland, Lord Salisbury,
Lord Granville, Lord Aberdare, Mr. Siemens, and
Mr. Armstrong. This was the fourth occasion
on which he assisted in a similar capacity, the
others being as bearer of Sir J. W. Herschel, of
Sir C. Lyell, and of Mr. Darwin.

As has already been noted, the reduction of
the National Debt was a measure to which Sir
John gave much attention. Mr. J. G. Hubbard
writes to him asking him to look at a
letter on the subject which Mr. Hubbard had
written to the *Times*. He particularly enquires

whether Sir John would prefer Mr. Childers' *fixed* charge Plan, under which the redemption of Debt would increase from, say, £6,000,000 in 1885 to £9,000,000 in 1895, and to £13,000,000 in 1905, or a fixed redemption, say of £7,000,000 in permanent operation through the form of Terminable Annuities. The latter was Mr. Hubbard's proposition.

Sir John replied :

15 LOMBARD STREET,
21 *June* 1883.

MY DEAR HUBBARD—I did not answer your note yesterday, as I thought I should perhaps have seen you at the House.

£7,000,000 does not seem to me enough to devote to the repayment of debt under existing circumstances.

I am very sorry that the Government will not have the advantage of your support, for it seems to me that the importance of reducing debt somehow is much greater than the exact method which is adopted.—Believe me, yours very truly,

JOHN LUBBOCK.

Right Hon. John G. Hubbard.

The final words of the above letter : " the importance of reducing the debt somehow is much greater than the exact method which is adopted," are worth notice, because they are so very typical of the exceedingly practical way in which Sir John always set himself to the realisation of any of the very many plans which he took in hand. As has been said of him, he was " singularly adroit." He would take the means which seemed best to him, but if he failed of success by those means he would immediately turn, with remarkable suppleness and dexterity, and recommence the attempt to attain his end by some other means. It was largely this quick ability to shift his front, while keeping the same objective, that enabled him to be so extraordinarily successful in passing his measures through Parliament. He never attached much importance to method : it was the thing to be accomplished, it mattered little how, that seemed to him to signify. As in his literary work, it was substance, far more than form, that he attended to.

In August of this year *Punch* did him the honourable impertinence of selecting him as the subject of one of the " Fancy Portraits," No. 96, under the semblance of a large bumble bee, with really a very tolerable likeness of Sir John making its head and thorax. Beneath was the legend :

SIR JOHN LUBBOCK, M.P., F.R.S.

How doth the Banking Busy Bee
Improve the shining hours,
By studying on Bank Holidays
Strange insects and wild flowers.

It is really rather apt, as a testimony to his incessant diligence.

In September he went on a little tour of visits in Scotland and the north of England, of which the following is the brief itinerary as noted in his journal : " Aug. 31st, Naworth Castle. Sept. 1st, with L. Stanleys along the Roman Wall; 13th, Guisachan (presumably with the late Lady Ashburton) ; 17th, Loch Luichart ; and 24th, Haddo House (with Lord Aberdeen)."

On October 9 he was at Knowsley again, with Mrs. Mulholland and Miss Lubbock, to meet the Gladstones. His diary of October 11 records : " Had a walk with Mr Gladstone. He thinks the Greeks derived their belief in immortality mainly from Egypt. Iphigenia was, he considers, not a Homeric myth, but belongs to a later period."

It was in the autumn of this year that he went for the first time to Rushmore, the place of Major-General Lane Fox Pitt Rivers, and it is about this date that we may begin to note entries in the diary which seem significant. For example : " Saturday Nov. 17th. Went down to the Pitt Rivers'. Sunday 18th. In the morning walked with Miss Fox Pitt. Monday 19th. I had a good deal of talk with Alice Fox Pitt." In December we find this young lady a guest at High Elms, and several references about her, all in a highly appreciative strain. Nor was it long before she returned on another visit, for she passed some days with them about the time of the New Year.

Huxley had been the Rede lecturer at Cambridge in 1883. Sir John was invited to succeed him in the lectureship for 1884. He did not feel that he had leisure at this time to accept the invitation, though he did so when it was renewed two years later.

He relates a dexterous use that he made, in a speech at Accrington, of an amusing little anecdote which may be new to some, though, no doubt, with a chestnutty flavour to others : " Dec. 1st. Went to Huntington's meeting at Accrington. He spoke capitally. The meeting sang heartily and melodiously till we came in. Shuttleworth made a very nice short speech introducing Mundella and me. I was quite taken aback by the warmth with which they received me. I

introduced, *apropos* of the floods of Conservative
oratory, a story of Miss Baring's about an
American publican who said that the Falls of
Niagara would be all very well if it were not for
the poverty of the material."

The introduction of a new Reform Bill brought
into prominence the question of the best method
of representation.   Sir John Lubbock had taken
great interest in it, being strongly in favour
of a proportional representative system, and it
was on January 16 of 1884, in Mr. Beaumont
Lubbock's house in Clarges Street, that the
Proportional Representation Society was formed.
Sir John states his main argument in favour of
the system thus lucidly :

It is obvious that the present system leaves much to
chance.   Suppose, for example, there are 12,000 voters,
of whom half are Radicals and half Unionists, in three
Constituencies.

If the votes are divided as follows :

	Constituency A.	Constituency B.	Constituency C.
Radicals . . .	3000	1500	1500
Unionists . . .	1000	2500	2500

it is obvious that the Unionists would have two seats and
the Radicals only one.   But if the votes happened to lie
as follows :

	Constituency A.	Constituency B.	Constituency C.
Unionists . . .	3000	1500	1500
Radicals . . .	1000	2500	2500

it is clear that though the numbers are the same the
Radicals will have two seats and the Unionists only one.
Many of those who defend the present system do so
under the belief that, if not altogether just, it merely
gives the majority somewhat more than their share.
This however is quite a delusion.

Suppose, then, in the preceding illustration the
Unionists had 6250 votes and the Radicals 5750 ; the
Unionists would have a majority of 500.   Of course,

if the two parties were spread evenly, the Unionists would carry every seat, and the minority, though so large, would not have a single representative. On the other hand, if the majority were somewhat concentrated, as in the following example :

	Constituency A.	Constituency B.	Constituency C.	Total.
Unionists .	3000	1625	1625	6250
Radicals . .	1000	2375	2375	5750
	4000	4000	4000	

the Radicals, though a minority, would secure two seats out of three.

The two great requisites in representation are that while the majority should rule, the minority should be heard, and it is evident from the foregoing example, that our present system fails to secure either requisite.

Sir John's view was very fully shared by Mr. (now Lord) Courtney, who urged it on the Government, and as the Government insisted on retaining the present system, Mr. Courtney sent in his resignation.

It was decided to form a society to bring the matter before the country, and at the first general meeting, on March 5, Sir John was elected President.

A test ballot was held in the House of Commons to show the practical working of the methods, and Sir John wrote articles in the *Pall Mall* and in the *Daily News* to explain it.

In the autumn they held a series of meetings, at which test elections were held. These elections added very much to the interest, and showed, at all events, that the system was quick, simple and easy in practical working.

An address was sent out as follows and largely distributed :

HIGH ELMS, HAYES, KENT,
February 2, 1884.

SIR — A Society has recently been formed for the purpose of bringing together all those who, while desiring that the majority of the Electors should have their due preponderance, are also anxious that the minority should be fairly represented.

The present system notoriously fails to secure this, nor would the plan of equal electoral districts promise in this respect much better results.

But, however this may be, if additional seats are given to large constituencies, the question of proportional representation becomes one of great practical importance.

The Society is not pledged to any particular plan or system, and it is proposed to hold a meeting of all those who (assuming that the system of single seats be not adopted) would favour some form of proportional representation, in order to determine the best system for adoption, and the mode of bringing the subject before Parliament and the country.

I have been requested by the Committee to invite you to join the Society, and give it the advantage of your advice and co-operation.

If you are willing to do so, may I ask you to sign the enclosed Post-card and return it to the Honorary Secretary.—I am, your obedient servant,

JOHN LUBBOCK.

Proportional representation has not yet made the way in this country that its advocates have hoped, but on the Continent it makes striking progress, being adopted by Denmark, Switzerland, and Belgium. The following letter to Sir John is from the aged statesman who was instrumental in its introduction into Denmark :

COPENHAGUE, *le* 17 *août* 1885.

MONSIEUR—Ayant eu l'honneur de recevoir votre billet du 30 juillet, je regrette beaucoup que l'état de ma santé ne me permet pas de répondre d'une manière satisfaisante aux questions que vous avez bien voulu m'adresser. Je dois me borner à dire que je n'ai pas changé d'opinion sur la méthode proportionnelle adoptée chez nous et pratiquée en Danemark depuis 30 ans sans la moindre difficulté. Je crois toujours que la loi danoise donne une solution satisfaisante de la question électorale, surtout pour des élections de 5 à 7 députés dans des circonscriptions convenablement choisies, et je crains que des préjugés trop enracinés s'opposeraient encore de longtemps à y introduire des améliorations sensibles. Car je n'ai jamais prétendu que la loi danoise donnât la solution définitive du problème.

La vraie liberté électorale exige, selon moi, que les électeurs du pays entier puissent se réunir librement, sans être parqués dans des circonscriptions plus ou moins arbitraires, et qu'un certain nombre d'électeurs, fixé par la loi, ait le droit d'élire un représentant.

Agréez, Monsieur, l'expression de ma considération la plus distinguée.   C. ANDRE.

Sir John's diary of this date gives abundant evidence that although he was so variously busy he could still find ample time for much social enjoyment, constantly meeting his friends, going to their houses, and entertaining them at his own. Indeed, the visitors' book at High Elms would bear sufficing witness to this, in the week-end parties that assembled there. It would not be easy to find a name distinguished in science that was missing, and his guests included very many of the highest distinction in other walks of life as well.

There is ample evidence, too, that he was preserving the sound body, together with the sound mind, to a degree not usual with a man just touching his half century in age. The diary of February 17 records a game of fives—himself and Norman against his son John and nephew Hugh. He also records, with pride, that he and Norman were victorious. But a prouder note of triumph still is sounded in a like connection

in November of the same year, when he played
three games with three of the boys, taking each
in turn as his partner, and won every game.
Mr. Philip Norman has assured me that as a
young man his activity in the fives court and his
ability at the game were quite exceptional. He
was still, and up to the end of his life, of a
slender, light figure, well compact, with no
superfluity of flesh, and nearly always in good
health. He was very temperate and never smoked.
On Monday August 4 in this year, being one of
the Bank Holidays that he had instituted, we find
him playing in a cricket match at High Elms, and
most appropriately scoring a triumphant 44 not
out !

On February 19 he has a note which will rouse
a responsive echo in many hearts. " Went to
Pygmalion and Galatea with Mrs. Pitt Rivers,
Miss Fox Pitt, and a small party : admired Miss
Anderson very much." Who that saw that most
beautiful performance will not have shared in
that admiration for the then Mary Anderson,
now Madame Navarro ?

On March 18 his daughter Amy, the widow of
Mr. Mulholland, married Mr. Van Zandt.

But there are many evidences in the story of
his life at this moment of the imminence of a
similar event which should touch him far more
closely. Entries in the diary of the early part
of this year show very frequent meetings, at
Rushmore and in London, with Miss Alice
Fox Pitt, and on April 12 he proposed to
her and had the happiness of being accepted.
He makes a characteristically naïve comment in

his diary of his " surprise " to find that his
children were not greatly astonished to hear of it.
Apparently he had deemed the progress of his
wooing to be more secret and discreet than it
really had been.

They were married on May 18, going to France
and Switzerland for the honeymoon and returning
on June 13. They took rooms at first in Queen
Anne's Mansions, and, of course, had the country
house at High Elms.

Conceivably it might be thought that all
auguries were not ideally favourable in this union
of a high-spirited young girl, for such was Miss
Alice Fox Pitt, with a middle-aged savant. It
was, however, from the first a union of the most
true, tender, and devoted mutual affection, an
affection which seemed to increase continually, if
that could be possible, with the passage of the
years. They were married in the same year that
Rolfe, his youngest son by the first marriage, left
Eton and went to work in Mr. Golding's office in
the City. Doubtless Miss Fox Pitt, by her upbring-
ing, was more disposed than many a girl of her age
and character to give the due meed of admiration
to the extraordinary qualities and abilities of her
husband. General Pitt Rivers was a man of
wide interests, with a special bent towards
archaeology, and his daughter would have been
educated in an atmosphere in which due honour
was paid to the distinction of men of learning.
And we have to remember, too, the very exceptional character of this particular man of learning
whom the young lady's charm had fascinated.
He was wonderfully youthful both in mind and

body for his years, and with his slight figure did not look near his age. But the great quality which made for domestic harmony and mutual love was the beautiful serenity of his mind. One who afterwards was associated with him in business informed me that when there was some question of Sir John's coming in as a joint director, he was rather fearful of a man known to be so frequent a sufferer from the gout. He was afraid lest the irritable temper that usually accompanies that fell torment might be imported into the business with the new director. When he came to know Sir John better, the knowledge was in the nature of a revelation to him as to the possible triumph of the controlling mind over the suffering body, even when the suffering was due to such a temper-trying cause as this.

Parliament reassembled on October 23, and Sir John at once gave notice of a resolution respecting Proportional Representation, and of a Bill limiting the hours of labour of young people in shops.

On November 24, however, Mr. Gladstone got rid of the Representation motion by moving on the Thursday that the House should adjourn till Monday. Nevertheless, Mr. Courtney and he spoke in favour of Proportional Representation a few days later (December 4) on the second reading of the Redistribution Bill.

On December 15 they held the first of a series of meetings on Proportional Representation. This first meeting was in Princes Hall in London, followed by others at Manchester, Nottingham, Liverpool, Norwich, Leicester, Greenwich, etc.

During the session he sat on the House of Commons Committee with reference to Westminster Hall. It appeared that the roof was mainly that of Richard II., the repairs having been few. Many of the stones still bear the original mason's marks.

He had extraordinary experiences this year in the possible length to which after-dinner speech-making can run. The first occasion was in Edinburgh and the second in Cambridge. On April 16 he had been in Scotland for the Tercentenary of the University of Edinburgh. The University gave him an honorary degree. They considerately sent him a list of the speeches. At the Banquet he proposed " International Commerce," coupled with the healths of M. de Lesseps and Sir R. Morier, but owing to the length of some of the preceding speeches his turn did not come on till past midnight, and of course, under the circumstances, he only made a very short speech.

He had travelled down to Edinburgh with Lord Leighton, who apologised for not talking much, as he had an important toast to propose on Art. Sir John said, " Well I have also to speak. Mine will be the forty-second speech, and yours is the forty-fifth, so I should not trouble myself much."

Before the dinner Sir R. Morier came to him very anxiously and begged him to be careful what he said, as he was negotiating a commercial treaty with Spain and the Spaniards were rather touchy. " Oh," said Sir John, " mine is the forty-second speech of the evening, so I shall not come on till after midnight and you may be quite easy, I shall say nothing to put up the backs of the Spaniards."

In December he went to Cambridge for the Peterhouse Sexcentenary, and at the dinner returned thanks for the House of Commons. It was a very long business. At 12.30 Sir Frederick Bramwell had to return thanks for " Applied Science." The whole speech may be quoted. It was this : " At an earlier hour there is much that I should like to have said about applied Science, but as it is nearly one o'clock the only application which strikes me as at all appropriate would be the application of a domestic lucifer to a bedroom candle." With this he sat down, and Lowell, the American Ambassador, who was opposite, scribbled on a menu and chucked across to him the lines :

> O wise Sir Frederick,
> Who thy wit could catch,
> Hold thee a candle
> Or supply thy match ?

Sir John continually added, as the opportunity arose, to his landed property about High Elms, and in this year bought Cockshot Hill and Farnboro' field, which now form part of the estate.

An interesting note in the diary is that under date October 18 : " Called on Lady Stanley of Alderley, and while there Gladstone came in. He said that when in 1874 he proposed to do away with the Income Tax, he expected to do so partly by economy, but partly, also, by an increase in the Death Duties."

When we consider the present weight of the Income Tax and that of the Death Duties also, these words will not be read without a sigh that our burdens seem so little likely to be lightened.

He adds in the diary of the same day : " I took Alice, Willy Fox Pitt, Marcia and Violet Lane Fox to the Savoy to see the *Sorcerer* and *Trial by Jury*. Did not care for either."

It has to be confessed that the last comment is typical of his attitude towards most dramatic performances. He could not endure the misunderstandings, generally between husband and wife, which are the basis of most modern (and ancient also, perhaps) theatrical representation. They distressed him.

He was much more interested in the performance of Van, the puppy, who, he reports, was learning to pick out cards tolerably. He still had his ants, all set out in their glass-houses and pursuing their incessant activities in the study, and he also had an observation hive of bees fitted in with their exit through the window. At this time he notes that two of his ants were ten years old, and they survived as old friends till fourteen and fifteen years of age respectively. At the death of one of these illustrious insects, which was recorded in some of the scientific journals, a French paper had a paragraph "profoundly sympathising with the great scientist on the loss of his aged and valued relative."

CHAPTER XIX

MR. GLADSTONE'S HOME RULE BILL (1885–1886)

(Age 51-52)

In the early spring of the following year Sir John
and Mr. Courtney conducted " Proportional Representation " meetings at Leicester, Nottingham,
Greenwich, Lambeth, Islington, St. Pancras,
Liverpool, Tower Hamlets, Norwich, Oxford,
and Clapham. In almost every case they held
an illustrative election, and he claims that " the
actual experience was even more conclusive than
any verbal explanation." In many cases they
ended with a resolution in favour of the system.
At Nottingham the local Liberal leader, Alderman Gripper, announced his intention of moving
an amendment. Few doubted that he could
carry it in his own town and against two strangers.
He put his case well, but to the general surprise
his resolution was lost by a large majority.

At the Lambeth meeting the Secretary of the
Liberal Association also came down intending to
move an amendment. He did not dispute the
theoretical arguments, but was under the impression that the system was too complicated
and difficult for actual use. The results of the

illustrative election, however, surprised and convinced him ; so that far from moving an amendment he offered to second, and did second, the
resolution in favour of the system.

By way of making sure of the correctness of
the arithmetical calculation that he had applied
to Proportional Representation, Sir John consulted Sir G. Stokes, stating the case thus :

HIGH ELMS, HAYES, KENT,
Feb. 3*rd*, 1885.

MY DEAR PROFESSOR STOKES—The opponents of
Proportional Representation continually object that,
under the system we have proposed, much would depend
on chance.

This of course might be entirely obviated by dis-
tributing the second votes in proportion, but we have
not thought this necessary because the chance is so
small.

According to our calculation, supposing a Constituency of 25,000 Electors, returning 3 members, and that
a candidate receives 10,000 votes of which one-half are
marked in the second place for a candidate " B " and
one-half for " C," and suppose that 4000 have to be
distributed, the element of chance would generally
affect the result by less than 20.

Your authority on such a question would of course be
accepted as conclusive. Will you therefore allow me
to ask you whether this is so, and also to state what the
odds would be against the result being affected by
chance to the extent of 100.—I am, yours very truly,

JOHN LUBBOCK.

Prof. Stokes, M.A., D.C.L., etc.

To this enquiry Sir G. Stokes replied :

I have carefully calculated the chances, and quite
verify your result. I find that the average difference
from 2000 in the votes assigned to B or C in the case
you mention would be as nearly as may be 16, and that
the odds against the difference being as great as 100
would be in round numbers 44,000 to 1.

The following is from Mr. Hare, who independently invented the " Single Transferable Vote " System, which Sir John thought the best of various plans by which Proportional Representation could be effected :

CHARITY COMMISSION, WHITEHALL,
October 23rd, 1885.

DEAR SIR JOHN LUBBOCK—I fear I cannot assist your friend, Mr. Brown, in solving the various problems which he suggests on the subject of Proportional Representation. At my advanced years, and with official duties daily to perform, I have really given up the consideration of details in the method,—leaving the question to younger and clearer heads. If I were replying to Mr. Brown, I should be able to do little more than refer him to the rates of distribution of votes set out in the 4th Edition of my Treatise—the 18th, 19th, and 25th clauses of my draft Bill contained on pp. 31, 161, and 188 of this (4th Edition) of my Treatise on *The Election of Representatives* (Longmans, 1873).

My cardinal principle has always been to secure for the electors the most complete expression of their opinions in their choice of candidates. The view of most of my political critics has been less in favour of the electors than of the candidates—how will they succeed, or how they may fail ?

Not long ago, a member of Parliament (I think it was Mr. A. Arnold) asked me this question : Suppose the Birmingham voters put Mr. Bright's name first, and Mr. Chamberlain second, and the votes are given only to Mr. Bright,—would not your plan exclude Mr. Chamberlain ? I said, " Of course, but——" He would hear no more,—that was enough to show the injustice and absurdity of my system. I should have answered that if there were enough voters to make up two quotients in their favour, all those taken from Bright would be given to Chamberlain, and secure his return— if there were not enough, they could return but one ! There must be accidents and chances in all the business of life.—He that begins a business first, has a better chance of success—as they who get to the door of a meeting-room or theatre, where a crowd are seeking admission, and all have an equal right, will yet probably be the most successful in entering.

I have just received, from Bruxelles, the Report of the " Conférence Internationale pour la Représentation Proportionnelle." It is really very interesting to all of us who have taken an interest in the subject. I was very glad to see your letter (p. 222) expressing your warm sympathy with their object.—Ever yours sincerely,
THO. HARE.

The following explanation of the Belgian system is from M. d'Hondt, a professor in the University at Ghent :

11, RUE DES SŒURS NOIRES, GAND,
13 *septembre* 1885.

CHER MONSIEUR—J'espère que vous aurez bien reçu l'exemplaire que je vous ai adressé de l'exposé du système practique de représentation proportionnelle adopté par la Comité de l'association Belge.

Ce système pratique est adapté au mode de votation Belge.

En supposant qu'en Angleterre les noms de tous les candidats doivent être imprimés par ordre alphabétique sur des bulletins officiels remis aux électeurs au moment du vote je proposerais dans ce cas pour votre pays, le système suivant :—

Rien ne serait changé à la forme du bulletin de vote.

Les candidats d'un même parti ferait avant les élections une déclaration officielle, aux termes de laquelle ils se *présentent ensemble*. Les partis seraient ainsi nettement tranchés, et cela est indispensable attendu que la représentation proportionnelle suppose absolument des partis ne pouvant nullement être appliquées aux individus.

Chaque électeur aurait autant de voix qu'il y a de sièges à conférer. Il pourrait en disposer comme il le voudrait au profit d'un ou de plusieurs candidats. Il inscrirait dans la case à coté du nom du candidat, en chiffre, le nombre de voix qu'il veut lui donner.

La somme des voix obtenues par les candidats d'un parti, constituerait le chiffre électoral de ce parti.

La répartition des sièges entre les partis se ferait à l'aide du chiffre diviseur, comme dans le système Belge.

Dans chaque parti, à concurrence des sièges qui lui serait attribué à la répartition les candidats ayant le plus grand nombre de voix seraient élus.

Lors du meeting de Woolwich où vous m'avez fait l'honneur de me conduire, j'ai remarqué que le peuple anglais tenait énormément à ne pouvoir *voter que pour un candidat.*

Mais le fond de la pensée, je crois, était de vouloir la *parfaite égalité des électeurs* entre eux et de protester contre le système du scrutin de liste, tel qu'il est appliqué en Belgique et en France, où les listes incomplètes et les candidatures isolées sont nécessairement sacrifiées.

Dans le système proposé où *chaque* électeur a autant de voix que de sièges, et où il peut disposer de ces voix en faveur d'un ou de plusieurs candidats l'égalité des électeurs est parfaitement sauvegardée.

Je pense donc qu'il ne froisserait pas l'esprit public anglais.

Je me suis fait un devoir de vous adresser la présente comme réponse plus complète à la lettre que vous m'avez l'honneur de m'écrire le 30 Juillet dernier.

Agréez, je vous prie, Cher Monsieur, l'assurance de mes sentiments aussi distingués que dévoués,

V. D'HONDT,
Professeur à la faculté de droit de l'Université de Gand.

à Sir John Lubbock, Président de l'association reformiste anglaise,
High Elms, Hayes, Kent.

On February 5 Sir John was at a Proportional Representation meeting at Liverpool, from which he was hurriedly called home, and on the 6th his eldest child, by his second marriage, Ursula, now Mrs. Adrian Grant Duff, was born.

We find him lecturing on the 12th and again on the 15th of the month on " Leaves," and he notes that about this time he commenced his work *On Seedlings.*

This was at the beginning of the time of England's terrible anxiety about General Gordon's mission in the Soudan. Sir John had an article on the Soudan in the *Contemporary* for April. The excitement in the House was not diminished by an omission inadvertently made by Mr. Gladstone in reading out of a telegram from Cairo that " the French Consul has left," and there stopping, not observing that it went on " further papers for our consideration."

Sir John writes in his diary on February 19 : " Parliament met. Gladstone made a very unsatisfactory statement. I am all against going to Khartoum unless we mean to stay there." It is evident that both on the Egyptian question and on Home Rule for Ireland there was not the same harmony of opinion between himself and Mr. Gladstone as had been the case for many previous years.

There is rather an interesting note, too, in the diary for April 23 : " We had some talk in the House about arbitration, and eventually, at the request of Whitbread, Rathbone, and some others, I wrote to Lowell and asked him to see me on Friday morning, which he did. He said he knew no reason why the United States should not arbitrate, and if I thought there was a sufficiently strong feeling he would telegraph out and ask. In the afternoon Whitbread and I saw Lord R. Grosvenor (the chief Whip), and told him what had been done. Of course he could say nothing definite, but expressed his own impression that it was quite a move in the right direction. On Monday I again saw Lord Richard,

but, understanding that the Government opposed
arbitration, we decided to do nothing for the
moment."

On May 2 Sir John was at the Royal Academy
dinner, returning thanks for Science.

In the House of Commons he carried the
second reading of his Shop Hours Regulation Bill,
but was unable to get any day for the Committee
Stage. He carried resolutions for two Committees, one on Forestry and one on the system
of election of School Boards. The Committee
on Forestry elected him Chairman, and unanimously recommended the establishment of one or
more Forest Schools, but nothing was done, and
for many years Great Britain remained the only
important country in Europe without any such
school.

The evidence given before the Second Committee was strongly in favour of Proportional
Representation.

He also spoke in the House on Egypt, on the
Soudan Expedition, on Proportional Representation, on the Education Vote, on Finance, etc.

On May 16 he started with Lady Lubbock for
a little tour in the Dolomites, returning on June 8
to find that the Government had resigned. They
had a big family gathering, of no less than nineteen, at High Elms, on the occasion of his sister
Harriet's coming over to England from Canada.

On July 18, he writes: "Went with an
excursion from the Working Men's College to
Cambridge. They showed us everything, as far
as possible in a day, and we, including Alice,
dined in Trinity Hall. During dinner a succession

of people came to look at us from the gallery, and we were told afterwards that it was because only three ladies had previously dined in Trinity Hall— viz. Queen Elizabeth, Queen Caroline, and Queen Victoria ! "

On the 25th of August he went to Scotland with Lady Lubbock, paying a round of visits. They stayed for a fortnight, first with the Galloways, and then with the Lyells, at Kinordy, where he was interested in seeing capercailzie for the first time. Thence he went on to Aberdeen for the British Association meeting, where he read a paper to a very large audience on Ants, Bees, and Wasps, and took other active part in the meeting. From Aberdeen they went, with the Rayleighs, to Haddo, and from Haddo, by way of Nairn and Invergarry, to Loch Hourn to stay with Mr. and Mrs. Robert Birkbeck. " Very glad to get to Mary's at last," he writes, on September 21 (Mary was his sister, who was married to Mr. Robert Birkbeck). " Joyful meeting ! "

They arrived home on the 27th. Sir John notes, " Comfortable journey. Found all well."

On October 1 he was at Birmingham, un-veiling the statue of Sir J. Mason, the founder of Mason's College. The *Birmingham Gazette* of the following day spoke of " the splendid address of Sir John Lubbock, full of suggestive force. It cannot be read without awakening ideas which strengthen and broaden as the mind dwells upon them. It was an eulogium on the benefactor he came to honour, but it was much more. It was a sermon on science, finished, fervent, and fearless. . . . He ennobled his subject and gathered the sympathies, as he awakened the interest, of every thinker who heard his address." [1]

During the autumn he lectured at Toynbee Hall and the City of London College, and spoke for friends during the General Election at several places.

He was himself re-elected on November 24 without opposition.

He devoted much thought during the autumn to the preparation of the famous list of " best 100 books," which he first published as a lecture to the Working Men's College in Great Ormond Street, and afterwards incorporated in the *Pleasures of Life.* He consulted many friends on the subject, generally by word of mouth, but in some cases by letter.

The following is the reply of Mr. John Bright :

ONE ASH, ROCHDALE,
Nov. 3rd, 1885.

DEAR SIR JOHN LUBBOCK—Your list of books rather surprises me. They are far too " far back " and too learned for me.

I read a good deal, but am not a learned reader. Lately I have been reading Jowett's *Plato*—and most of it seems to me a dreadful puzzle.

You will be shocked at these remarks but will forgive them.

I have recently been interested in bringing out a new edition of Dymond's *Essays on the Principles of Morality.* It is published by Routledge & Co. and is not costly— not more than 5s. for the volume. If you can add this to your list I shall be glad.

I will not undertake to suggest anything more. You will admit my modesty if not my wisdom.—Always sincerely yours,   JOHN BRIGHT.

---

[1] *Birmingham Gazette,* October 2, 1885.

He told me, later, how immensely surprised he was to find that so widely read a scholar as Sir Stafford Northcote should be ignorant of the very existence of such a work as the *Meditations of Marcus Aurelius.* The following letter is from him, who had by that time taken the title of Iddesleigh.

PYNES, EXETER,
November 25th, 1885.

MY DEAR SIR J. LUBBOCK—I am afraid I cannot make any useful suggestions with regard to your list of books. I do not feel as if I fully realised your conception.

There are in your list about a dozen books which I humbly confess to not having read myself,—Marcus Aurelius, Epictetus (barely glanced at once or twice), Confucius, Spinoza, Wake, Mahabharata, Ramayama, Shahnameh ; and I am afraid I must add Miss Martineau's two books, and that I could not stand an examination in Lewis.

By so much, at least, do I fall short of your standard and feel myself disqualified for passing a judgment. Of the remainder of your favourites I would say that I divided them, as Miss Edgeworth makes Frank divide human wants,—into " Man's must wants " and " Man's may wants." Or to take an Aristotelian distinction, I should regard some of them as being important ἁπλῶς, to all persons, and under all conditions of life, and others as important ἡμῖν, to some persons or under some conditions only.

Of course you do not contemplate the reading of these books only. Your pupil would have studies of his own, which would carry him far afield, and which at the same time would take up so much time as to make it difficult for him to complete your prescribed course. But you think that there is a certain amount of book-knowledge which every man (*qua* the new county elector ?) ought to acquire in order to enable himself to understand the mental condition—past and present—of the world he lives in, irrespectively of his individual place and occupation therein. Very good : this is knowledge which is one of Man's " must wants," which he requires.

Such knowledge should, I think, be confined to as small a list of books as possible ; but the books should be representative. Now it strikes me that your list is at once too big and too little. Look at your classics. —It is a large order to prescribe the whole of Homer, of Hesiod, of Aeschylus, Sophocles, Euripides, Aristophanes, Herodotus, Thucydides, and Xenophon, Aristotle's *Ethics* and *Politics*, Plato's *Republic* and the *Phaedo*, to say nothing of Plutarch's *Lives* and Aesop. You may say, this course is necessary to give the student an adequate idea of the wondrous Greek literature ; and for giving a truly adequate idea it may be so : but, even so, you don't give enough. Pindar is as essential as half the plays of Euripides or half the books of the *Iliad* ; and the omission of Demosthenes is incomprehensible. Surely a few orations might take the place of the *Hellenics* of Xenophon. Then what a loss is the father of pastoral poetry, Theocritus ! and I should say a word for Lucian too.

How do you treat the Latin Classics ? Where are Livy ? and Tacitus ? (They are perhaps excluded as historians ; yet you keep Herodotus and Thucydides.) Of course, I see you have the *Agricola* and *Germania*. You are constantly dipping your feet into historical waters, but not stepping boldly. But I leave history for a bit, and go back to poetry. Where is Lucretius ? and where is Juvenal ? and where is Ovid ?

Now as to the Moderns, I almost refuse to enter upon the consideration of a list which does not include Chaucer ! Of course he must be expurgated for general reading ; but with the excision of three or four tales and of a very few passages, he stands at the head of English literature. Of course in the phrase " English Literature " I don't include the few world-wide reputations like Shakespeare : but, out-taken Shakespeare, I really don't know a writer with so many charms, or one who so brings home to you the life of his day, or who touches the tender feelings so effectively, or who has such an eye for the beauties of Nature.

I have not time to go through your list of Moderns ; and I want to say a word about the exclusion of history. Surely we could not understand, far less appreciate, any other books, except perhaps books of pure science, without some acquaintance with history. It is essential to have some sort of historical frame to set the pictures in. But if it is indispensable in some form or other, why not pick out at least a few specimens of the best types of history,—perhaps even a few types which show what should be avoided ? Gibbon's *Decline and Fall* may be as faulty as you please,—but how grand ! Hume, Clarendon, Sismondi, Grote, and so forth, and even the untrustworthy brilliance of Macaulay, are masters who have established at least the same kind of right to exhibit their works in the World's great library that Rafaelle, or Leonardo, or Turner, or Landseer have gained for their pictures in the world's great galleries. That they look at their subject from different points of view, and treat it on different principles, is not a reason for excluding, but for including them. And see how you violate your own rule by admitting such books as Macaulay's *Essays*,—very one-sided history.

Please forgive this rude and crude string of observations, which I have not time to reduce to shape.—Believe me, yours very faithfully, IDDESLEIGH.

Sir John Lubbock, Bart, M.P.

It is indeed remarkable that so distinguished a classical scholar should not have read Marcus Aurelius. Sir John urged him to do so, and his opinion of the book is expressed in a note from Lady Iddesleigh, saying that she had asked Lord Iddesleigh to let her answer Sir John's note. Lord Iddesleigh was " enchanted with Marcus Aurelius," and had already read some of it with the greatest pleasure.

On November 25 came the unwelcome news of the defeat of Mr. Sydney Buxton at Peterborough, quickly followed by that of many others on the Government side.

When the new Government was formed, some of the papers discussed the probability of the offering of the Chancellorship of the Exchequer to Sir John, but I do not know whether the offer was even tentatively made. In any case it is not to be thought that he would have contemplated for a moment the possibility of taking office, under Mr. Gladstone, as a Home Ruler.

The year ended for him with a quiet family party for Christmas.

On January 9, 1886, he gave, at the Working Men's College, his lecture on Reading, which contained his list of best 100 books. He writes, on January 21, that "there has been a great deal in the papers about my 100 books." That same 21st of January was the day of the first meeting of Parliament for the momentous and remarkable Session in which Mr. Gladstone was defeated on the Home Rule Bill. Sir John notes that "The Home Rulers took all the seats below the gangway, so I had to move above, where, however, they also mustered in great force."

They were living this year, for the Parliament season, at 33 Belgrave Square.

He had an article on Books in the February issue of the *Contemporary Review*, and observes that the Education Commission was taking up a great deal of his time. Nevertheless, as soon as Parliament met, he introduced the Shop Hours Regulation Bill, which limited the hours of labour of young persons under 18, to 74 a week. He got it through the second Reading on February 18, and it was referred to a Select Committee of which he was appointed Chairman. The Committee took a great deal of evidence, and not only reported in favour of the Bill, but suggested a general Bill for Early Closing.

The opponents of legislation on the question

induced the Lord Mayor to call a general meeting of London shopkeepers, expecting to carry a resolution against any such measure as he had proposed. Sir John attended and asked for a hearing. Having explained how matters stood, he moved an amendment in favour of his Bill and quoted, as illustrating the hard lives of shop assistants, and especially of women, the Norfolk epitaph :

Here lies a poor woman, who always was tired,
For she lived in a world where too much was required.
Weep not for me, friends, she said, for I'm going
Where there'll neither be cooking nor washing nor sewing.

I go where the loud Hallelujahs are ringing,
But I shall not take any part in the singing.
Then weep not for me, friends, if death do us sever,
For I'm going to do nothing for ever and ever.

" This quotation," he observes, " carried the meeting and the amendment." Variant readings of this epitaph are extant, but the gist of it is the same in all.

Sir John was much pleased by the high appreciation of Mr. Ruskin of the merit of the illustrations of foliage in his book on the "Shape of Leaves " :

" DEAR SIR JOHN," Mr. Ruskin writes, " I only waited to answer till the book came. You know how glad Lady Lubbock would make me in coming too, only I cannot be sure that Mrs. Severn is here to see she is comfortable—she's sure to be here anyhow by the time you would care to come. We shan't have a flower for you for weeks, though the bees were out a week ago— *now* there's 8 inches of snow. The delightful book did come this morning through snow and all. The leaf drawings are quite the best I ever saw in their kind, and I'm ever so jealous—and eager to read—but I'm dread-

fully afraid of being told that leaves are only made for
aphides—not for trees—or me.

"Do you never get angry with the uses that other
people put your discoveries to ?   I wish you and Huxley
would sometimes say ' I never meant *that*.'—Ever your
affectionate   J. RUSKIN.

   "Sir John Lubbock, Bart."

Of course most of the political talk at this
time was of Gladstone's Home Rule Bill, and it
was the subject of numerous conversations and
meetings between Sir John and other members
of the Liberal Party. The meetings usually
were made the occasion of men's dinner-parties ;
Lady Lubbock being unable to act as hostess ;
but occasionally we find a note such as that
under February 6, "Breakfasted at Grillions,
sat next E. Stanhope, went home with Derby,
and had a long talk with him about the situation.
Afterwards to Hartington and Goschen—all strong
against Home Rule."

On Saturday 20 he records : "Had a men's
dinner-party—Goschen, Bramwell (Lord), Millais,
Browning, Ebrington, etc." There were those
at this dinner of whom good conversation on
other than the political topic of the day might be
expected. Again a week later, he had another
men's dinner—" Archbishop of Canterbury, Aberdare, Tweedmouth, May, Rawlinson, Bramwell
(Sir F.), Roscoe, Courtney, Goldsmid, Cozens
Hardy, Milman, Paget, A. Kinnaird, Brassey,
and Leslie Stephen."

The Saturday after there was yet another
dinner without ladies, when his guests were,
" Dean of Westminster, T. Bruce, Sir H. Vivian,
Lefevre, Romanes, Carruthers, Sir R. Welby,

Walter Pye Smith, Lechmere, Rathbone, C. S. Hodgson, H. R. Grenfell, and G. Howard."

On March 30 was born his daughter, Irene, now Mrs. H. Pelham.

As soon as Mr. Gladstone's Home Rule proposals were fairly well known, a requisition was presented to the Lord Mayor requesting him to call a public meeting of citizens in the Guildhall. This was held on April 2, and Sir John moved the first resolution of protest against the Bill, which was carried with great enthusiasm.

Mr. Gladstone introduced his Bill on April 8 in a very eloquent speech, which has become historical.

Sir John voted with the majority which threw out the Home Rule Bill on the second Reading. Having regard to the extremely Liberal character of his Constituency, he had grave doubts whether this vote would not cost him his seat. Under the circumstances it was natural that his re-election should be challenged, and in Mr. Frederic Harrison he met a most formidable opponent.

The election was fought with great good humour, and resulted in his winning the victory by nearly three to one—1314 to 516. The Constituency contained above 500 medical men, of whom 495 voted for him and only 43 for Mr. Harrison.

For some years he had been President of the West Kent Liberal Association, and was surprised one morning to see in the papers a copy of a resolution purporting to have been passed by the Council in favour of Home Rule. No notice of such a resolution had been given, and consequently he wrote to protest. He received a letter of excuse from the Secretary, admitting that, strictly speaking, both the President and all the Vice-Presidents of the Association should have been summoned to the meeting of the General Committee when the resolution supporting Mr. Gladstone was passed; but that it was so seldom that they were able to have them present that the summons had not been sent to them. The business for which the meeting was called was mostly routine, and the Chairman was the responsible party for having the resolution put. The secretary promised that in future due notice should be given him of any important business to come before either the Executive or the General Committee.

Some further apology and explanation were offered, but the result was that the President, Treasurer, several Vice-Presidents, and some other members of the Committee withdrew from the Association.

Cardinal Manning, as has been seen, was an old friend of Sir John, and always one of his warmest supporters in the Early Closing Movement. The following may be given as a sample of several letters expressive of his views on this subject :

ARCHBISHOP'S HOUSE, WESTMINSTER,
25th April 1886.

MY DEAR SIR JOHN LUBBOCK—It was my fixed intention to attend the meeting of to-night in support of your Bill on behalf of our over-crowded people. But I find it out of my power.

My earnest support on behalf of your Bill has grown day by day as I have seen the letters in opposition to it ; and I am sorry not to be able to say this to-night ; but

you will say it for me.—Believe me always, very truly
yours,   HENRY G., Card.-Archbishop.

On May 25, in recognition of his efforts on
their behalf, Sir John was entertained at a dinner
by seven hundred tradesmen.

The third Reading of the Bill was carried in
the House by 81 to 17 on June 18.

It has been noted that he was invited, two
years previously, to deliver the Rede lecture—
at that time in succession to Professor Huxley—
at Cambridge. His engagements had then prevented him from assenting to the request, but
this year the invitation was renewed by the
Vice-Chancellor, and Sir John felt himself able
to accept.

He was invited to be President for the year
of the Watford College of Science, and gave his
presidential address on September 26, and also
accepted the Presidency of the Walsall Literary
Institute.

Lord Randolph Churchill had written to him,
in the end of August, asking him to allow his
name to be put forward as a member of a Royal
Commission on the currency and the " alleged
depreciation of silver." He was obliged to reply
that being already a member of the Education
Commission, it would be impossible for him to
attend the meetings of both, but he suggested
that Lord Randolph should confer on the subject
with Lord Cross, who was Chairman of the latter
Commission. The result was an arrangement
that he should be free from attendance at the
meetings of the Education Commission, and
should be present only when their report was

being considered. In this way he was left at liberty for the Currency Commission, and accepted Lord Randolph's suggestion.

The following correspondence between them has reference principally to the unsatisfactory condition of the gold coinage :

Confidential.

TREASURY CHAMBERS, WHITEHALL, S.W.,
December 16th, 1886.

DEAR SIR JOHN LUBBOCK—

" *Recoinage of light Gold* "

I have given much attention to this matter during the recess and venture to trouble you confidentially with the rough outline of a scheme I am prepared to recommend to Parliament in the event of its securing the favourable consideration of the banking community.

My object has been to recoin the light gold, and maintain the coinage permanently on a sound basis without cost to the taxpayer or loss to the " last holder." This I provide for by the abolition of the half-sovereign, and by a small and limited issue of one pound notes. I enclose a summarized calculation of cost and profit. I also contemplate using the surplus profit of £45,000 per annum accruing from the operation for the purpose of abolishing the duty on silver plate and paying the drawback.

Your opinions on this question as the leader of the London Banking interest will be most valuable to me, and I do not shrink from troubling you, for I know the question has for long greatly interested you.—Believe me to be, yours very truly,

RANDOLPH S. CHURCHILL.

The plan is :

1. To recall the half-sovereign.

It is estimated that there are £20,000,000 of half-sovereigns in circulation, which are light to the extent of about £220,000. These half-sovereigns would therefore produce as bullion £19,780,000.

The removal of a fractional coin such as the half-sovereign must be expected to cause a certain demand for silver. Experience can only show the extent of that demand, but for the purpose of stating the argument, the Chancellor of the Exchequer assumes that ¼th of the half-sovereign circulation would be replaced by silver, *i.e.* £5,000,000. £5,000,000 in silver would cost, say, £4,000,000.

2. The Chancellor further proposes to issue gradually 5,000,000 or 6,000,000 one pound notes. This issue would be against securities, and would be managed by the Bank of England in its Issue Department. The £20,000,000 of half-sovereigns would therefore be replaced by £5,000,000 silver, say, 6,000,000 one pound notes, and £9,000,000 sovereigns new coined : and the gold recovered from the recalled half-sovereigns £19,780,000 would be (?) by 9,000,000 sovereigns and £4,000,000 spent in purchase of £5,000,000 silver. The balance, £6,780,000, if invested in securities at £3 per cent would produce about £204,000.

A sum would thus be provided by means of which the sovereign-circulation, deficient to the extent of half a million, could be restored, and a fund created sufficient to provide :

(1) for the making and maintenance of £6,000,000 notes and

(2) for the maintenance of the gold coinage for the future.

To this Sir John replied as follows :—

ATHENAEUM CLUB, PALL MALL, S.W.,
23rd December 1886.

MY DEAR LORD RANDOLPH—On my return from Lancashire I have found your letter, which arrived during my absence. Please therefore excuse my delay in replying.

I should be most happy if I can be of any use to you as regards the circulation, and would come and see you at any time if you would care to talk it over.

There would, I fear, be considerable reluctance to part with the half-sovereign. The 5 shilling piece has never been popular, and the difference between the sovereign and the half-crown is inconveniently great.

I think also that many would object to the issue of £1 notes, at any rate without a parliamentary enquiry, and it would be difficult to limit the amount. This is a question which I should be specially glad to talk over with you, as it is rather intricate.

There is another mode by which, I think, the light gold might be provided for without loss to the Exchequer.—I am, yours sincerely,

JOHN LUBBOCK.

The question of bimetallism was one to which he had given much attention, but it is hardly of a kind that appeals to the general reader. The following letter from Mr. Riversdale Grenfell, arising out of its consideration, is a singularly lucid statement of a matter which appears very intricate to the minds of ordinary mortals :

COPPER OFFICE,
27 UPPER THAMES STREET, E.C.,
20th December 1886.

MY DEAR LUBBOCK—As far as I understand the cost of production theory it runs on all fours with the Ricardian theory of rent.

a	. . .	£1 per oz.
b	. . .	2 ,,
c	. . .	3 ,,
d	. . .	4 ,,

If the whole demand of the world can be supplied by A and he chooses to sell at £1 : 19 : 0 per oz. the price would be £1 : 19 : 0, and the others would work at a loss or give up producing.

If A could not supply the world, but a fresh demand ensued, B might come in up to £2 : 19 : 0, when the effect would be that A's profits would increase £1 per oz. And so on to the others.

If the demand were far below A's power of production, then he would reduce the amount produced down to the Demand, but he might still get £1 : 19 : 0 if the Demand were a constant quantity. Of course this supposition is absurd, because what A would do would be to reduce the price between £1 : 19 : 0 and £1 till he stimulated the demand.

At this point the letter switches off with startling abruptness to :

Dean Stanley

You, or Fitch, I forget which, told a story on Sunday about Lord Beaconsfield and Dean Stanley, which I think Walrond would very much like to have for his life of the Dean. " No dogmas, no deans." I did not catch the whole of it, but if you could send it to Walrond, he would be very much obliged.—Yours truly,

H. R. GRENFELL.

On October 9 Sir John started with Lady Lubbock for a tour in Greece. By the way, at Paris he paid visits to M. Pasteur and M. Renan.

On the 22nd they made an expedition to Marathon, but the excessive heat spoiled their enjoyment of the historic battle-field. The presence of Dr. and Mrs. Schliemann added very much to the pleasure of their time in Athens. They made the acquaintance of Miss Tricoupi, by whom they were very favourably, and of Mr. Tricoupi, by whom they were not quite so favourably, impressed.

On the 26th they started for an expedition by Corinth, Tiryns, Mycenae, Delphi, and Thebes. Sir John writes that he was surprised to find to what miserable villages these celebrated cities had fallen.

On December 16 he was at Knowsley for an Early Closing Conference at Liverpool, and went on to Preston, where he delivered the address which was afterwards expanded into the first two chapters of *The Pleasures of Life.* The occasion was the distribution of the prizes to the students at the Harris Institute at Preston.

It had for a long time been the custom in the City to make advances on " Dock Warrants." This was done to the extent of millions, and Dock

Warrants were always supposed to give a clear title to the goods. Suddenly the mercantile community was startled by a decision in the Courts to the effect that this was not the case. Sir John was applied to to pass a Bill which should bring the legal position into conformity with the view of it which City men had always taken. There were some technical objections raised by eminent lawyers, because in effect it made the Warrants a more complete security than the goods themselves would have been. The merchants and bankers in the House, however, were so unanimous in favour of the Bill that it became law.

Towards the end of the year he received an invitation from the Lowell Institute to give a course of lectures in Boston, and it was with very great regret that he felt obliged to decline. The calls on his various activities were more than sufficient at home, and his response to them was extraordinary. He thought nothing, as on October 4, of running down to Glasgow for an Early Closing meeting. Even this year he was again playing fives with his sons, and men young enough to be his sons, when at High Elms. He notes on April 30, his birthday: " Have great reason to be thankful for so many blessings, and hope I am grateful." Nevertheless, he has the rather mournful comment in regard to this year : " The Home Rule split makes a kind of constraint among old friends." It was a sundering of hearts which so extremely friendly a man could not fail to feel acutely. He also suffered a grievous loss this year by the death of his old friend Professor Busk, of whom he writes on August 10 :

" Received the news of poor Busk's death. He has been a kind good friend for many years, and his example was one to do every one good. He was not only able, but most good and kind. His friendship was certainly one of the greatest privileges of my life." This is very high praise from Sir John Lubbock who, in spite of all his kindliness, was by no means given to praise without discrimination. His final note for 1887 is that : " In Parliament I did not speak often, but succeeded at length in carrying the Shop Hours Bill, which limits the hours of labour of young persons in shops to 74 hours a week."

In the course of the year he had to part with his dog " Van," the subject of his experiments, which a London life did not suit. He returned it, therefore, to Mr. Tidman, at Chislehurst, from whom he had procured it. The next morning, as Sir John was returning to London, to his great surprise, as soon as the carriage door was opened, in jumped " Van " !

CHAPTER XX

" THE PLEASURES OF LIFE " (1887)

(AGE 53)

DEAR SIR — We have been considering the proposal
you were good enough to make to us this morning in
regard to a book of miscellaneous essays to be entitled
The Pleasures of Life, to contain among other papers
your address upon the pleasures of reading. We are
inclined to think that such a book, if it does not bear
the appearance of a mere re-issue of papers which have
appeared elsewhere, but is substantially a new book,
forming an organic whole, would have a very fair chance
of success. Whether it would have a permanent sale,
as your scientific books have had, we hardly feel prepared
to say.

The above is an extract from a letter of the
firm of publishers which brought out several of
Sir John Lubbock's scientific books, and also,
eventually, the proposed *Pleasures of Life* to
which it refers.

It was not a great many years after this that
I heard my wife, sitting next to Lord Avebury at
dinner, tell him that she had been informed that
Jessica's First Prayer had been translated into
more languages than any other book except the
Bible. I do not know whence the information
came—that does not matter, nor whether it is

accurate—the interesting point is Lord Avebury's
answer. " I wonder," he said, " whether it has
been translated into more than *The Pleasures of
Life* ? "

This is the book, this which has been so many
times interpreted into a strange tongue as to
defeat the destruction of the Tower of Babel,
of which the publishers could write thus tentatively, cautiously, doubtfully ; and I must say
that had I been their reader for the occasion, it
is just in such a way that I should have made
my report on the book. With Sir John Lubbock's
name on the title-page, it was perhaps just worth
publishing—yes. Without a well-known name
to help it along—no. The result bore striking
witness to the wonderful gift of Sir John for
knowing " what the public wants." He had
been so much in touch with the reading public,
by the many addresses and lectures that he had
delivered, that his opportunities in this direction,
perhaps, were greater than those of publishers
or their readers, but even he was astonished
by the extraordinary popularity which the book
achieved. Within a comparatively short while
it sold to the extent of a hundred thousand
copies, and it sells still in I do not quite know
how many languages. And of almost all his
books it was probably the one that was compiled with the least mental effort. Already we
have noticed Sir John's way of reading a
book, never without a slip of paper in it, which
served as a marker of his place, and at the same
time as a sheet on which he might make note of
passages which caught his attention, either copy-

ing them out, if they were brief, or marking their first and last words. Then those slips were given to the secretary, who would collate and type out the passages referred to, and in this extremely easy manner a book like *The Pleasures of Life* would be quickly compiled. There was no originality—Sir John expressly disclaimed all intention of producing an original work. The *flair* that he displayed, however, both in this and in later collections of the same time, showed an original genius that would have made the fortune of any journalist. I do not at all know what the profits were of this, or his other books of many editions ; but no doubt the fortunes of the journalist and of the banker are reckoned differently. What might seem a small matter to the latter would be a sum of some importance to the former. No importance whatever appears to have been attached by Sir John to what must surely have been the very considerable pecuniary result of his various writings.

The aim that Sir John had in the compilation of this book is best given in his own words prefatory to the first and second series of the *Pleasures*.

" Having been when young," he writes in the preface to the first series, " rather prone to suffer from low spirits, I have . . . taken the opportunity of dwelling on the privileges and blessings we enjoy . . . and I reprint here the substance of some of those addresses . . . hoping that the thoughts and quotations in which I have myself found most comfort, may perhaps be of use to others also."

In the preface to the second series of the *Pleasures*, he observes, after noting some other criticisms passed on the first essays, that " Some have complained that there is too much quotation—too little of my own. This I take to be in reality a great compliment. I have not striven to be original." He continues : " If, as I have been assured by many, my book has proved a comfort, and has been able to cheer in the hour of darkness, that is indeed an ample reward, and is the utmost I have ever hoped."

I have made rather a point of the ease with which Sir John gathered these compilations, because some, even of his warmest admirers, have commented adversely on the making of these books as a waste of time in the case of one whose time might have been employed to greater advantage in various other ways, and have wondered that he should attach such a high value, as he evidently did, to the result. But the time spent on them was, as I have tried to show, but trifling, and as for the result, I think that Sir John would justify himself in regarding it of some importance. He knew what the public wanted, but he always had a care that it should be the highest of its want that he supplied in such books as *The Pleasures of Life*. He collected into a convenient and readable form the thought which he deemed that others would appreciate, and how right his judgment was as to their appreciation the sales of the books in all lands show sufficiently. I believe he might find his perfect justification in the contention that those popular books have helped many men and women of many nations to think more worthily and to live more happily. It is difficult to say what human work is justified if such result as this may not be taken to approve it. Possibly, so far as Lord Avebury's repute as a writer is concerned, it is to be regretted that he is known more widely as the author of these composite books than of such serious and original work as is contained in *Prehistoric Times*, in *The Origin of Civilisation*, and the books which record his studies in the intelligence and the biology of the lower animals, and in the laws which control growth in plants.

Does it seem surprising, even when so few of the directions of his industry as the above are named, that the characteristic of Lord Avebury's mind and life which has been most often re-marked is his wonderful versatility ? In one of the multitude of letters of appreciation and of sympathy received by Lady Avebury after his death the line occurs : " He touched life at every point." I think, if we carefully study his career and know his life, we shall be obliged to realise that this is a statement which has to be taken with much reserve ; that it is, in fact, a eulogy more generous than just.

His versatility was extraordinary—that is above all dispute—but it had its limits, and these limits were strict. It is part, as I think, of that economy of power and of time which enabled him to achieve so much, that he should have set himself these limits. If we consider his outlook, we have to see that many human interests were not represented in it at all. All the beauties of Nature and of scenery were objects of keenest love and interest ; but he was little attracted, as I think, by the beauties of art. He might give it the careless appreciation of one naturally perceptive of fine colour and form, but he paid it no study : I had almost said that he wasted no time on it. I do not know, indeed, that in his case this might not be said with perfect truth, for surely it could only have been a cause of regret and of loss to his work in the world, had he made any further division of his talents. As it was, it appears that he practised a very wise economy in diverting his attention to none of the modes of art. Music only attracted him in its simplest forms, and even the forms of beauty in literature, so far as they are concerned with the expression only and not with the thing expressed, stirred little response in him. It is of a piece with that indifference to the classics which his tutor had bewailed at Eton. Amidst the lamentations the good man had struck the note of hope that the boy might become " a sounder scholar." Vain hope that was never realised ! It is questionable whether pure scholarship could ever have taken real hold on a mind so constituted and so preoccupied with the more practical subjects of knowledge : in the circumstances among which his further development took place, it was impossible that he should fall under that particular kind of intellectual charm. Metaphysical philosophy had equally little attraction for him.

Leaving Eton as he did at such an early age and going straight into the City, he had none of the years of comparative leisure which are almost

a necessary condition to the acquirement of a
taste for the arts, and less still would he be able
to find time for the acquirement of the art of
leisure itself.

Working without haste and without rest, his
mind was ever thoughtful, never inclined to day-
dream. If he permitted himself—if, we may
say indeed, he knew—the joy of reverie, it was
always reverie deliberately directed, aimed at a
preconceived target—therefore, maybe, better to
be called by some different name. I have mentioned before that one of his sons told me that
when he was taking the young fellow for the first
time into the City, to introduce him to the business, he said, " I have always found it a good plan
to have a book in my pocket with me, to read at
odd moments. It is wonderful how much you
can get through in that way " ; and accordingly,
in the turmoil of the " Tube," he drew forth a
book from his pocket and began reading it with
a concentration which enabled him perfectly to
detach his mind from the bustle and noise about
him.

So, too, when his children, and, later, his
grandchildren, were in the room and playing
games of the most uproarious kind, he would be
peacefully absorbed, it may be, in a German
geological treatise, far remote from them all, in
an atmosphere of his own making.

I shall not, I hope, be misunderstood when I
write that I am in a sense glad to be compelled,
for truth's sake, to modify the eulogy which
would suggest that he took all knowledge for his
province. His intellectual province was indeed

a very spacious one, but had it not the limitations
noted above, had the eulogy quoted been equally
just as generous, it could hardly be possible that
this character sketch were of a very human being,
as Lord Avebury most essentially was : it would
rather suggest the superhuman in its range and
its attainment.

I do not know whether any reader of the above
will be disposed to reply with the objection—
" How can you speak of a man as indifferent to
the charms of art and of music, etc.', when he has
touched on these so well and shown such just
recognition of their value in his *Pleasures of
Life* ?   How can you speak of the indifference to
literature of one who has given us so delightful
a book (translated, too, into so many languages)
as the *Pleasures of Literature* ? "   The answer
would be that it is perfectly true that he had this
adequately full appreciation of all that these
pleasures of art and music might mean to
humanity, probably as full an appreciation as it
is possible for a man to have to whom they did
not make their emotional appeal ; but that this
admission is not in any way inconsistent with the
assertion that to him they did not make any such
appeal.   It is possible for one man to have no
ear for music, or for another to feel himself quite
unattracted by field sports, and yet both the
first and the second can hardly fail to realise that
there is a large section of mankind to which music,
another to which field sports count for very much,
and for whom they have even to be rated among
the chief enjoyments of life.   In such a manner
was it possible for Sir John to estimate very ade-

quately the increase of the sources of pleasure given to mankind by appreciation of arts which did not touch him very closely.

I have thought that it was not possible to present Sir John Lubbock's intellectual character in any true light to the reader without making some insistence on these limitations to his still very extraordinary versatility, but there is one, and a higher side, the moral, of his character which it is possible, as it seems to me, to admire without any restriction whatever. And I write these words in the fullest sense of their extraordinary significance. One who was a friend of Sir John almost from the childhood of both of them said to me, " I do not believe that he once, in the whole course of his life, did a thing that he thought to be wrong." That is praise so high that it is hardly conceivable that it can be justly bestowed on any human being. I knew him over a less extended, but still a considerable period, and of my own more limited knowledge should endorse this very remarkable dictum. He appeared to have attained the ideal height of perfection at which temptation to do that which the reason and the conscience condemn ceases to assail a man. For that very cause, because the good action was that which always seemed natural and even inevitable for him, it almost appeared to have lost its meritorious character. Of course, the apparent absence of temptation was but the result of a very unusual power of control developed by lifelong exercise. It was the art which conceals art exhibited in relation to the ethical problems.

Sir John received enough letters to fill a big volume relative to these *Pleasures of Life*. I have made selection of a very few of them for the present work, in order to give a general idea of their tenor. They came from all parts of the world, from all grades of people—royal personages, men of culture, working men, women, even children. It amused me much to find, when I came to look over some of them, that the first in order was the following from a governor of the Bank of England !

BANK OF ENGLAND,
30th June 1887.

MY DEAR LUBBOCK—I have just bought, after having read, *The Pleasures of Life*—I was quite fascinated with it—but you have omitted one pleasure—*Tobacco*—please to remember it when you publish a second edition.

It amused me to find this placed in the fore-front, because if there is one amiable human weakness for which he had very little sympathy, it was just this, of smoking. He was a very temperate man in every way, and I do not think that he ever tasted tobacco smoke except vicari-ously, from the pipes of others ; and of this he had ample experience afforded him by his brothers and sons. I believe, however, that Mr. Chamber-lain is the only man who ever was known to light a big cigar after dinner at his table. No one else ventured on more than the mild cigarette. Sir John never, in my hearing, found fault with smoking as a habit, but I am sure that tacitly his face was set against its encouragement.

The next letter is from a shopman on whom Sir John Lubbock, by his legislation restricting the hours of toil in that profession, had laid other claims for gratitude beside that which this book involved :

> DEAR SIR—I feel under a debt of gratitude to you for having induced me by your *Pleasures of Life* to read your *Beauties of Nature*. This work led me to read Geikie's *Geology* and a number of the *Best Hundred Books*, with the result that I now seem to live in a new world, and subjects which before seemed dry are now intensely interesting.
>
> I have read 38 books out of your final list, but cannot say that I appreciated all.
>
> Some of Montaigne's essays are still unread. The *Shi King* I could make but little of, and *Locke on the Understanding* is a little too heavy for me yet.
>
> Formerly I was one of the unfortunate class of drapers' apprentices who had to take their recreation before 7.30 A.M. and do their reading between 8.30 and 10 P.M., and am consequently a warm admirer of your efforts for early closing.
>
> You will gather from this that I have had no classical education, and therefore appreciate such introductions as " Dr. Gillies' to Aristotle's *Ethics*." I greatly missed something of the kind in reading Demosthenes and had to search for it in a classical dictionary and a Greek history. The reader has to infer from the oration the charges Demosthenes is rebutting, and I think cannot follow the argument so well in consequence.
>
> Again thanking you for the new interests you have awakened in me by the perusal of your books.—I remain, yours gratefully.

The following is one among several proposals for a translation into an Indian dialect :

> DEAR SIR—I have read your *Pleasures of Life*, and except the last essay on " The Destiny of Man " have liked it so much that I asked my friend, Mr. W. S. Caine, M.P., to introduce me to you, but he does not know you sufficiently well to introduce me to you, and so I introduce myself and venture to address this letter. I am son of a magistrate and landed proprietor of the North Western Provinces of India, reading for the Bar here.

The object of my introduction was not to waste your time by call, but to talk on your book.   I wonder if you have read Persian literature.   If you read *Sadi Omar-i-Khyam*, and other Persian Philosophers, I think you would find a vast field to your interest, as your inclination is very much like theirs.

Urdu literature, unfortunately, is very limited, and it would be a pity that the advantages of your book may be limited to English readers, I have therefore thought to translate it in Urdu, but as I am short of time, and besides anything in the form of book cannot have a wide circulation *at once*, therefore if it is translated and published in the newspaper in chapters first and then in the form of a book, a great number of people would be benefited by it.   I therefore wish to ask your permission to translate and to send it to some best paper in India.

Hoping to be excused for the liberty I have taken.

This is of a similar tenor, proposing translation into another dialect :

Sir John Lubbock, Bart., M.P., F.R.S.,
    D.C.L., LL.D., London.

HONOURED SIR—I had the good fortune through the kindness of a friend to come across your esteemed little volumes entitled *Pleasures of Life*, and have been advised to render them into Gujrati.   I therefore make myself bold enough to trespass upon your valuable time and to request the favour of your kindly according me your kind permission to render your valuable works in Gujrati, for which act of kindness and grace I shall feel myself deeply obliged.—Yours faithfully.

A Japanese version is suggested :

TOKYO, *May 10th*, 1903.

MY DEAR SIR—Allow me to write you not acquainted.

I have had the honour and liberty to introduce to the Japanese society your great work, *The Pleasures of Life*, which doubtless has caused no small effect on the present intellectual and moral requisites of this country.

I had intended to send to you some copies of my humble translation to make it acquainted by its noble author, whereas, owing to my not being familiar with

the *mœurs* of your society, I have been hitherto hesitated
to fulfill the task : while, by the hint given by Mr.
Masaki, translator of your another work, I am very
happy now to do the task long intended.—Greeting your
health and prosperity, I am, dear Sir, yours most
sincerely,   NOBUNORI HONDA.

Address :
   Nobunori Honda
   Lecturer & Secretary of the Waseda-Daigaku,
   (Waseda University), Tokyo.

I think that Sir John appreciated the following from a working man, evidently of superior
intelligence, as highly as any that he received :

SIR—I have for some days been thinking how much I
should like to write you on the subject of the grand little
book you have written entitled the *Pleasures of Life.*

Although I am only a working man and my means of
purchasing books very poor, still I manage to get a
glimpse of works which are beyond my reach to purchase,
through the medium of our fine Reference Library of
which I often avail myself when I can find time.   I have
just been to have a look at the *Pleasures of Life* and I
am prompted to write you my sincere thanks for having
produced such a book which I feel sure will be read with
interest, pleasure and advantage by many thousands of
working men.   I consider it a book that will inspire us
with better thoughts as to the many advantages which
are within our reach if we will but make the necessary
effort to enjoy them.   You are right, Sir, when you say
many are deterred from reading what are termed stiff
books for fear they should not understand them, but
for a working man I consider the cultivation of a love of
reading will indeed prove to be a blessing as in a good
book he has company that will be of lasting benefit to
both himself and his family, and company that will not
attract him from his home for pleasures of a doubtful
character.   I speak from experience when I say this,
as I am fully aware of the many temptations that beset
the path of the workman.   I have for many years taken
a pleasure in reading, beginning with that great triumph
of this 19th century, the daily newspaper, till I acquired

such a taste for reading that I am not happy unless I see what is going on in the world. Let the masses of the people study their homes, and make the family hearthstone the sacred altar that it should be. We of this grand old country of ours now enjoy many blessings of which our forefathers never dreamt. And through the efforts of our great Liberal statesmen we shall doubtless go on to still further progress. I am not one who thinks that the old country is played out. I believe there are great things in store for us under the wise and generous rule of our able leaders. Take as an instance, that great undertaking, the Ship Canal, which I hope shortly to see begun in Manchester. I feel sure, Sir, you will not consider me presumptuous in addressing you my thanks and admiration for your many efforts to better the condition of that class of the community to which I belong, but perhaps will be rather pleased to hear from one of them who by his energy and perseverance has, at least intellectually, improved his position. I take it from my life that worldly possessions are not essential to a man's happiness, my ideas have always been that the improvement and cultivation of that divine gift to the human family, the brain, the greatest and best source of happiness, and without which man is little better than the brutes.

Apologising for thus far troubling you, I trust I shall ere long be able to purchase for my sole use and enjoyment the whole of your able and interesting works.— I am, Sir, yours obediently.

Mr. Lecky, Mr. Walter Pater, and other men of letters wrote to him very appreciatively about the book. Sir George Trevelyan's letter may perhaps be quoted as among the most interesting :

WALLINGTON, CAMBO, NORTHUMBERLAND,
July 8th, 1887.

DEAR LUBBOCK—I always delight in your books, the nearer they approach pure literature the more,—and this seems to approach it closest. I am taking it out to read, where it should be read, on the grass and under trees, and I shall begin with the Chapter on Friends, knowing that you always act up to what you write.

We had our Jubilee yesterday, and very pleasant it was.—Ever yours sincerely,　　G. O. TREVELYAN.

Later in the day.

The Happiness of Duty is most admirable and comforting. But the book is all good. I will put down one or two thoughts different parts suggested.

As to reading on a railway, my experience is different from yours. It is then that I can read quickly and steadily great masses of sustained writing, *e.g.* on two journeys between this and London I read with exceptional interest Lecky's account of the French Revolution and his account of the Irish Parliament in his 2nd vol.

In dwelling on the importance of tolerance with relations and friends, it is important to recognize what I am satisfied is a frequent and noble cause of difficulty : the unwillingness of a man to put himself on a higher plane than those he loves, and accept and acquiesce in their moral and intellectual defects as he would those of strangers. The young cannot do this : hence the frequent arguments and quarrels of the young. Life teaches the lesson to the wise, and a hard and sad one it is.

All that about education is excellent—teaching *con amore*. My second boy had a passion for science, and little taste, apparently, for literature. Sadly I recognized that in our barbarian household I could help him nothing. But I took care that the half-hour in which we did Horace was the pleasantest of the boy's pleasant day. And he has got one of the great Harrow prizes younger, and in a lower form, than has been done for 50 years, during which so many really great composers flourished there. The piece was slight : but had real value as poetry. Ah me ! I wish I had more to teach him !—Ever yours,　　G. O. TREVELYAN.

CHAPTER XXI

" NATIONALITIES " AND POLITICS (1887)

(AGE 53)

THEY again took 33 Belgrave Square for the
season. Parliament met on January 27, and
Sir John at once introduced three Bills—one for
the Earlier Closing of Shops, one to amend the
law relating to Public Libraries, and one to
facilitate the formation of open spaces in large
cities.

The first was blocked and he was unable to
make any progress with it ; the other two became
law.

The object of the Public Libraries Bill was
partly to encourage the formation of libraries
in villages by permitting lending libraries, and
abrogating the necessity for a separate building ;
and secondly to enable Unions to adopt the Act.
He also spoke on the Education Estimates, on
the Savings Bank Bill, and on the British Museum
Vote.

He had been for some years a member of the
Public Accounts Committee, and this year the
Government asked him to undertake the Chair-
manship.

The House of Commons Committee on Public

Accounts fulfils very important functions, which are little understood by the general public. The whole of the National Accounts are audited by an important official, the Comptroller and Auditor-General, who reports to Parliament if any sums have been paid without the authority of Parliament, or have been placed to a wrong account.

This report is referred to the Committee. The Committee then investigate every item criticised by the Comptroller, and report to the House of Commons. At the time of Sir John's chairmanship the Committee used to meet every Wednesday at 3. They sat round a horse-shoe table, with the Comptroller at one end, the representative of the Treasury at the other, and the representative of that Department of which the accounts were under investigation at a small table in the middle. There was often a species of triangular duel between the Comptroller, the Treasury, and the Department—all keen for the public service and all men of great weight and experience.

On difficult points it was frequently necessary for the Chairman to interview all three, sometimes several times, so as to be very clear in the report he laid before the Committee, and to express it in a way which should cause as little friction as possible.

The office therefore occupied much time and thought. It is of course, like all such appointments, unpaid.

He appears to have found the work much to his liking, and his relations with the Committee, the Comptroller (Sir C. Ryan), the Treasury, and the heads of the various public departments were always pleasant and cordial.

It may be interesting, as a means of indicating the position which Sir John Lubbock at this date held in the popular estimation (perhaps it should be observed that *The Pleasures of Life* had not then been published), to quote the following " order of merit " from the *Pall Mall Gazette*, which had been instituting a series of competitions on various subjects among its readers. It is to be noted that the verdict is nominally in respect of " Men of Letters," but obviously the jury did not confine themselves very closely to this restricted point of view.

The subject of one of our recent competitions was, it will be remembered, to name the forty living Englishmen who should first receive " immortality " if an Academy of Letters on the French model were to be established in this country. The competition proved very popular, and answers came in from all parts of the country and all classes of persons. The following list, in which the names are given in order according to the number of votes recorded for each, may be taken, therefore, as embodying the popular verdict on the several claims to " immortality " of our living men of letters :

1. W. E. Gladstone.	13. Archdeacon Farrar.
2. Lord Tennyson.	14. Prof. Max Müller.
3. Matthew Arnold.	15. Sir John Lubbock.
4. Prof. Huxley.	16. W. Morris.
5. Herbert Spencer.	17. Cardinal Newman.
6. John Ruskin.	18. W. Besant.
7. J. A. Froude.	19. Leslie Stephen.
8. Robert Browning.	20. B. Jowett.
9. John Morley.	21. John Bright.
10. Prof. Tyndall.	22. Frederic Harrison.
11. E. A. Freeman.	23. W. Black.
12. E. A. Swinburne.	24. Justin M'Carthy.

On March 19 an interesting letter from Sir John appeared in the *Times* on the so-called " Nationalities of the British Islands." It elicited also some interesting correspondence.

March 18, 1887.

To the Editor of the *Times*.

SIR—I observe that the supporters of Home Rule place in the forefront of their argument the assertion that " we have within the compass of the United Kingdom no less than four real nationalities." By this do not suppose that allusion is meant to the modern and, so to say, accidental divisions between England and Scotland in the first place, England and Wales in the second, or to the silver streak between England and Ireland, for we are hardly so degenerate as to reverse our old boast and allow the waves to rule Britannia. In fact the addition of the adjective " real " is of course intended to give emphasis to the declaration, which no doubt means that there are in the United Kingdom four distinct races, and that the existence of four distinct races is reason why we should permit one of them to have a separate legislature and a separate Executive. It is, therefore, worth while to enquire what the facts really are. As regards South Britain, it will be generally admitted that, omitting the question of pre-Celtic races, Wales and Cornwall are predominantly Celtic, with a considerable Norman intermixture ; that certain districts are mainly Scandinavian ; that our population is built up of three principal elements—Celtic, Saxon and Scandinavian.

In Ireland the population of the East and North is

---

mainly Saxon, in the North-West Celtic, while in the extreme South-West the basis is Iberian, akin to the population of parts of Spain. Very many of those who imagine themselves to be Celts, and the natural foes of the Sassenach, are descendants of English colonists, even in Munster and Connaught. The Parnells, Grays, Moores, Burkes, Fitzgeralds, M'Mahons, Barrys, Butlers are Anglo-Norman.

I pass to North Britain. Here we are met at once by the curious fact that the Saxons were in Caledonia before the Scots. In fact the Scots were an Irish tribe. Ireland, says Bede, " was the original country of the Scots." " Ibernia propria Scotorum est patria." " Scotia was originally Ireland," said Bozius,—" Scotia, quae tum erat Ibernia." The Scotch came from Ireland says Marianus, " Scotus de Ibernia insula natus." Ireland, says Chalmers in his great work, was " known at the end of the third century as the native country of the Scots, and in after ages by the name of Scotland. This appellation was afterwards transferred from Ireland to Scotland "; and he asserts, as the result of all his enquiries, that no permanent settlement of the Scotch in Caledonia took place till towards the close of the sixth century.

In fact, down to the middle ages, if a person was called a Scot, it was meant that he was born in Ireland. I must not overwhelm you with quotations, but, having given several of the earliest authorities, perhaps you will allow me to quote two of the latest. Mr. Bonwick says, " the real Scotia was Ireland, whose name got transferred to North Britain," and Mr. Taylor in *Words and Places,* remarks that " the Scots, this conquering Irish sept, which appears to have actually colonized only a part of Argyle, succeeded in bestowing its name to the whole country." Argyle is indeed the country of the Gael or Irishman.

In the north of Scotland, the Orkneys and Shetlands, the population is mainly Scandinavian, Sutherland being so named as the Southern portion of their territory. In the east and south the population is mainly Saxon. Edinburgh is a Saxon city, built by Edwin, king of Northumbria, and called after him.

Of the great Scotch families the Baliols are named from Bailleul or Beliol, in Normandy, the Camerons

from Cambronne, the Bruces from Yorkshire, the
Stewarts from Shropshire, the Hamiltons from Hamble-
ton in Buckinghamshire, the Lindsays from Lindsay in
Essex, the Sinclairs from St. Clair in Normandy, the
Comyns from Comines in Flanders. Some even of the
Highland clans are Teutonic. The Gordons, says
M'Laughlan, the Frasers, the Chisholms, etc., are
without any trace of a connexion with the Celts, and
originally without doubt of purely Teutonic blood. So
are the Macaulays, while Maclaughlans, Kennedys,
Macdonalds and Munroes are Irish, and the Elliotts,
Frasers, Maxwells, Mathesons and Keiths, English.

" The great heroes of Scottish history," says Bonwick,
" Bruce and Wallace, were of English origin." The
Lothians, says Hume, were " entirely peopled with
Saxons."

Thus then, in Scotland, as in England, the east is
mainly Teutonic, the west mainly Celtic.

Huxley and Beddoe have both pointed out, and it
will be generally admitted, that the people north and
south of the line dividing England and Scotland are
practically identical. On the other hand, so far from
Scotland being inhabited by a single homogeneous
people, the struggle between the east and west was
bitter and prolonged. A MacDonald burnt Elgin in
1420 ; and, says Burton, " It will be difficult to make
those not familiar with the tone of feeling in Lowland
Scotland at that time believe that the defeat of Donald
of the Isles (at Harlaw) was felt as a more memorable
deliverance even than that of Bannockburn."

I maintain, therefore, that the defence of Home Rule,
on the ground that there are four " real nationalities "
in our islands is entirely without foundation. If,
however, we are to be divided at all according to blood,
the division would not be into England, Scotland,
Ireland and Wales. The main division in Great Britain
would be not from east to west, but from north to south ;
the Saxon division would include the greater portion of
the east of England, the east of Ireland and of Scotland ;
the Celtic division would comprise most of the west of
Ireland and west of Scotland, with Wales and Cornwall ;
the Scandinavian the north of Scotland, several maritime
districts on the west, Westmoreland, Cumberland and
Pembroke, while the extreme south-west of Ireland

would be Iberian. The exact limits would give rise to an endless number of bitter disputes. Indeed so much intermingled are the different races that one of our highest authorities, Dr. Beddoe, after careful and prolonged study, says : " With respect to the distribution and commixture of race elements in the British Isles we may safely assert that not one of them, whether Iberian, Gaelic, Cymric, Saxon or Scandinavian, is peculiar to, or absent from, or anywhere predominant in any one of the three kingdoms."

This being so, I submit that any argument in favour of Home Rule based on the existence of distinct nationalities falls utterly to the ground, while the effect of rousing race antagonisms, from which we have suffered so terribly in the past, and which are now happily latent, can only add to our political difficulties and tend to weaken the British Empire ; while, on the contrary, if we recognize the undeniable ethnological fact that the English, Irish and Scotch are all composed of the same elements, and in not very dissimilar proportions, it would do much to mitigate our unfortunate dissensions and add to the strength and welfare of our common country.—I am, Sir, your obedient servant,

JOHN LUBBOCK.

The following is some of the more interesting of the correspondence which this letter produced :

18 LENNOX GARDENS, S.W.,
31st March 1887.

MY DEAR LUBBOCK—Touching the said Archpirate Maccus—a bilingual document (Bodl. MSS. Wood, 1 fol. 68. b) being a grant by King Edgar to the Monastery of Glastonbury—is signed in the following order :

Ego + Edgar rex tocius Britanniæ.
Ego + Eggiva ejusdem regis mater.
Ego + Edward (their son).
Ego + Kynadius rex Albaniæ.
Ego + *Maccusius archipirata.*
Ego + Dunstanus Dorobernensis eccl. archiepiscopus.
Ego + Oswald Eboracensis eccl. primus.
Ego + Athelwoldus Winton eccl. minister et Glastonie
eccl. quondam monachus.

Ego + Brithilin Fontanensis episcopus.
Ego + Alpharus dux domine mei Sanct Marie.[1]

You will find this charter printed in Dugdale's *Monasticon*, vol. i. p. 43 (Ed. 1817).

Then as to rowing King Edgar on the Dee :

" On making his annual sea voyage round the island King Edgar found, on his arrival at Chester, eight sub-kings awaiting him, in obedience to the commands they had received, who swore to be faithful to him, and to be his fellow-workers by sea and land." (Lappenburg, *History of England under A.S. Kings*. Thorpe's translation, vol. i. p. 125.)

The same story is given in the *Chronicon de Melros*, but I have not a copy to refer to here. Maccus is therein called the " King of many islands."

The " eight " was manned as follows :

> Kenneth of Scotland.
> Malcolm of Cumbria.
> Maccus of Man and the Hebrides.
> Dyfnwall of Strach Clyde.
> Siferth ⎫
> Jago ⎬ of Wales.
> Howell ⎭
> Inchill of Westmoreland.

I believe the story to be utterly without foundation, but, even as a fabrication, it probably deals with cotemporary potentates.—Yours very truly,

HERBERT EUSTACE MAXWELL.

I think both you and the Duke of Argyll tend to minimize the Celtic predominance of blood in Ireland. You find thousands of natives bearing English (Teutonic) names without, I believe, a drop of English blood in them. This arose in great measure from the statutes passed from time to time obliging the Irish to assume English names, *e.g.* ſionać Shinnach, now Fox (a translation of ſionać) ; Faiþće (Faithchy, Fahy), now Green ; Coiȝþiće (Coigriċhe), now L'Estrange ; ðonnán, now Brown ; ciaþ, now Black, etc., etc. But the more purely Celtic we admit them to be, the more hopeless would be any attempt to give them self-govern-

---

[1] We, of course, would write these feminine genitive endings "ae," but why "mei"—not agreeing in gender ?

ment. I am glad to see the Duke of Argyll quoting
Prendergast. I copied those two passages out of him
last year, and they are valuable as written by one of the
Nationalists. You will forgive my insisting on the risk
of minimizing the distinctly Celtic nature of the Irish
population. Temperament, features, history, all combine to support their claim to be regarded as Celts to a
far more complete degree than either Highlanders,
Galloway men or Welsh. In Man, where the speech is
Celtic, the people are mainly Norse, so they are in Lewis,
but in Skye, Celtic.

From the above it appears that the place, in
order of precedence, of the Archpirate of the
period was just one above that of the Archbishop.
It had been suggested that the said Maccus was
an ancestor of the Maxwell family, but Sir Herbert
seems inclined to disown him.

Professor Huxley writes on the same subject :

4 MARLBOROUGH PLACE, N.W.,
July 24th, 1887.

MY DEAR LUBBOCK—I am afraid that my Unionist
proclivities are also sufficiently notorious to damage
my chance of being regarded as an unprejudiced witness
in respect of the ethnology of the three Kingdoms.

But, luckily for me, I said my say on the subject
fifteen or sixteen years ago in a Sunday lecture on " The
Fore-fathers and Fore-runners of the English people "
delivered on January 9th, 1870. There is a very good
report of it in the *Pall Mall Gazette* of the 10th.

It brought a nest of hornets about my ears, English
and Irish. I summed up the points which I thought
most important in an article " On some fixed points in
British Ethnology," which is reprinted in my *Critiques
and Addresses*—an interesting volume which for some
reason or other the British public has never properly
appreciated—though they go on buying other productions of mine which, so far as I can see, are not a bit
better.

I have my hands full just now ; but I will turn over
your suggestion in my mind.

As to the facts of the case, I imagine that there can be

no doubt of the absurdity of the nationality plea on ethnological grounds.

The greatest absurdity of all is the supposition that the people on the North and South sides of the Scottish border, from the Humber to the Forth, are nationally distinct—in any other than an artificial, political sense.

I hope you will be able to come to the "X" —Athenaeum, July 30th.—Ever yours very faithfully,

T. H. Huxley.

Mr. Isaac Taylor writes :

Savile Club, 107 Piccadilly, W.,
March 26th, 1887.

Dear Sir—I have been greatly interested in the discussion in the *Times* on the Races of Britain, in which you have done me the honour to quote some things I have written.

If you have any thought of putting your letters into more permanent form—a magazine article, for instance— I should be glad to have an opportunity of correcting and supplementing my old work of twenty years ago.

E.g. I now think it can be proved that the Angles were nearer in race to the Danes than to the Saxons. That there were three, if not four Jutish settlements. That in Yorkshire, Angles and Danes occupied alternate townships—interspersed, but not fused. *E.g.* in my own parish, and in several neighbouring parishes there are two townships—one Angle and other Danish. The Landnamabok affords curious evidence of the mixture of Gaels and Norsemen who colonized Iceland from Ireland. The Manx runic inscriptions afford curious evidence of the mixture of Scandinavians and Celts in the Isle of Man.

Dr. Beddoe's recent book you know, but his facts and tables remain to be interpreted, and will, I think, supply you with a strong argument from the "Pictish" side. The king of Scots with his handful of Gaels ruling over Pictland was like the Scandinavian Russ ruling over Slavs at Kiev or Novgorod.—Believe me, yours faithfully,

Isaac Taylor.

The City of London Liberal Association was partly Unionist and partly consisted of Home

Rulers. The leaders of both sections determined to remain united for the present.

Each of the Metropolitan Liberal Associations sent representatives to the Central Radical "Caucus." The City Association nominated Sir John as one of their delegates, and after some hesitation he consented to serve, thinking that he would thus maintain the right of Liberal Unionists to regard themselves as Liberals, and in the fond hope that some day a reunion of the old party might be possible. This position he held for some years, but being the only Unionist on the "Caucus" he thought it better not to attend the meetings.

On May 20 he started with Lady Lubbock and their two daughters for a short holiday in Switzerland, and stayed at Weggis on the Lake of Lucerne. On June 7 they went to see the landslip at Spiringen. "It was a wonderful sight, the mountain side was still crumbling, and every now and then great masses came crashing and roaring down, every now and then leaping high in the air and throwing up great clouds of dust." He remarks that it helped to enable him to realise, however faintly, what the greater landslips at Goldau, and still more at Waldhaus Flims, must have been like.

The following is a charmingly expressed invitation from Mr. Ruskin :

BRANTWOOD,
14 *June* '87.

DEAR SIR JOHN—And will you *really* come ? It's so wonderful to think that you can forgive me all the ill-tempered things I have said about insects and evolution and—everything nearly that you've been most

interested in—and will see the Lake Country first from
my terrace, where, however, Darwin has walked also.
And it *is* a terrace—a mere nook of turf above a nest of
garden—but commanding such a piece of lake and hill
as can only be seen in England.

I shall be here all the year, and whenever you can
prevail on Lady Lubbock to seclude herself from the
world—(there is not a house south of us on either side
the lake for four miles)—and on Miss Lubbock to take
up her quarrel where we broke off—irreconcilable—you
will find Brantwood gate wide on its furthest hinges
to you.

You will have to put up with cottage fare—and
perhaps—with a couple of days' rain. I have only a
country cook—and when it rains here, it does not know
how to stop. For the rest, if you come when the roses
are yet in bloom and the heather in the bud, you will not
be disappointed in Wordsworth's land.—Ever affectionately yours, JOHN RUSKIN.

Mr. Ruskin had made some whimsically
ferocious, or ferociously whimsical, attacks on
Sir John's list of best hundred books. Commencing one of two articles in the *Pall Mall Gazette*,
he writes : " Putting my pen lightly through
the needless, and blottesquely through the rubbish
and poison of Sir John's list, I leave enough for
a life's liberal reading, and choice for any true
worker's loyal reading . . ." and so forth. Mr.
Ruskin was keenly antagonistic, moreover, to
the scientific views of the school to which Sir
John belonged. " I've been made so miserable,"
he writes to Miss Susan Beever, from C.C.C.
Oxford in 1875, " by a paper of J. Lubbock's on
Flowers and Insects, that I must come and
whine to you. He says, and really as if he
knew it, that insects, chiefly bees, entirely
originate flowers ; that all scent, colour, pretty
form, is owing to bees ; that flowers which insects

don't take care of have no scent, colour, nor
honey. It seems to me that it is likelier that the
flowers which have no scent, colour, nor honey,
don't get any attention from the bees. But the
man really knows so much about it, and has tried
so many pretty experiments, that he makes me
miserable."

Ruskin's whole attitude towards the men of
the Darwinian school might be described as that
of a man who said that " all truth is beauty,"
opposed to men who said that " all beauty is
truth." He would define truth in terms of
beauty ; they, beauty in terms of truth. But
beneath their differences there was a warmth of
personal affection between him and Sir John.
The gentleness of each must appeal to the other,
and again, despite their differences, they had a
mutual appreciation. Sir John speaks delightedly
of Ruskin's description of the grape hyacinth as
" a cluster of grapes and a hive of honey distilled
and compressed together into one small boss of
celled and beaded blue." Elsewhere Sir John
writes of Mr. Ruskin : " He was a man of singular
charm."

Nevertheless, for all the warmth of the invitation, much to the credit both of proposed
host and guest, who had known how to differ
from each other acutely, without rancour, I do
not think that Sir John found time to accept it.
His days, indeed, are fully accounted for.

For their autumn holiday they took Bambrough Castle, and were fortunate in having Mr.
Clark, the great authority on English Castles, as
a guest. He made Bambrough his headquarters

for a fortnight, during which time they paid
visits to the Duke of Northumberland at Alnwick,
and to Lord Tankerville at Chillingham, besides
making excursions to Warkworth, Dunstan-
borough, and some of the other border castles.

At Chillingham Sir John records that he
" was fortunate enough to have a very good view
of the wild cattle."

He lost an old friend this year, as already
noticed, in one of his aged queen ants, which
died towards the end of July. " She has been
with me," he writes, " ever since December 24,
1874. She hid herself in a corner, as they usually
do when about to die, but the other ants brought
her out and put her in her usual place among
them as if they could not realise that she was
dead."

In September Mr. Craig Sellar had written to
him, at the request of Lord Hartington, asking
him for suggestions as to a constructive policy
for the Liberal Unionists to lay before the country.
Sir John replied as follows :

High Elms, Beckenham, Kent,
13 Oct. 1887.

My dear Craig Sellar—I have received your letter,
and send you, as requested, my views, for Lord Hartington's consideration.

It seems to me that the economic condition of Ireland
during the present century has scarcely received sufficient
consideration, and I enclose a copy of my letter to the
Chairman of my Committee, in which I have referred
to this more in detail. You will find the passages
marked.

In no country where the population had fallen from
8,000,000 to 5,000,000 in 40 years could the Government
be popular.

If the present discontent had no such explanation, I

confess I should feel much less hopeful ; but now that the population is more in relation to the resources of the Country, I hope the people may be more comfortable and consequently more contented ; though of course, this will require a long time.

In standing out for " one Parliament " we occupy tangible ground, and I should be sorry to agree to any *legislative* assembly in Dublin, because in the first place, I believe that such a concession would greatly weaken our position in Britain ; and secondly, so far from removing difficulties, it would only give the Parnellites a leverage for further demands.

Separation seems to me a lesser evil than Home Rule.

I do not see that we are called on to frame any new constitution. It is clearly no use to suggest half measures which would not satisfy Parnell.

It is, I think, for them to tell *us* what they want, and then we can consider it.

If they were to have a separate legislative body, and yet sit in the Imperial Parliament, it seems to me clear that we must also have a separate Legislative Body for Britain, for we could not allow them, in such a case, to interfere with our special affairs.

But in that case, I take it, we must also have a Supreme Court to determine, as the highest authority, what were, under the new constitution, to be the powers of the separate Legislatures and of the Imperial Parliament.

The Home Rulers do not seem to recognise this, and yet to it they will inevitably be driven.

Trevelyan says that the old Bills are dead, and that concessions have been made which ought to remove our difficulties. For my part, I have no idea what the present policy of the Gladstonians is.

We should, I think, try to elicit what they now propose, and we can then consider it ; but it is no part, I think, of our duty to construct any new constitution.

I am sorry the Government have proclaimed the League.

I think it would have been better to punish boycotting and petty persecution under the Crimes Act, and I would levy fines on newspapers.

In the next session, I think we should suspend

members, whether English or Irish, who interfere with
the decency of debate.

I hope I have not written at too great length, and
please remember that I am writing at all because you
ask me to do so.   Probably a few minutes' conversation
might make my views clearer.

I will only add that while these are my opinions as
at present advised, I recognise the difficulty of the
situation, and Lord Hartington is far better able to
judge what is wisest for us to do under existing circumstances.

A. Craig Sellar, Esq., M.P.

In the same month he and Lady Lubbock
were at Eaton, the Duke of Westminster's, for
a lecture which he gave at Chester.

Certainly, in his own estimation, in spite of his
various work and studies, the year was principally
notable for the extraordinary appreciation shown
by the public of his *Pleasures of Life*.

CHAPTER XXII

INSTITUTION OF THE LONDON COUNTY COUNCIL (1888)

(AGE 54)

In 1888 Sir John took 39 Berkeley Square on a lease for five years.

On February 7 he attended a meeting at the Memorial Hall in support of Early Closing. Parliament opened on February 9, and he at once introduced the Early Closing Bill, a Bill on behalf of the Collecting Friendly Societies, and also a Bill to amend the law relating to factories.

The Early Closing Bill provided for the general closing of shops, with some exceptions, at 8 P.M., but he intimated his willingness in Committee to accept some extension for London if thought desirable. The principal London doctors and clergy of all denominations, including the Archbishop of Canterbury, the Bishop of London and Cardinal Manning, petitioned in favour of the Bill, which, nevertheless, was thrown out on Second Reading (May 2) by a large majority. This convinced him that it was impossible to have one fixed time, and that each locality must be left to decide for itself.

He was re-elected Chairman of the Committee of Public Accounts, and on March 7 was elected President of the London Chamber of Commerce.

He went down to High Elms, with Lady Lubbock and the children, on May 11, until the end of the month, and there is a note in his diary of the 29th : " We have had a peaceful time here. I have given myself a good rest, reading and doing my proofs of *The Senses and Intelligence of Animals.*" Another man might have written, instead of " a good rest, reading, etc.," " been hard at work, reading." But Sir John's idea of a " rest " was ever a change of toil.

On June 10 the eldest son, Harold, of his second marriage, was born.

They took a house at Lyme Regis for the so-called autumn holiday, where he was working mainly at a second part of *The Pleasures of Life.* During September he went to Bath for the British Association meeting, and stayed with Mr. and Mrs. Dunn at the College. He read a paper on the habits of the Solitary Bees and Wasps. One day was devoted to an excursion to Stanton Drew.

From Lyme Regis they went for a short visit to the Harcourts at Malwood, in the New Forest. Mr. John (now Lord) Morley was of the party. On September 26 Sir John notes in his diary : " Had a long and interesting talk with Harcourt about Home Rule. He would give Ireland, and, if desired, Scotland, power of managing their own special affairs, and yet thinks we should allow Scotch and Irish members to vote on ours. This, it seems to me, England would never assent to. At the same time he considers that the

Imperial Parliament must retain the finance, and that a supreme court would be necessary. He thinks that if there was a General Election now they would carry every seat in Scotland, and several in the North and the Eastern counties. I do not believe this. He says Parnell would be thankful to get anything! He did not give me the impression, however, of being very sanguine."

The following day they were back at High Elms, and on October 2 he writes : " Just as we had settled ourselves in the drawing-room after dinner, C—— came in and announced, ' Your ladyship's room is on fire,' as coolly as if he had been announcing dinner. Fortunately no great harm was done."

There was a late autumn session this year in November, and he spoke on the Education Estimates and on various Bills. The political situation was, of course, very difficult. On November 27 he notes : " Lunched (or break-fasted ?) with the Courtneys at eleven. John Morley and Miss Potter there, the former very frank about Ireland. He has not given up his Land Bill, and, I thought, admitted that Home Rule with the Irish members at Westminster was quite indefensible."

Two days later he was entertained by the London shopkeepers at a dinner at Willis' Rooms, and was enthusiastically received by his hosts.

He had suffered yet another loss in the autumn of the year by the death of his sole surviving old queen ant, at the venerable age of fifteen years. The death of her royal companion, at the age of fourteen, has already been recorded. It is believed that these are the oldest known insects. All this year the editions of the first series of *The Pleasures of Life* continued to be brought out almost as fast as the publishers could produce them, and his other books were constantly being reissued and translated into fresh languages and dialects. The following letter from Sir John's lifelong friend, the great botanist, Dr. Hooker, is an appreciation of *The Senses of Animals*:

THE CAMP, SUNNINGDALE,
Oct. 25th, 1888.

MY DEAR LUBBOCK—I had hoped to have finished *The Senses of Animals* before I wrote to thank you for your thoughtful present.

I am quite fascinated by it, and thank you most heartily for what is to me a most valuable repertory of facts previously quite unknown to me, and put together in the most instructive way. It was a happy thought of yours to take up the subject, and a happier con-summation to have dealt with it so lucidly. I rejoice in my previous ignorance, in that it has brought me face to face with so much of fascinating interest.—Yours affectionately, J. D. HOOKER.

The event of greatest importance, however, during this year, in which Sir John took active part, is probably that referred to in his diary of December 13: " The Liberals and Conservatives have both asked me to stand for the London County Council, and I have accepted. I should not have done so if the request had not been practically unanimous, the leaders of all parties having signed it."

It is possible, even so, that had Sir John foreseen all the additional labour that it was to bring into his already crowded life, he might have declined, but had he done so it is certain that the

infant institution would have lacked its principal
and most valuable preceptor in teaching it the
right performance of its at first little understood
functions.

Fortunately, it is no part of my task as Lord
Avebury's biographer to relate the genesis of the
London County Council out of the Metropolitan
Board of Works. Mr. Justin M'Carthy, in his
admirable *History of our own Times*, points out
how especially fortunate the new body was in
the varied ability and high eminence of its first
members. " The first Chairman," he writes,
" whom the County Council appointed, was no
less a man than Lord Rosebery, the second
Chairman was Sir John Lubbock, one of the most
able and highly-cultured men in the House of
Commons." And again, after a list given to
show the many talents represented in the Council,
he writes : " Sir John Lubbock could speak for
the interests of the bankers, and also for the ideas
of thinking men." We may, no doubt, acquit the
author of any malice or intention in the rather
charming irony which puts the " thinking men "
into this acute antithesis with the bankers.

Four seats on the County Council were allotted
to the City of London, and for these there were
six candidates. The result was declared, on
January 18, as follows : Lubbock 8976, Rosebery
8032, Cohen 3925, Clarke 3622, Shaw 2752,
Johnson 729. The first four therefore were
elected, Sir John heading the poll. The first
meeting of the newly-formed body took place on
the last day of the month, when Sir John was
voted into the chair *pro tem.* He notes : " I had

been rather anxious about the meeting. However, it went off very well; the members were very well behaved." The Progressives had returned eighteen out of nineteen candidates that they had put forward. On February 1 the meeting, adjourned from the previous day, was resumed. On the 11th the second formal meeting of the Council was held, at which Lord Rosebery was elected Chairman for the year, with Sir John as Vice, and Mr. Frith as Deputy.

The *Times* said with regard to the original voting :

By far the most interesting and important of the returns published yesterday of the elections to the London County Council is that for the City of London. Alike in its choice of representatives and in the number of votes recorded for them the City has established its claim to be regarded as the leading constituency of the new County.

Sir John Lubbock heads the poll with 8976 votes and Lord Rosebery follows with 8032, the two other successful candidates, Mr. Benjamin Cohen and Mr. Henry Clarke, being several thousand votes behind. This is altogether as it should be. Sir John Lubbock has every claim to be chosen as the first representative of the City of London on such a body as the County Council.

As Lord Rosebery said in his graceful speech at the declaration of the poll, the electors have rightly placed at the head of the poll one who not merely possesses personal and hereditary connexions with the City of London, but is also a man of great talent and high public spirit. They have done equally well in placing Lord Rosebery second on the list.[1]

The calls which the County Council made upon him, for some while during which its procedure was being determined, seem to have been in-

[1] *Times*, January 19, 1889.

cessant. On February 21 he notes, " Opening of Parliament. First I had (as almost every day now) a County Council Committee, then I went to the opening of Parliament and brought in two Bills, one enabling local authorities to establish a weekly half-holiday for shops, and the other my Factory Acts Bill." In May he further introduced a Bill to amend the Public Libraries Act. On March 2 he notes again : " Have had a heavy week of County Council Committees," and yet again on the 12th of the month, " County Council . . . it is really taking an immense amount of my time." These observations on the part of a man to whom work was so welcome, show how heavy the demands must have been, especially when he was attending the meetings from High Elms. It was not till March 5 that they came up to Berkeley Square.

He brought out his second series of *The Pleasures of Life* in May. The following typical little note is an acknowledgment from Cardinal Manning :

ARCHBISHOP'S HOUSE, WESTMINSTER, S.W.,
May 18th, 1889.

DEAR SIR JOHN LUBBOCK—I thank you much for your book. The first part I read with much pleasure, and I am sure that I shall enjoy the second.

Your witness against Dismalism, the first-born of Pessimism, is very valuable. Life is full of pleasure to all who honour it.

I send you a dry return for your refreshing fruit.

Let me know when your Committee meets.—Believe me, always, very truly yours,

HENRY E., Card.-Archbishop.

The very day after the publication of the second series of *The Pleasures of Life*, in the spring of this year, the publishers had written to him saying that they must print another edition of two thousand, as the first was already sold out ! There was only one paper, as he observes, that was sarcastic at all in its criticism, and, he adds, " the passage on which they are most severe is not mine at all, but a quotation from Plato ! "

On his birthday, April 30, the Liberal members of the County Council sent him a round robin, wishing him many happy returns.

In the beginning of June he and Lady Lubbock went off, as usual, for one of those Swiss tours which enabled him later to write the *Scenery of Switzerland.* They went over the Ghemmi to Visp, Zermatt, Lausanne, Geneva, Mâçon, Paris, and home to High Elms on the 22nd.

A week afterwards he writes : " Dr. Nansen, the Greenland explorer, came to breakfast. We had also Aberdare, Herschell, Flower, F. Galton, Lyell, Roscoe, Sir H. Maxwell, and Bates." I quote this entry because it indicates how Sir John kept up, almost to a later date than any one else, the breakfast-party habit. It is a form of hospitality on which opinions will vary much, perhaps somewhat with the eupepsia or the reverse of the breakfasters. To Sir John, who regarded himself as guilty of something rather like slothful indulgence if he did not begin the day as early in the morning as half-past six, the half-past nine breakfast came at an hour at which he was very ready both for refreshment and for conversation. There were others of a different habit of life who did not find their

conversational energies at their best on these
occasions. I know there is somewhere, though I
cannot lay hands on it, an amusing letter from
Mr. Joseph Chamberlain in answer to an invitation from Sir John to breakfast, in which he says
that he regards that meal as an anachronism,
that at an early hour in the morning, such as
2 or 3 A.M., he would be delighted to meet and
converse with Sir John and his other guests, but
that such an hour as that proposed for breakfast
he considers ought to be consecrated, by civilised
humanity, to sleep.

It was a curious friendship that existed
between men so different as Sir John and Mr.
Chamberlain, but it was founded on a strong
mutual esteem.

In Sir John Lubbock's opinion, the provisions
of the " Declaration of Paris " did not go far
enough, and thinking that it would be desirable
to assimilate the law relating to property at sea
during times of war to that on land, and so make
ships free of capture and seizure, he brought the
question up before the Council of the London
Chamber of Commerce. The Council agreed
with his view and passed a unanimous resolution
in that sense, asking him to convey it to the
Prime Minister (Lord Salisbury) and engage his
support.

He saw Lord Salisbury, who was quite of the
same opinion,˙but was afraid that France would
not concur, and asked him to consult Lord
Lytton, then our Ambassador at Paris. This he
did, and Lord Lytton wrote in reply as follows :

PARIS, *July 12th*, 1889.

MY DEAR SIR JOHN—I must apologise for having left your letter of the 8th three days unanswered ; but the subject of it was too important for hasty reply.

Personally, I have always thought that the Declaration of Paris went either too far, or not far enough ; and that, having precluded ourselves from issuing letters of Marque, or seizing enemies' goods under neutral flags, we made an immense mistake in opposing the Exemption of private ships from capture. I believe that our acceptance of this principle at the time would have secured the adhesion of America and Spain to the Declaration of 1856. But, as matters now stand, the difficulty of obtaining its adoption by the other Maritime Powers of Europe (especially if such a proposal were to emanate from us) lies in the obviousness as well as the magnitude of the advantage we should derive from it. We have the largest navy and the largest carrying trade : and I fear that no European Power which approaches this question from the point of view of *a possible belligerent* would *now* be disposed to centuple the strength of our large navy by relieving it from the necessity of protecting our large carrying trade.

Without actually making the proposal, I cannot ascertain for certain how it would be received by the present French Government. But I have the strongest impression, that at the present moment, it would have no chance of a favourable reception.

I am collecting, and hope to be able to send you shortly, the opinions of French Jurisconsults on the expediency of treating private property at sea like private property on land in time of war. These opinions, if in the main favourable, might perhaps be usefully cited in any international discussion of the question in the event of a propitious occasion for raising such a discussion. But they would have no influence over the French Government in its practical consideration of the question from a belligerent point of view : and that is the point of view which would be of paramount importance to any French Government at the present moment. In the event of War between France and England, or between France and any other country looking to the naval support of England, it would undoubtedly be the object of France to tie up our navy as much as possible, and to destroy or divert our carrying trade. The exemption of our carrying trade from capture by French Cruizers would render this object unattainable.

In any such proposal directly emanating from us, the French would at once smell a rat ; and they would meet it with the stock arguments, that private property stands by sea and land in totally different relations to the War Power : that trading or passenger ships may, in time of war, be easily converted into transport ships, or even into war ships for the repair of a naval disaster ; and that therefore such ships cannot be exempted from the risk of capture without thereby augmenting an enemy's naval resources in exact proportion to the magnitude and importance of his mercantile marine. And, moreover, that an enemy's mercantile marine being the natural recruiting ground of her navy, its liability to destruction is a no less natural condition of belligerency.

The French are now living in constant apprehension of a war with Germany which might possibly assume European proportions, and which would in any case be to France a life and death struggle. The action or inaction of the Naval power of England is one of the contingencies which they are bound to take into account in their preparations for such a struggle. They have spent millions on the augmentation of their land forces, and are beginning to think more about their navy. No French Cabinet could survive a popular impression that it had taken any step calculated to weaken the offensive power of the country, by land or sea, in the event of war ; and the French carrying trade is insignificant as compared to ours. The main object of every French Cabinet is to avoid exposing itself to Parliamentary attack—and the present French Cabinet is on the eve of a general Election, the results of which may possibly change the whole constitution of the State. It would be idle to attempt any serious negociation with a weak and unpopular Government in this position. Whatever the present French Cabinet might agree to would most probably be rejected and cancelled by the next Parliament ; whilst on the other hand, an unfavourable declaration of opinion by the present Cabinet might prejudice the chance of raising the question under more promising conditions hereafter.

For all these reasons I would in any case advise the
postponement of overtures here till we have seen what
the French Elections bring forth. But even from a
Government less frightened than the present . . . I
fear we should have but a very poor chance of obtaining
the participation of France—in the present state of
Europe, to the proposed extension of the Declaration
of Paris. In 1856 France and England were allies, and
the foreign policy of France was directed by a strong
personal ruler. In this Country no parliamentary
government could have carried the Cobden Treaty.

It is most reluctantly that I come to these conclusions.
For the extension of the Declaration of Paris in the sense
you advocate would now be of incalculable benefit to
us, and I should esteem myself most fortunate if I could
contribute to the attainment of that object.

If I may venture a suggestion as to the *modus operandi*,
I would recommend an endeavour to get the question
raised by some minor Power (Belgium or another) in a
general conference on some cognate matter. It would,
of course, in that case be advisable to have secured
beforehand by confidential negociation the concurrence
of a majority of other States. I don't see how America
could refuse to give up Privateering if the other Maritime
Powers agreed to exempt private ships from capture ;
although I apprehend that it would be impossible to
waive the right of search and seizure for contraband,
and the question of what constitutes contraband in
different circumstances would always remain a very
disputable one. I don't know whether advantage could
be taken of the Brussels Conference on the S.T. to make
some attempt in this direction. But if the object is
kept in view, other opportunities may occur.

If the proposal emanated from some minor Maritime
Power it would provoke less opposition than if coming
directly from us. And, put forward by such a Power
on purely humanitarian grounds, it would appeal more
plausibly to the French Democracy. It is just possible
that rather than figure as the only Power irreconcilably
opposed to so great a mitigation of the reform of Maritime
War, France would in that case agree to it. I can't say,
however, that I think the prospect promising. All the
considerations which render it desirable for us to obtain,
if possible, such a recognised alteration in the conditions

of Maritime war while Europe is still at peace, would
probably indispose France and Russia towards any effort
on our part to bring it about.—Yours, my dear Sir John,
very faithfully,　　　　　　　　　　　　　　LYTTON.

He sent the letter to Lord Salisbury, who
replies :

MY DEAR SIR JOHN—Many thanks for letting me see
the enclosed, it is a very interesting and a very convincing
letter.

I am afraid that in proportion as wars tend, as they
are doing now, to be wars for existence, the laws of war
will be liable to change in a retrograde sense.　The very
acuteness with which each belligerent feels the enormity
of the stake he has laid down, will dissuade him from
sacrificing any sensible advantage in deference to considerations of a less pressing character.—Believe me,
yours very truly,　　　　　　　　　　　　　SALISBURY.

Early in August a strike broke out in the
Docks, and he was urged, by several interests
involved, to try to effect a settlement.　In
various social matters he had co-operated with
Cardinal Manning, and knowing the Cardinal's
great influence with the men, he wrote to him as
follows :—

15 LOMBARD STREET, E.C.,
8th August 1889.

Private.

MY DEAR CARDINAL MANNING—As I understand,
the contention of the Strikers is that though the rate of
5d. (per hour) would give higher rates than unskilled, or
even agricultural labourers obtain elsewhere, still that
practically the men do not get it because the employment
is so irregular.

Do you think that could be met by the Dock Companies forming a list of labourers who should be paid 5d.
with a guaranteed minimum per week ?

If you were disposed to suggest this to Mr. Burns and
Mr. Champion, I would, if you liked, go with you, and
if they agreed would do my best to induce the Docks to
assent.—I am, yours sincerely,　　　　JOHN LUBBOCK.

Mr. Sydney Buxton who, as Member for Poplar, was naturally much interested in the matter, was away for his holiday, but his constituents telegraphed to him to return. The following letter from Mrs. Buxton indicates the trouble he and Mrs. Buxton had in their return journey :

WESTPORT, 23rd *August* 1889.

DEAREST FATHER. . . . Sydney and I have been having a very nice time here ; but now to our very great disgust, we have been telegraphed for home to London. There are some strikes going on in the East End, and Sydney has a good deal of influence with the men, as he has helped in arbitrations before, so when they telegraphed begging him to go back, he thought we ought. I think he is quite right, but it is a great nuisance. I felt inclined to stamp and swear when the telegram came. We have to be back on Saturday morning, for the great meeting in the afternoon—and to do it, we had yesterday to drive 43 miles, with one broken-kneed horse all the way ! It certainly was what our carman called a " long, slow, thravel " : but there wasn't any other animal to be had. We were staying at a most delicious place called Renvyle, on the Galway coast. It is a very pretty quaint old house, slated all over outside, and panelled with oak inside, standing in the midst of lovely scenery, and with very good shooting—of a rough sort—all round. It belongs to a Mrs. Blake, a distressed Irish landlady, who, not being able to get her rents, very pluckily turned her house into an hotel, and so makes her living. It is altogether most comfortable, though Mrs. Blake, herself, might become a nuisance in time. Yesterday she discovered from Syd's telegram that he was an M.P., so all the while we were packing, she kept dashing into our room with new arguments about the Agitation— flourishing the bill she was making out for us in one hand, and a report of her evidence before the Parnell Commission in the other. But she was very hospitable and nice to us, in spite of our telling her we were Parnellites. I always say I am a Parnellite in this country, as I don't choose to let Sydney fight the landlord class all by himself : and indeed I am a great admirer of Mr. Parnell's, if that constitutes a Parnellite.

I am afraid we shan't be able to come to H.E. in October, as we shall be fixtures at Cromer from the middle of September till near the session : but if we might come in January, it would be very nice. We are looking forward much to seeing you all in September.—With best love, your loving daughter,

Con. Buxton.

Early in September a meeting was called at the Chamber of Commerce to consider the subject, at the instance mainly of Sir J. Whittaker Ellis, who made a special appeal to Sir John to attend it. Sir Whittaker pointed out that the traders were getting a little impatient at the enforced stoppage of business, and that it would be most useful if Sir John would come and exercise his influence with them. Considering the endurance shown by the strikers, it was most important to maintain a patient bearing, but, on the other hand, it could not be denied that it would be worse than foolish not to make some move to put an end to the present disastrous state of things.

Sir John replied to the appeal that he would be at the Bank in Lombard Street, and would be happy to come to the meeting on a summons being conveyed to him. The traders met at twelve, and sent a message asking him to come over. He found they had before them a proposal to appoint a deputation to wait on the Dock Directors and to point out—

1. That the Strike was causing great inconvenience.

2. To urge them to put on sufficient hands and clear the ships.

3. That if they were prevented from doing so by violence they should apply to Government for a force to prevent interference on the part of the Strikers.

The first two resolutions were passed, and they were discussing the third, to which there was a good deal of opposition, when Sir Whittaker Ellis, who was in the chair, asked Sir John to express his view on the subject. He replied that he had come prepared rather to listen than to speak, that probably they knew more than he did, but that he thought the last proposal was a somewhat desperate remedy, and he could not but hope that it would be dropped. On the other hand, if they went to the Docks with the first two suggestions, the Directors would certainly say, as regards the first, that they were aware of and deeply regretted the inconvenience ; and as regards the second, that if Mr. Burns' pickets were removed they would have plenty of labour in five minutes. He thought, therefore, that this course would do no good, and indeed doubted whether the moment was one in which they could take action with advantage. He did not like to suggest to them to retrace their steps, but he thought that the best course would be to keep this committee together, to be ready to act, and to ask the Lord Mayor to interview the Dock Directors and the leaders of the strike, and see whether some satisfactory solution could be arrived at in that way. This suggestion met with general approval, and was unanimously adopted.

The following account of the proceedings is from notes left in Sir John's own hand.

After considerable discussion the meeting passed a unanimous resolution requesting the Lord Mayor, the Governor of the Bank of England,

and Sir John Lubbock to confer with the Dock Directors and the men, and attempt if possible to arrange a settlement of the dispute.

Accordingly, he wrote to the Lord Mayor and the Governor of the Bank asking when they could meet.   Next morning he received from the Lord Mayor a note asking him to come to the Mansion House, which he did at once.

Cardinal Manning, the Bishop of London (Dr. Temple), and Mr. Buxton were there.

The contention of the men was, that though the nominal rate of wages might be sufficient, yet, as a matter of fact they lost half their time standing outside the Dock gates, and were not actually in receipt of remuneration for more than three days in the week.

Cardinal Manning and Mr. Buxton contended, therefore, that the demand for an increase, under these circumstances, was reasonable.

Sir John, however, urged that a mere increase of wages would not meet the evil.   It was not a question of wages, but of organisation.   A mere increase would attract more hands, who could then be employed for a still less proportion of their time, so that though the expense to the Dock Companies would be greater, the earnings of the men might be no more than at present, because they would spend even more time waiting idle at the gates.

He proposed, therefore, that in the first instance they should confer with the Dock Directors. This was rejected, but the Bishop of London was in favour of submitting Sir John's suggestion to the men.   Eventually it was agreed that the

leaders of the men should be invited to the
Mansion House, and that the Committee should
adjourn till they came.

Sir John thereupon returned to the Bank and
heard no more till a quarter to four, when the
Lord Mayor came in hurriedly and begged him
to go with him to the Dock House. Sir John
was surprised, and said that they had not yet
seen the men. It appeared, however, that the
Lord Mayor, Mr. Buxton, and Cardinal Manning
had seen them, without summoning either him
or the Bishop. They claimed to have laid Sir
John's suggestion, which they themselves did not
favour, impartially before the men, by whom it
had been declined. That being so, the Lord
Mayor, Cardinal Manning, and Mr. Buxton determined to go to the Docks and urge the Directors
to concede the demands of the men at once.

Sir John said that under the terms of their
resolution in the morning he considered that he
ought to have had the opportunity of conferring
with the men and of laying his views before them;
that the traders in their meeting of the day
before very wisely suggested that they should
confer with the Dock Directors before coming
to any decision, and, moreover, that they had
not heard the views of the Governor of the
Bank.

He told the Lord Mayor that he thought they
were bound to hear the Dock Directors before
coming to any decision.

The Lord Mayor, however, intimated that he,
Cardinal Manning, and Mr. Buxton had made up
their minds.

Under these circumstances Sir John protested, and declined to accompany the Lord Mayor.

The Dock Directors were more than a little indignant, thinking that the Lord Mayor should have heard both sides, and positively refused the proposal.

Next week the Lord Mayor again begged Sir John to attend a meeting at the Mansion House. The leaders of the men attended, and eventually a compromise was arrived at, and Cardinal Manning agreed, notwithstanding his great age, to go to Poplar and lay the proposition before the men.

The following is Mr. Buxton's account of the Cardinal's interview with the representatives of the men :

THE MANSION HOUSE, LONDON, E.C.,
Sept. 11/89.

DEAR SIR JOHN—I write this at the request of Cardinal Manning—and I have read it over to him.

Yesterday evening, as arranged, he and I met the whole of the Strike Committee (with few exceptions) at Poplar.

After a very prolonged and animated discussion, and very great opposition *at first* on the part of many of the men present, probably of the large majority, the enclosed resolution was ultimately passed—practically unanimously—and signed by the Executive Committee.

In yours and the Lord Mayor's inevitable absence from town, Cardinal Manning and myself saw Mr. Norwood privately this afternoon, and laid the resolution before him.

He will officially lay it before his Board at 2 o'clock to-morrow—until which time the matter is absolutely private.

The proposition is practically that which we urged on the men on Monday, and which it was understood you would be prepared, in conjunction with the Lord Mayor, to press on the Board, if the men would accept it in writing—and this they have now done.

" That this meeting empower Cardinal Manning to
inform the Dock Directors that the men are willing to
meet them half-way in the matter of the time at which
the payment of 6d. and 8d. is to begin and to accept
Monday 4th November as the date."

Cardinal Manning will see the Directors to-morrow,
when the proposition will be discussed ; and he is *very
anxious indeed* that, if you could possibly see your way
to it, you should, in order to strengthen his hands, send
him a telegram to-morrow (Thursday) *before* 2 o'clock
(addressed perhaps to the Mansion House) to the effect
that you trust the proposition will be accepted by the
Directors.

From our interview with Mr. Norwood, we feel pretty
confident that he will urge on his Board the acceptance
of the proposition ; and your assent would greatly
strengthen his hands also.

The Directors will simply say Aye or No to the proposition ; for we have informed Mr. Norwood, of that
which we feel absolutely certain, that, on the part of the
men, November 4th is the irreducible minimum—and
Mr. Norwood thought himself that this Board would not
haggle over intermediate dates.

This is thus a real chance of ending the Strike, which
if it passes away cannot we fear recur.

We are writing in a similar way to the Lord Mayor,
who is also unavoidably out of town till Friday—and we
hope he will also telegraph approval.—Yours affectionately,   S. Buxton.

While he thought that the Dock Directors
had been very uncourteously treated, and the
whole matter not at all well managed, he considered, on the whole, that the Company would
do wisely to accept the compromise, and telegraphed in this sense.

The Dock Directors agreed, and the strike
ended, but the Company took steps to organise
the engagement of the men in the manner
indicated in his letter to Cardinal Manning.
The Directors, he subsequently heard, had in

fact been considering such a system at the moment when the strike broke out.

With Lady Lubbock he attended the British Association meeting at Newcastle, staying at Jesmond with Mr. and Mrs. Robin Hoare. He read two papers—one explaining the differences of the forms of the leaves in the two English species of *Viburnum* (guelder rose), the other on the peculiar form of the oak leaf, quite unlike that of any of our other trees.

One of the objections urged against his Early Closing Bill was that it might be inconvenient to working-men. He sent a copy therefore to Mr. H. Broadhurst, M.P., Secretary to the Parliamentary Committee of the Trades Union Congress, and asked him to be so good as to ascertain the views of the Trades Unions. Mr. Broadhurst replied that " his Committee had expressed approval of a general effort being made to shorten the hours of shop assistants, and that they would be glad to offer Sir John such assistance as they could give." Far from considering that working-men would be put to any inconvenience, the Congress, when appealed to, agreed to support the measure.

On October 30 he took the chair at the London Chamber of Commerce dinner to Lord Dufferin.

November 8 he was at Stockport opening the new Technical School, and on November 14 gave away the Heriot-Watt College prizes at Edinburgh.

A week later he and Lady Lubbock started on a hurried visit to Rome, where, under the guidance especially of Professor Lanciani and Professor Pigorini, they saw all the most interesting discoveries and excavations which had been made since Sir John's last visit. He records that " I cannot hear of a single bronze sword " (though there were many bronze ornaments) " having ever been found in Rome. Stone implements are also very rare, indeed almost entirely absent."

They returned home on December 9, " after a bad passage."

On December 12 he received a message from the Lord Mayor asking him to come to the Mansion House to aid in settlement of a dispute which had arisen between the Gas Companies and their workmen. The matter was one of much difficulty, but in the end a satisfactory arrangement was arrived at. Cardinal Manning was present, with his invaluable experience and influence to aid the cause of peace. " Eventually," writes Sir John, " we settled all the points amicably except one or two which both sides referred to the Lord Mayor, the Governor of the Bank, and me. The South Metropolitan Gas struggle only remained. Mr. Livesey was present and told me he had all the men he wanted. On the other hand, the Secretary of the Union stated positively that he would find it impossible to get another ton of coal."

The termination of that long fight will perhaps be remembered—how the Company entirely beat the men, and then dictated to them generous terms which made the concern an object lesson in the way of a successful experiment in profit-sharing.

The recurrence of those Labour disputes, prejudicial not only to masters and men, but to

the whole commerce of London, led to the formation by the London Chamber of Commerce of the
London Labour Conciliation and Arbitration
Board, the success of which seems to have been
mainly due to the energy and tact of Mr. G. B.
Boulton. Twelve employers were nominated by
the Chamber of Commerce—the different sections
being arranged in twelve groups—and twelve were
nominated by the London Trade Unions arranged
in twelve similar groups, to which were added
two nominated by the Lord Mayor and by the
Chairman of the London County Council. Sir
John was a member of the Board from the
commencement and took much interest in the
work. The advantage of this body over other
Conciliation Boards is that the latter generally
have, on opposite sides of the table, two dia-
metrically opposed interests — employers and
employed. In the London case, however, a
dispute would directly affect two representatives
only and the other twenty-four would be able to
exercise a comparatively unprejudiced and in-
dependent judgment.

Sir John states that in his opinion the Board
" worked well."

An excellent criticism of *The Senses of Animals*,
given by one of the reviews, indicates in a few
words the secret of the popular success which it
achieved immediately :

In Sir J. Lubbock's new book on *The Senses of Animals*
he sensibly adds to *The Pleasures of Life* by collecting
information perfectly new to the unscientific majority
of mankind. He enables us, not indeed to ascertain how
animals " envisage " the world but to be certain that
their world is extremely unlike ours. Take a beast

which has eyes in its back, ears in its legs, and which sings through its sides. How different must be the phenomena that surround that animal from those which greet us in our pilgrimage.

The second part of *The Pleasures of Life* ran through four editions during the year. The first passed through six more editions, and was translated into Russian, Swedish, and French, besides appearing as a "Tauchnitz." There was also a German translation of *The Senses of Animals*, a Spanish translation of *The Origin of Civilisation*, and a new edition of *The Origin of Insects*.

At the end of the year he received this complimentary announcement from Lord Salisbury :

HATFIELD, 29 *Dec*. '89.

MY DEAR SIR JOHN LUBBOCK—It is with extreme satisfaction that I am authorised to inform you that the Queen has been pleased to direct that you should become a Member of the Privy Council on the approaching New Year's day.

It is with no ordinary pleasure that I find myself the instrument of making this communication to you.— Believe me, yours very truly, SALISBURY.

CHAPTER XXIII

CHAIRMANSHIP OF LONDON COUNTY COUNCIL
(1890)

(Age 56)

Towards the end of the eighties there are fewer
references in Sir John Lubbock's diary to the
games of fives which he had been able to enjoy
for many more years than such violent exercise
as they demand is permitted to most men. Some
years before this his brother Henry had removed
from the High Elms kennels a pack of beagles which
he had kept there for a long while. The brothers
used to go out in the early morning before
starting for business and have a run with them.
Nevertheless, though the kennels of the little
hounds were no longer there, the master occasionally brought them over, and Sir John several times
records that they had a hare hunt. But in 1889
the beagle pack was given up and we hear neither
of the hare-hunting nor of the fives any more.
The game that began to assume the place of these
more athletic exercises for Sir John was the less
violent one of golf. Taking up the game when he
did, it was not to be expected that he would
become a great player, but a keen player he

certainly was ; and steady up to the point that he attained. He made a nine-hole course in the park at High Elms, and it used to astonish me, time after time, to see the accuracy with which practice had enabled him to gauge the strength required to run the ball up, as he did, from long distances, to the small putting greens, over the ground, left in its original state of rough pasture, of the park. I would attempt a pitch stroke, which had the air of being rather more scientific, but was generally a relative failure as regards the important point of bringing the ball to rest anywhere near the hole. Sir John would push the ball up, with a running stroke of the putter, estimating the final result of all the multitudinous bumps with an accuracy which made it look like an inspired fluke every time.

A very good account, with an admirable general idea of Sir John's procedure in the study of his insects, is given by Sir Edwin Arnold in a lecture which he delivered in the early part of this year in Japan.

" Take the example," he said, to his Japanese audience, " of one whose name you will know and honour, Sir John Lubbock. I have the privilege of his friendship, and have watched those daily researches of his by which he has thrown so much interesting light upon the habits of ants, bees and wasps, as well as on the structural marvels of the floral and the forest world. If you have read his delightful books and could afterwards see the simple arrangements which have produced them, those among you who are naturalists would be encouraged to attempt similar great and

illuminating things for us in your richly-gifted
Japan. Wishing to find out the sense of colour,
and to estimate the preference for different
flowers displayed by bees, you see Sir John sitting
with watch and pencil in his garden at High Elms.
On the turf lie pieces of paper, all equal in size
and smeared with an exactly equal amount of
honey, but variously tinted. In the summer
sunshine the bees come and go, attracted by the
honey. Selecting their favourite hue—because
they take the coloured paper for flowers—they
alight in numbers upon one of the squares, leaving
the others comparatively neglected, and thus in
a few hours we have obtained an answer from
the hive itself, as clear and businesslike as the
popular vote which you will soon give for your
new Imperial Parliament.

" Sir John showed me, not long ago, the little
apparatus where his ant cities were kept. Tier
above tier in shallow boxes, isolated by water,
and closed by a double lid of glass and wood, he
feeds and studies there the various species of
that wonderful insect. He drew back the wooden
lid from one large ant city, which revealed to me
through the glass its tiny people in their daily
life. There, in the central cell, was the Queen,
imposing, majestic, isolated ; courtier ants stood
round, always respectfully facing her majesty ;
and attendants brought the pupae, or ant babies,
in procession before the sovereign. Slave ants,
dark of hue, performed in gangs the hard work of
the city for the lighter coloured kwazoku and
shizoku of the community ; and small white
wood-lice, quite blind, ran about the by-ways

carefully cleaning up all dirt and litter. You may think I am romancing, but far more wonderful facts reward such an observer as Sir John Lubbock. Individuals in an ant city number from half a million to a million, and, incredible as it may seem, they all know each other. Imagine anybody recognising every single face in Tokyo ; but these ants, whose brain is smaller than a pin's head, can surely do this ! All this, for which I personally answer, discloses a new sense in these minute creatures ; while experiments made with the light-rays lying beyond the red and violet, totally invisible to us, prove clearly that many small living things are quite as perfectly aware of those hidden beams as the magnetic needle is sensitive to the polar current which we cannot feel. No doubt to the eye of the dragon fly, or of the Dytiscus beetle, altogether another world than ours is represented by the ordinary face of nature, near and far. These facts carry the thoughts of the educated European as far downwards into the lower regions of biology as the star photographs lift it upwards in the celestial regions. And everywhere alike he now sees at work the same grand principle of evolution."

Later in the year Sir John had a short letter of much suggestive interest from Professor Wasmann, the great German entomologist, to whom he had sent a copy of *The Senses of Animals*.

9–5–90.

DEAR SIR—I have received yesterday your letter and the book and feel very much obliged for your kindness. Although I have studied already the German translation of your interesting book, I am nevertheless very glad to possess the original from yourself.

The details about Laura Bridgman and your experiments on "Van" have given me peculiar interest. They seem to prove that there exists some essential difference between the mental faculties of man and superior brutes ; the poor girl could get with one sense to a notable degree of human intellectuality, but "Van" could improve by the use of his five excellent senses only so far as to combine sensitive images, according to the combinations given by your own intelligence. This seems to me very remarkable. But I fear we do not agree about the definition of "instinct" and "intellect."—I am, yours very sincerely,   E. WASMANN.

Mr. Andrew Reid asked him to write an article (I believe for the *Westminster Review*) on the Home Rule question, but he did not feel able to treat of it in the manner which would meet Mr. Reid's views, and replied to him to that effect. Mr. Reid, however, would at first take no refusal and renewed his request, to which Sir John replied :

HIGH ELMS, FARNBOROUGH, R.S.O.,
KENT.

DEAR MR. REID—I am afraid I could write nothing which you as a Home Ruler would care to insert.

Political agitators have I believe inflicted a gigantic loss on Ireland, which I see has been recently estimated by Mr. Giffen at no less than £150,000,000.

My objection to Home Rule is, however, in great measure from an English point of view.

If Irish Members are to have a Parliament of their own and then to sit at Westminster, I agree with Sir G. Trevelyan that they will not only be "masters of their own parliament in Dublin, but they will be our masters at Westminster as well."

One of the most important provisions in Mr. Gladstone's Home Rule Bill was that Ireland should contribute a fixed sum to Imperial Expenditure. That being so, we should I think be mad to allow them to vote on Imperial policy, as they might involve us in an immense expenditure, the whole burden of which would fall on us.

If Irish members are to be left to manage Irish affairs, then surely we ought to be left to manage ours.

But if there are to be separate Legislatures for Gt. Britain and for Ireland, as well as a supreme Parliament, —that would be *not* Home Rule, but Federalism.

I have over and over again expressed my opinion that Federalism is not open to the same objections as Home Rule, though it presents of course great difficulties. But it is unnecessary to discuss them, as Federalism has not been proposed by any leading English Statesman.—I am, yours faithfully,

JOHN LUBBOCK.

Presumably it is Mr. Reid, who, on the back of this letter, has made the following note :

This letter is so well put together, cutting out very sharply the blocks of stone, that I do trust you will let me publish it. I can then publish Mr. Gladstone's communication as it is written to me, and your reply to that. Mr. Parnell may also join in the matter.

I cannot very well publish copy of Mr. Gladstone's letter unless you consent to references to you which he makes, and which I must leave out. There can be no objection, if you wish, to your seeing his letter any more than there can be to Mr. G.'s seeing yours, for they are both on public matters.

After the turn of the year we find Mr. Reid following up this correspondence with some further letters which have for their purpose to draw Sir John once more into the Gladstonian fold. He commences by congratulating Sir John on being a member of the Privy Council. He points out what a powerful assistance Sir John might bring to the Home Rule cause if he could be induced to reconsider his attitude towards it, and goes on to say that he would very much like to ask Mr. Parnell if he does now, or ever did, insist upon a fixed contribution. Mr. Gladstone,

Mr. Reid says, had informed him that he was perfectly ignorant of any wish or statement of Mr. Parnell's of the kind. He quotes Mr. Gladstone's own statement, as follows :

2. I am not aware of a single rag or shred of evidence to sustain the statement that Mr. Parnell requires the pecuniary liability of Ireland for Imperial charges to be disposed of by a fixed sum, or that this question is dependent on the perfectly distinct question of retention at Westminster.

3. Mr. P.'s not bound to open his mind to me . . . yet were I to make an assertion on the matter it would be the direct reverse of this.   (No. 2.)

.   .   .   .

4. What " Gladstonian " has explained away Home Rule or brought it below this meaning that there should be an Irish parliament for affairs properly and exclusively Irish ?

Mr. Gladstone writes further :

This letter is not suited for publication : but the whole statement of it may be used as from me.

Mr. Reid further says that he is attempting, in the *Westminster Review* in February, " to clear some of the snow away," and admits that the Liberal road to Ireland through an Irish Parliament and back again to the Union is not as clear as it should be.

Two more letters pass between them, Mr. Reid sending to Sir John Mr. Gladstone's letter referred to, and expressing the hope that some basis of reconciliation between their views may still be found ; to which Sir John replies :

HIGH ELMS, FARNBOROUGH, R.S.O., KENT,
17 *January* 1890.

DEAR MR. REID—Many thanks for your very kind letter.

I had always hoped for, and do not yet despair of,

reunion in the Liberal party. Personally it has been to
me a matter of deep regret not to be able to follow Mr.
Gladstone in his Irish policy.

I trust that further discussion may have a good
result and have always avoided anything which could
widen the breach.

I have no objection to your publishing my letter, nor
of course to Mr. Gladstone reading it ; but in that case
I should like to see his reply.

Mr. Gladstone then asks whether, seeing that
Sir John so strongly objects to the "fixed sum,"
he would fall into line if it were not to be "fixed."
Mr. Reid, while forwarding this question, says
that he believes the leaders of the Liberal party
to be all tending towards Federalism. Upon
which Sir John writes :

HIGH ELMS, FARNBOROUGH, R.S.O., KENT,
24 January 1890.

Private.

DEAR MR. REID—Many thanks for your too flattering
letter.

If we are to keep our existing financial union, no
doubt one great objection is removed, and as you will
see by the enclosed I have always said that Federation
does not appear to me open to the same fatal objections
as Home Rule.

I could not indeed advocate it because there are
obviously great difficulties for which I do not yet see a
solution.

You speak of my recent "political fellowships,"
but in the City and in West Kent as well as in my own
constituency, a large majority of those who led the
Liberal party in the good old days are Unionists.

You, yourself, say that the Liberals who have
hitherto differed from us on this point are now abandon-
ing Home Rule and tending to Federalism, an admission
on their part that we have been right so far.

If Mr. G. puts forward any new plan which I feel
I should be justified in supporting I would most gladly
do so, as my severance politically from him has been to
me personally a matter of deep regret.

Two more letters, neither striking any very novel note in the well-worn controversy, passed, and that, as it seems, was the end of the correspondence. No more attempts appear to have been made to shake Sir John from his position.

The Duke of Argyll, in March of this year, gave an address on Economic Science, in the course of which he enunciated a view which he believed to be Mr. Darwin's, on the origin of the human race. Sir John Lubbock took exception to it, as being an inexact interpretation of the great master's meaning, and the following friendly little war of words was waged between himself and the Duke :

39 BERKELEY SQUARE, W.,
8th March 1890.

MY DEAR DUKE OF ARGYLL—I have read with much interest your address on Economic Science, but am greatly surprised at the statement that in Darwin's opinion, " Man originated with one parent."

This is so much the reverse of what I understood from him to be his opinion that I should be greatly obliged if you would tell me his exact words and the date of his letter.

The subject is one of so much interest, and Darwin's views carry so much just weight, that I hope you will forgive me for making the request.—I am, yours very sincerely,   JOHN LUBBOCK.

His Grace the Duke of Argyll.

March 10/90.

MY DEAR SIR JOHN—You know that it is said of Scotchmen that they always answer a question by asking another ! Why does it surprise you that Darwin assumed the Human race to have begun at one spot, and with one pair ? Has he anywhere said the contrary ? I don't recollect any one passage in which *either* that, or the opposite theory is *distinctly formulated.* But I certainly always understood that he assumed with *all* species that each form had originated *at a given place* and *spread from that.*

It was on this understanding of his underlying assumption, that many years ago I wrote to him asking what was the ground on which he made it.

His reply was—what I described—a reference to the *Doctrine* of *Chances*.

I forget the year, but I am sure I have kept the letter —although I am not sure that I know where to find it.

If similar forms, or rather identical varieties, have had *separate origins*, both as to time and place, a serious hole would be made in his theory : but he may have changed his view in later years. You do not imply that he has distinctly *voted* in favour of Black, Yellow and White Adams—originating at different places. On the contrary you speak of what " you *understood* from him to be his opinion "—which seems to refer to conversation.

But I should like much to know whether you have any *written* evidence that he believed in more "Adams" than one.—Yours very truly, ARGYLL.

39 BERKELEY SQUARE, W.,
13 *March* 1890.

MY DEAR DUKE OF ARGYLL—I quite concur with you that in Darwin's opinion each species originated in one centre, but not I think from one pair.

As I understood him external circumstances led to changes eventually resulting in a new species, but these circumstances in most cases affected a large number of individuals.

I have not his books or letters with me here, but when I go home I will look up his letters.

I saw him, however, so frequently that we generally talked on such questions ; this being much easier than writing.—Believe me, yours very truly,
JOHN LUBBOCK.

His Grace the Duke of Argyll.

The diary for April of this year is rather painful reading, by reason of its frequent reference to his sufferings from gout and struggles against it. Nevertheless he managed to be in London frequently, and to be active in scientific lecturing and in business. On April 26 he is better but "still lame." He goes on : "An American named Hittel has been making a book on morality. He dwells principally on seven moralists, whom for short he indicates by initials thus—A, Marcus Aurelius ; B, Bentham ; C, Cicero ; E, Emerson ; F, Franklin ; L, Lubbock ; S, Seneca." Sir John, in making this entry, puts a very large note of admiration after " Lubbock," at finding himself in this company.

On the 29th he records : " Got a boot on for the first time. London County Council meeting. Then to House, both Half-Holidays being down, but Tanner talked them out." Nevertheless, in spite of his personal pain and Dr. Tanner's loquacity, he is able to note on the following day, being his birthday, that " I have great causes for thankfulness."

On July 15 Lord Rosebery resigned the Chairmanship of the London County Council, and the Committee of the Progressives proposed to put forward Lord Ripon. It was found, however, that some of the Progressives were determined to support Sir John Lubbock, and as it was known that he would have the unanimous vote of the Moderates, it was clear that Lord Ripon must be defeated. Naturally, therefore, he declined to allow himself to be nominated. The extreme Radicals, though they put forward no candidate of their own, saw fit to vote against Sir John. He was elected on July 22 by 63 votes to 30. The organs of the extreme Left, however, protested that he was only a *locum tenens* and that they would turn him out at the annual election in November. All this was not very

encouraging ; it would have been difficult in any
case to follow Lord Rosebery ; the Chairmanship
of the London County Council was no easy post ;
the action taken by his opponents rendered it
even more difficult, and gloomy prophecies were
not wanting. But when November came it was
found that all opposition had melted away and
his re-election was unanimous. As he himself
remarked, " It is sometimes more gratifying to
be re-elected than to be elected."

The speech in which he returned thanks for
his election in July throws a clear light on the
difficulties of his position :

GENTLEMEN—I have summoned this meeting in
response to a requisition signed in accordance with our
fifth rule, in order to clear off our Agenda paper before
we adjourn for the holidays. Under the circumstances,
and as we have so much work before us, I will not detain
you more than one or two minutes, but before commencing the business of the day, I am sure you will
allow me in a few words to assure you how profoundly I
feel the honour you have conferred on me, and the high
post to which you have elected me. It has been said,
I know, that I am not sufficiently progressive, and that
I shall not be able to maintain order. As regards the
first point, I might under other circumstances have said
something, but I believe that to maintain the harmony
and efficiency of our proceedings it is a primary duty of
the Chairman to forget party, though I know that on
the point we are not at all agreed.

As regards the second point, I will only say that the
Council has maintained, and I believe will maintain, its
own order. Doubts, indeed many doubts, as to my
fitness and qualifications I have myself felt, and, having
regard also to my Parliamentary and other duties, I
should have hesitated still more, but that the election
only lasts until November. In Lord Rosebery I have an
admirable example, but one difficult indeed to follow.
To follow Lord Rosebery is in some respects a great
advantage ; but not in all. No advantage in this world

—and I suppose it would be so in any other,—is without some drawback. In this case I know well that comparisons will inevitably be made between the present and the past. You will, I cannot but feel, often look back with regret upon the past. Still, I am sure that I may ask for indulgence—that I may rely on your generous support, because I know that it is the aim and object of us all, not merely to maintain the dignity of the Council, but to fulfil to the best of our abilities the duties we have undertaken, and the important trust which our fellow-citizens have confided to us.

Lord Farrer was elected Vice-Chairman, and as subsequent letters will show gave most loyal and valuable support.

When Sir John followed Lord Rosebery as Chairman of the County Council of London it was, as he himself said, inevitable that comparison between their respective leaderships should be instituted. Sir John did not fulfil, so well as Lord Rosebery, the popular ideal of a captain of men. He had wonderful gifts as a persuader of men, a capacity to win them round, by patient reassuring, to his own view, but I do not know that he had that indescribable, sometimes called magnetic power which would lead them to follow him even on courses in opposition to their own view. This, as I imagine, is of the essence of the power of what is meant by a leader and a captain. It is not to be inferred from this that Lord Rosebery ever thus led his County Council colleagues in opposition to their better reason. The difference between Lord Rosebery and Sir John in the chair of this important body was, as a member of the council expressed it to me, that Lord Rosebery was more prompt in his rulings, but Sir John was the more safe. Others, however, have

spoken to me of Sir John's quick dexterity as a
chairman. We may at least be sure that he
acted as an exceedingly efficient president of this
newly-formed body.

It was at this time that the following notice
was circulated among the members of the Linnean
Society :

LINNEAN SOCIETY, BURLINGTON HOUSE,
LONDON, W., 25 *July* 1890.

A Meeting of Fellows of this Society has been held
with a view of securing a Portrait of the Right Hon. Sir
John Lubbock, Bart., M.P., P.C., late a President of the
Society. It was proposed by Sir Joseph Hooker,
seconded by Mr. A. W. Bennett, and unanimously
agreed that a Committee be appointed to take steps for
carrying out this object.

In August he and Lady Lubbock went for a
tour in Switzerland, going first to Mauvoisin in
the V. de Begn. On the 15th he notes that he
found Aquilegia Alpina. Thence they went to
the Bel Alp to be near the Tyndalls.

During their absence some structural alterations were made at High Elms, the large hall
being formed by throwing together a passage
and a smaller room. Lady Lubbock, for it was
to her initiative that these alterations were
due, always showed extraordinary talent in the
decoration of the rooms and in their furniture,
both at High Elms and in their other houses. It
was a department which Sir John, very wisely,
left solely to her.

He had been interested in the idea that the
date of the Ice Age might be inferred approxi-
mately from data given by astronomy and had
consulted Sir Robert Ball, later the Astronomer

Royal, on the subject. Sir Robert, however, replies negatively, in an interesting letter :

OBSERVATORY, CO. DUBLIN,
24 *Sept.* 1890.

DEAR SIR—I am much obliged for your kind letter.

As to the *date* of the Ice Age I do not think the astronomical data can help us much. The formula that Croll used does not admit of such an extreme application or " extrapolation."

But I have lately been studying with the greatest profit and delight Wright's *Ice Age in North America*, a book which Cronkey recommended to me. He points out that the Niagara Gorge has been cut *since* the ice, and that Lake Erie was formed *by* the ice. The time required to cut seven miles from Lake Ontario to Niagara seems to be the most reliable method of measuring the date of the Ice Age. At a foot a year (Lyell's estimate, I believe) this means 35,000 years, but Wright gives good grounds for his opinion that it may not be more than 7000 !

As the facts which my little book is intended to set forth are (in the main) beyond a question, I thought it wiser to avoid matters about which there could be much uncertainty. I am half inclined, however, to attempt a summary of Wright's views, and if I do so I will trespass on your kindness to look over what I say. A few years ago I spent a week at Niagara, and the novelty of Wright's views makes me long to go there again. This year I was in Norway and the contrast between the Fiords *before* the Ice and Niagara Gorge *since* is very striking.

Wright's book has interested me quite as much as Geikie's *Great Ice Age*, and that is saying a great deal.

The arrangement of my pages will show you that when I began I did not intend to trouble you with so long a letter. Pray excuse it—and believe me, yours truly, ROBERT S. BALL.

Sir John Lubbock.

The following is worthy of quotation for the interest of its subject-matter, though the " map " which it is its principal purpose to suggest is not shown.

HIGH ELMS, FARNBOROUGH, R.S.O.,
KENT, 31 *Oct.* 1890.

MY DEAR BATES—I have, as you know, long had an
idea that the preponderance of peninsulas pointing
southwards, for which no explanation has yet I think
been offered, may perhaps be due to the preponderance
of water on the Southern Hemisphere.

If we suppose, for instance, a tract of land running
north and south with a central mountain chain sloping
off on both sides, we might have an oblong tract of land

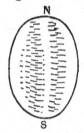

as above.   Now suppose the S end sunk, or the water
raised, it would assume a pear shape with the point
towards the S.

This seems to me to be the present state of our globe.
If the water had accumulated to the N end, the point
would have been to the N.

I write therefore to ask whether you could get for me
a map constructed (of the Northern Hemisphere first)
very roughly, assuming say an additional depth of water
of—

At the equator .	.	.	500
20° N. .	.	.	.	1800
40° ,, .	.	.	.	2500
60° ,, .	.	.	.	3500
70° ,, .	.	.	.	4000

Another reason for doing this very roughly at first is that I am not sure what depths of water should be taken.

This would test my idea. It might show the Rocky Mountains corresponding to the S. Andes ; Scandinavia to S. Africa ; the Ourals to India, while the mountains of N. China and Kamchatka seem roughly to reproduce the features of the Malay Archipelago.

I hope I have made my idea clear, if not please let me know.—Yours very sincerely, JOHN LUBBOCK.

The evidences of the various activities and speculations of his mind continue to mount up and seem inexhaustible. He notes, in the little summary in which, as usual, he jots down the main occupations of his year, that the County Council had made heavy calls on his time. Nevertheless, although he was Chairman instead of " Vice," I do not think that he found it quite so exacting as in its first year.

CHAPTER XXIV

VARIOUS ACTIVITIES (1891)

(AGE 57)

THE diary for 1891 opens on rather a delightful note. " January 1. Baby has not been very well. He said to Alice, ' If father knew his 'ittle boy was ill, he would come to him.' When I came home I asked him how he was. He said, ' Better. Not quite better. Not dead yet.' I asked him if he had any pain. He said, ' Little headache—in my head—that's a funny place.' "

Perhaps the inference is that a more familiar place for an ache was a little lower.

Early in the year Sir John had some correspondence with Mr. E. T. (now Sir Edward) Cook, at that time editing the *Pall Mall Gazette,* on the subject of the list of the best hundred books which that paper had published as a pamphlet. Sir John was invited at the same time to give a list of those which he considered to be the best ten modern books. His reply shows that he did not feel himself quite able to comply with the suggestion, but the alterations that he made in his own list of the " best hundred " are not without interest :

HIGH ELMS,
January 17th, 1891.

DEAR MR. COOK—I have been so much occupied with administration work for the last two years that I have not been able to keep pace with contemporary literature, and I do not feel that I could draw up such a list as you suggest.

I shall, however, read with much interest the opinions of others. When you reprint I really think you should give my real first list. The one you inserted as mine was compiled from the *Morning Advertiser*, and though the Report given there was admirable, it was not complete.

In justice, I may surely ask that my own list should be given. The omissions have caused me some vexation, for instance, I have been blamed for omitting the Bible.

I feel strongly on the point, and hope you will see the reasonableness of it.

The only changes I have since made are the insertion of Schiller's *W. Tell* and *Kalidases Sakuntala*, and the omission of Lucretius and Miss Austen.—I am, yours very truly, JOHN LUBBOCK.

Throughout his life Sir John took a great pleasure in trying to direct the minds of people who had not enjoyed his advantages to an intelligent interest in the scientific pursuits which had such a strong attraction for him, and I think it was as much with this end in view as any other that he and Lady Lubbock in the early part of 1891 gave the first of a series of what they called " Parish Parties." They let it be known in the schools and by means of the Parish Magazine that invitations to an evening party at High Elms would be sent to any of the Down or Farnborough people who cared to give in their names. About 150 came. The host and hostess put out specimens, photographs, microscopes, books, etc., and gave tea and coffee from 8 to 10. The party was very much appreciated.

In February of this year the Bank published its accounts for the first time. It was the first London private bank to do so, and they received many congratulatory letters, including one from the Governor of the Bank of England.

Shortly afterwards the Government asked Sir John to be Chairman of a Committee to settle the designs of the coins, those issued at the time of the Jubilee not being popular. The other members were Sir C. Fremantle, Sir John Evans, Sir F. Leighton, and Mr. R. B. Wede, Chairman of the National Provincial Bank. They invited several distinguished artists to send in designs. Eventually designs by Poynter and Brock were accepted and gave general satisfaction. Sir John was very strongly in favour of retaining the Rose, Shamrock, and Thistle. The Queen assented rather reluctantly, saying humorously that she thought there were " rather too many vegetables."

Later in the following year, Her Majesty again asked : " Is it likely that the coat - of - arms smothered in vegetables on the half-crown will be preferred to the very pretty coat-of-arms on the half-crown last adopted ? "

This spring the Chancellor of the Exchequer, Mr. Goschen, put forward some tentative proposals for an issue of £1 notes. Sir John opposed the suggestion in a speech to the London Chamber of Commerce, and again on March 16 at the Political Economy Club. It was not pressed further.

The project for the issue of the notes had a certain support from Mr. Gladstone. On April 11 of this year Sir John notes that he " dined at

Playfair's—sate between Lady Cook and Lady Winifred Gardner. After the ladies left I was next Mr. Gladstone and had some talk about £1 notes. He is rather in favour of them, but thinks there ought to be an enquiry."

Visits to the British Museum are of frequent notice in the diaries, and he had constant delight in taking his children to the Natural History Museum, the Zoo, and so on. After one of his British Museum visits he notes: "Lunched with Conny (Mrs. Buxton). She was telling Phyllis about the creation and Phyllis asked, ' Was I there ? ' ' Oh no,' said Kenneth solemnly, ' only grandpapa.' " Grandpapa, of course, was Sir John.

If it were possible, which I cannot imagine, to suppose Sir John in any circumstances in which he would not have worn all the aspect of being serenely at home, we might think that we should have so found him on March 9 when, as he records, he " lunched at the Garrick with Irving, Beerbohm Tree, Hare, Bancroft, and some other actors to discuss the Theatres Bill. It was interesting to meet them, but the conversation was mainly on the Bill." A few days later there is a note which bears witness to the interest which King Edward VII. always took in theatrical matters. " Sat. 14th, British Museum meeting. The Prince of Wales was very gracious, but attacked me about the Theatres Bill. I told him that the theatre people ought not to complain, as we were doing everything we could to meet their views."

In course of the same month, he concluded his sittings to Mr. Ward for the portrait which that painter was making for the Linnean Society. Sir John records his impression of it as being " very like, but, I think, too red."

I do not know the occasion of the following remonstrance, but presumably it was due to Sir John having done Lord Palmerston the injustice of denying him a *jeu de mot* which was rightly his :

BANK OF ENGLAND,
3rd June 1891.

MY DEAR LUBBOCK—On what grounds is the best joke I have ever heard made attributed to " a witty Manchester man " ?

The man who made it was Lord Palmerston, and to myself.

He had returned from a tour to Lancashire where he had been well received, and I, on meeting him, by way of something to say, called his attention to the distinction between the revenues and expenditure of Liverpool and Manchester, the latter spending much less on showy buildings, but on useful things quite as much. To which he answered, " Oh yes, it is the old story, ' light come, light go ' with Liverpool. They have the local dues, and if you change a letter it is explained in Deus nobis haec otia fecit,—Dues, etc."

I have often told the story, and I think at Manchester.
—Yours, H. R. GRENFELL.

By virtue of Sir John's efforts in composing the Dock Strike, the Coal and Gas Companies' difficulties, and other troubles between Labour and Capital, his good influences as a pacificator, in these conditions, became widely recognised and were much sought. Of this recognition the following appeal may be taken as good evidence.

HOUSE OF COMMONS,
June 11th, 1891.

DEAR SIR JOHN LUBBOCK—In common with many other of our fellow-citizens, we have noted the serious differences which have arisen between the omnibus

proprietors and their employés, differences which if
continued will be almost certain not merely to inconvenience the public, but to produce disastrous results
to employers and employed. In the belief that the
differences are such as might be adjusted by friendly
mediation, we as M.P.'s representing London respectfully suggest to you, as president of the London Chamber
of Commerce, and as a prominent citizen possessing the
confidence of the community, the advisability of your
offering to undertake to act in the capacity of a mediator.
—We are, yours faithfully,

W. RANDAL CREMER.
SYDNEY BUXTON.
JAMES ROWLANDS.
RICHARD K. CAUSTON.
GEORGE HOWELL.
E. H. PICKERSGILL.

" Possessing the confidence of the community "
is a phrase admirably descriptive of the popular
appreciation.

It is possible—I do not presume to know—
that the Reform Club, as a Liberal institution,
was at this time somewhat troubled between its
Home Rulers and its Unionists. In this year Sir
John was invited to become a special member of
the Club under the rule which permits such
invitation to be extended to any two members
annually " for marked and obvious services to
the Liberal Party."

No election, under the rule, had been held
since 1886, when the division occurred in the
Liberal ranks, and for the sufficient reason that
for the election of a candidate thus specially
invited the vote had to be unanimous. A *modus
vivendi*, however, had by this time been discovered,
by the election to the Club of one Unionist and
one Gladstonian annually. On this, the first

occasion of such election under the new rule, Sir John Lubbock and Mr. James (now Lord) Bryce were selected for the distinction.

At midsummer of this year Sir John gave up the secretaryship of the London Bankers, which he had held for over a quarter of a century. Lord Hillingdon conveyed to him the regret of the bankers and their thanks for his past services in a highly complimentary letter, and a little later Lord Hillingdon was himself elected as their chairman with Sir John as Deputy.

On August 5 he started for a little tour in Switzerland. At Geneva M. Correon joined him and they went together to Saas Fée. They found the glacier advancing and pushing up the turf, etc. Then over the Monte Moro to see the great moraine at Ivrea : then by the St. Bernard to Vevey and on to Homburg, where he met Lady Lubbock and the children. They went to see the Roman lamp at Saalberg and the Alt Konig where Brunhild slept in the ring of fire. " There are two great rings of stones," he writes, " but I saw no evidence of fire."

It has been noticed that in his diary the entries recording games of fives have quite ceased and are generally replaced by brief accounts of golf, but on September 14, at Homburg, he was playing lawn-tennis. A few days later the Empress Friedrich drove him out to see her new Schloss. " When we were alone," he says, " she spoke of her great sorrow and loneliness, poor thing ! We looked all over the Schloss and grounds, had tea and drove back. She talked very freely of European politics, and spoke with great affection

of England. She seems to have a very fair knowledge of wild flowers, and I tested her with some
of the less conspicuous species. She seems to
delight in flowers."

On the 22nd he notes : " Home by Bonn and
Brussels. It was a beautiful sunset. Harold
noticed it of himself and said, ' How pretty ! Is it
ours ? ' "

Almost his first act of any. public importance
after his return was his resignation of the Chairmanship of the London County Council, and
nearly all the papers had highly eulogistic
references to his conduct in the Chair of the
Council's business. The diary is a most curious
medley of entries which have a large public interest and value, together with such details as
" golf—69 and 71 " (this was at Cromer, where
he was staying at the beginning of October with
Mr. and Mrs. Sydney Buxton). It continues:
" Ursula caught a fine codling, which the children
had for breakfast." There is an entry of some
little interest, in the conversation about the Pope
which it records, on the following Sunday :
" Tricoupi, Sir J. Fergusson, Sir T. Sanderson,
Mundella, and Mrs. Stanley came for Sunday.
Sanderson said the Pope had personally a regard
for Victor Emmanuel. When he died they
brought the Pope the design for his tomb, which
the Pope approved, but said he could not sanction
it because the allegorical statues were all of
Pagan deities. There was nothing Christian
about it. So they took it away, altered Jupiter,
Apollo, etc., into Fortitude, Truth, etc., and
brought it back. The Pope was then satisfied."

When his resignation of the Chairmanship of the London County Council was brought before its members the regret expressed was universal, so much so that his diary of October 20 has the entry : "My colleagues on the London County Council presented me a memorial signed by every single one of them now in England, asking me to continue in the Chair until the end of our term of office. Under these circumstances I felt that I could not but consent."

Whether these feelings underwent any modification three days later, when, as he further notes, he "was in the Chair at the Licensing Meeting of the L.C.C. from 10 to 6.30, except half an hour for luncheon," we are not informed. It would not be much like Sir John to complain of hard work, but still such a tax as this on a man of his immense and immensely varied energies must have been felt heavily. It is really quite impossible, within the limits of tolerable space, even to notice more than a small fraction of the public work to which he gave himself so generously.

Sir John has stated that one of his greatest difficulties, in the whole course of his office as Chairman, arose in December 1891 when it was proposed by the General Purposes Committee to present an Address to the Prince and Princess of Wales on the approaching marriage of the Duke of Clarence. It appeared that some of the more extreme members intended to seize the occasion to make a personal criticism on the Prince, and it was felt that this would be a grave scandal. On the other hand, the notice had been printed on the Agenda paper, and to withdraw it would have been almost equally undesirable.

After conferring therefore with a few of the Chairmen of Committees, he determined to avail himself of the rule allowing the Chairman, if he thinks fit, to accept a motion " that the question be now put." It was arranged that as soon as the seconder sat down several members should jump up and move that the question be now put. This was done. The motion was put and carried, and the Address itself was then put and carried before the opponents had recovered their surprise.

They were excessively angry and threatened to move the adjournment. He said, " Certainly, but that on the motion for adjournment he would not permit any discussion on the Prince." Then Mr. Burns threatened a vote of censure. He said he " would give it precedence at the next meeting, that he knew he had done a strong thing, and could not complain if they abused him, but that on such a motion they could not attack the Prince "; on which Mr. Burns laughed good-humouredly and said he had the best of them all round.

He heard no more of the threatened censure, and had reason to believe that after a few days' reflection even his opponents quite approved what he had done. The above is but one of several instances which might be cited of an extreme dexterity in the management of meetings, which his frequent experience gave him, and of an audacity, concealed under a very gentle courtesy of manner, which often took the enemy off his guard.

CHAPTER XXV

RESIGNS CHAIRMANSHIP OF LONDON COUNTY COUNCIL (1892)

(AGE 58)

1892 opened sadly for the nation. Influenza was very rife, and one of its victims in the first month of the year was the young Duke of Clarence, the heir, after his father, to the throne. Sir John writes that at the first meeting of the London County Council they took only the unopposed business, as a sign of respect for the mourning of the Royal Family. It does not appear that unopposed measures were at all normal in the County Council just at that moment. Parties were divided with some evenness in their views on several vital points, such, for instance, as the mode in which loans for public works should be made to the vestries. Sir John was firmly in favour of advancing the loans in instalments, as had been done hitherto. His chief opponent was Mr. C. Harrison. On January 20 he notes that, " After a long discussion I carried in the Finance Committee a resolution against C. Harrison, recommending the Council to adhere to our instalment system as regards our loans.

We shall, I suppose, have a battle royal over it in Council next Tuesday." They did. Under that date he writes : " We have had a great struggle over our loans in the L.C.C. I moved a resolution in the Finance Committee that we should continue the policy pursued till now. This came up for confirmation. Campbell moved an amendment to leave everything open, but was beaten by four. Benn then moved an amendment to postpone the further consideration till March. This was carried by one vote, on which Farquhar, Antrobus, and Harben resigned their seats on the Finance Committee as a protest, and I believe one or two others will follow." On February 2 we seem to pass into a more peaceful atmosphere, for he is able to note, " A quiet Council. We had several loans, but so far the Vestries have all preferred the old system."

During this time of stress he had the direction of the affairs as Chairman without the support of his deputy, Lord Farrer, who saw eye to eye with him on all these points, but was, unfortunately, abroad. There are one or two of Lord Farrer's letters of the time which show how cordially he was with Sir John in spirit as a Moderate and opposed to the Progressives. Lord Farrer was laid up at Naples as the result of an accident on shipboard.

WEST END HOTEL, NAPLES,
11 *January* 1892.

MY DEAR LUBBOCK—Thanks for your note. I am getting on, but muscles and sinews are slow in resuming their functions, and I do not know when we shall be able to move, much less when we shall get back home— probably not before the Election. I wish I were with you to fight Charles Harrison, but it is out of the ques-

tion. It is to my mind a vital point. To lead the
ratepayers of London to believe that they can permanently shift the burden of taxation by postponing debt is
fatal to all sound Finance. It will veneer the mere
selfishness of casting burdens off ourselves on to posterity
with the false pretence that we are taxing Owners.
When the debt is postponed, it will be found that the
burden ultimately falls on the same class of persons as
at present, and that we have simply relieved present
ratepayers (occupiers or owners) at the cost of future
ratepayers (occupiers or owners).

I feel so strongly about this that I have written to
Benn to say that I shall probably resign my Vice-Chair-
manship by way of protest, if C. Harrison's proposal is
carried. Of course, I will not do this without hearing
from you.—Sincerely yours, T. H. FARRER.

Mr. Harrison's progressive policy did, however,
for the time being, prevail after a keen conflict.
Sir John, writing to Lord Farrer says, " I am
sadly vexed at the result." Lord Farrer's following letter must have given him some comfort :

WEST END HOTEL, NAPLES,
2nd February /92.

MY DEAR LUBBOCK—Your note of the 30th—just a
word. It is indeed an undignified and inglorious position
for the majority who have followed C. Harrison, but not
for you. Great as have been your services to the Council
throughout I don't think they have ever been so great
as on this occasion.

Did I tell you how much Lord Rosebery was pleased
with your letter, and your action generally. He says
the whole business will in the end weaken C. Harrison's
influence. I am not sure of this. But I think it may
lead a new Council to see, that if they choose leaders,
they must find some way either of letting the leaders lead,
or of letting them depart, and choosing others. It is
idle to ask Chairmen to carry out a policy of which they
do not approve.

I want to see your article on the Government of
London.

I am mending, and was able to hobble into the Museum

yesterday on the level, but am still very far from having the use of my leg.

The Government Commission on Water seems to me to be right in its terms, if it gets the right men.   There is nothing in it to prevent our Bill going on, I think.— Sincerely yours,   T. H. FARRER.

Under all the circumstances it is perhaps little wonder that Sir John definitely decided that at the end of his term of office as Chairman he would not stand again for the County Council. Pressure to reconsider this decision was put upon him from various quarters.   The City of London Liberal Association wrote : " At our Executive Committee to-day the most urgent wishes were expressed that you should stand again, and a resolution was passed and a deputation appointed to wait on you. . . . Great stress was laid on the advantage of your being spokesman of the Council in the House of Commons."

Nevertheless Sir John felt, I think, that he had done his full meed of public work in this particular direction, and was firm in his resolve not to stand again for the Council, though he did later consent to nomination as an alder- man.

On retiring from the Chairmanship he invited his colleagues to a dinner.   The following response to that invitation from Lord Rosebery, his pre- decessor in the chair, shows a full appreciation of the peculiar difficulties which the office had entailed on Sir John, as well as the writer's ap- preciation of the gallant way in which he had " crested the wave."

MENTMORE, LEIGHTON BUZZARD,
Feb. 6, 1892.

MY DEAR LUBBOCK—Your kind note greeted me on my return here from Italy yesterday. I should greatly like to assist at your dinner, as I also wish to assist at that to be given to you by the City Liberal Club. But, frankly, all depends on sleep with me just now. If I get two consecutive nights of fair sleep, I am all right; if, as too often happens, I have bad nights, I am all wrong. And it is so long since I have dined out, that I would ask you to let me leave it open till close upon the day. You do not need the assurance that I will if I can.

I have seen much of Farrer. He is wonderfully well and vigorous; sitting in the sunshine in a noble view; and pretty good on his crutches. . . . I am afraid you have had great trouble of late—alone in your chair without Deputy, or Vice in any form; and with Chairmen crumbling around you. But you have fairly crested the wave; and, not content with presiding over all London wholesale, and half London in detail, you have written (I suppose with your unoccupied toes) *two* articles on London subjects this month! You are a marvel.—Yours sincerely,   ROSEBERY.

Lord Farrer himself wrote his congratulations and regrets, to which Sir John replies: " Many thanks for your very kind letter. It has been a great pleasure to me working with you, and your advice and help have been invaluable."

The articles referred to by Lord Rosebery are the one on the " Government of London " in the *Fortnightly*, and the other on the " London Water Supply " in the *Nineteenth Century*. I think that Lord Farrer had assisted him with a few notes on the latter subject, for they are the subject of the reference in the first sentence or two of the following letter, of which the latter part refers to the *Senses of Animals*.

WEST END HOTEL, NAPLES,
January 3rd, 1892.

MY DEAR LUBBOCK—You will get in a day or two a few hasty notes which I had intended to be subjects of an article. I shall not, however, be able to do anything with it in the absence of materials, and I therefore send them to you, in case you should be able to make any use of them. Use them freely and destroy them; I have another copy. I have just finished your book, and feel what a vista it opens for future observation; it is clear that the thing now to do is to try to find out, as you have done, what animals really do see, hear and feel, rather than what their organs ought to enable them to do. What a world of possibilities the subject opens to us.

Another thing which strikes me much is that those very elaborate organisations, such as the eye, which seemed at first inconsistent with evolution, become,— with further knowledge and observation,—the strongest confirmations of it. Do you know Goethe's little poem beginning,—

Immer so vor vielen Jahren.

I always wanted Darwin to make it a motto for one of his books.—Sincerely yours,   T. H. FARRER.

It has been sometimes stated that the astronomical explanation of the cold of the Glacial period, which he adopted in *Prehistoric Times*, has since been disproved.

The following letter from Professor Bonney shows that one high authority at any rate shared his views. The Duke of Argyll's letter of a year later, acknowledging a copy of Sir John's *Beauties of Nature*, gives an indication of the Duke's views on one aspect of the question.

23 DENNING ROAD, HAMPSTEAD, N.W.,
Jan. 9, 1892.

DEAR SIR JOHN LUBBOCK—I do not remember to have seen—perhaps owing to my absence from London and general occupation with pressing matters for some time past—Bodmer's paper on River Terraces.

Please tell me where it appeared, and I will look it up.
Will you at the same time kindly inform me whether
Sir R. Ball's *Cause of the Ice Age* is the *first* volume
which has been published of the Modern Science series.
I have always been convinced that Croll was in the
main right, though I felt the great difficulty which Ball
has now proved to be a " Bogie." Still I am not satisfied
that the mystery of Geological Climate is wholly solved—
though we are now freed from our main difficulty. But
we have to explain the eocene climate as well as that
of the glacial epoch, and I am not sure whether his
" geniality " is equal to that.—Very truly yours,
T. G. BONNEY.

INVERARAY, *Jan.* 29/93.

MY DEAR SIR JOHN—Many thanks for kindly sending
to me a copy of your book on *The Beauties of Nature*—
just the sort of book I like best.

In cutting it just now I noticed that you accept the
theory of the " Ice Sheet " covering up the whole of our
Scotch Hills—as completely as the slopes of Greenland
are now covered.

I am myself persuaded that this Ice Sheet is as pure
a myth as ever arose out of Scientific theories.

But this is a long story, there were glaciers—at all
events coming down all the glens—no evidence that I
can see of anything more.—Yours very truly,
ARGYLL.

The following note from the spokesman of the
" staff " of the County Council bears witness to
Sir John's thoughtful kindness for all associated
with him.

I have had the pleasure of communicating to the
members of the staff in all the departments your kind
letter of farewell. They are much gratified at the
appreciative terms in which you speak of them and
their work, and are very sorry that the expiration of
your term of office has deprived them of a head, who in
dealing with them always displayed unfailing kindness
and courtesy. " And this is the verdict of us all."

On February 27 he gave the dinner, of which

previous mention has been made, to his colleagues on the London County Council. They buried all their controversies, the speeches were excellent and very cordial. Lord Rosebery was able to be present, and after the dinner wrote him a pleasant little note of appreciation.

DURDANS, *Feb.* 28, 1892.

MY DEAR LUBBOCK—I must write you a line of congratulation on your entertainment of last night. It was both genial and splendid—a rare combination ; all enjoyed themselves ; and there was not a jarring note. No public body has ever had a pleasanter Nunc dimittis. —Yours sincerely,   ROSEBERY.

Though he declined to stand again for the City, still, being urged on all sides to accept a seat as Alderman, he felt he could not refuse, and on March 15 he was elected at the head of the list—indeed, it was believed, unanimously. He made his acceptance conditional, however, on the understanding that he should not be expected to work on Committees.

In February we find the Secretary of the London Chamber of Commerce writing to him.

It was the unanimous desire of the Council, at their meeting on Thursday last, that you should be requested to be good enough to allow your name to be once more submitted for re-election as President, at the forth-coming Annual Meeting. I believe that, in this con-nection, Mr. Tritton has already informed you that the period of office of President usually extends over two years ; and that, as you have served only one year of the second period perhaps it may be possible for you, in view of the possible relaxation of your duties else-where, to complete the second period of your term of office as President. Some importance will, I believe you are aware, attach to the Congress of Chambers of Commerce of the Empire which will be held in June next, and it is specially in connection with this that the Council desire, if possible, to secure your services.

The Council will, I am sure, be extremely grateful if you are able to entertain this request favourably ; and personally, I need hardly assure you that I will do my best to take up as little of your time as possible. . . ."

This request he complied with.

He was much gratified by the following invitation to join " The Club," but feeling that it would not be possible for him to attend often, asked that his election might be postponed. A year or two later he did join " The Club."

THE CAMP, SUNNINGDALE,
Feb. 17.

MY DEAR LUBBOCK—You have doubtless heard of Hirst's death—a grievous loss to our little Club. Bates, too, on the same day.

I have been commissioned to ask whether it would be agreeable to you to be proposed for membership of " The Club," of which I enclose a card. It is the Blue ribbon of such-like Clubs (always excepting the X !) and holds the shades of Johnson, Goldsmith, Reynolds, Banks and a host of the like. Of course, *punctual* attendance is not expected, but a reasonable amount is. I need not say that your company would be much prized, and I am always anxious that The Club should contain a strong contingent of the best scientific men.—Ever affectionately yours,   J. D. HOOKER.

This year he was living at 117 Piccadilly for the Parliamentary season. The session was a heavy one, and he writes that on February 23 he was called out of his bed to go down to the House and vote.

On March 2 his son-in-law, Mr. Van Zandt, died with a wholly unexpected suddenness, leaving Sir John's eldest daughter for the second time a widow. He felt this tragedy very deeply, as is shown by the entries referring to it in his

diary.   Towards the end of the month Mrs. Van
Zandt came to stay with them.   It was but the
day before this tragic event that Sir John records
in his diary, like a schoolboy just off for the
holidays, " At last—my final Council over !   A
great relief.   Fardell proposed, Benn seconded,
and Russell and Thornton supported, a vote of
thanks to me in very kind and complimentary
speeches.   In some respects I am sorry, but it
has been a great anxiety, and I am glad it is all
well over."

The Council by this time was beginning to get
into its stride, and it had fallen to Sir John and
to Lord Rosebery to do much of the hard work
of the rough-rider in teaching it, at the same time
as they themselves learned, its paces.   During
this month of March he was much interested in
the commission to settle the new coins.   On the
10th he says, " We settled our Foreign Bondholders' report.   Afterwards we had our final
meeting of the Coinage Commission.   We have
agreed on designs, keeping Pistrucci's George and
Dragon, but for the rest adopting designs by
Brock, excepting the reverses of the Florin and
Shilling, which will be by Poynter."

Sir Charles Fremantle, at this time Master of
the Mint, was his Vice-Chairman on the Council of
Foreign Bondholders.   Sir Charles informed me
that he was most astonished to find how extensive
was Sir John's knowledge of coins.   I pointed
out to him that Sir John's antiquarian studies
had of necessity incited him to a study of many
of the ancient coins, so that this was really not
such a wonderful example of his versatility.   Sir

Charles had a most profound respect for Sir John's business ability, saying that they never were in a difficulty in any concern of the bond-holders which Sir John's acumen did not at once solve if they could catch him for a consultation. He remarked what a wonderful combination Sir John was of " thinker, almost dreamer, with acute man of business, keen on the main chance."

Thinker—yes ; but dreamer—surely no. On any subject that attracted his attention Sir John could concentrate most powerful thought, but the dreamer is rather one who allows his mind to wander, without special aim, as associated ideas suggest each other. This was not in the least Sir John's habit, and he would have regarded it as a sheer waste of time. He was the last man in the world to endorse either in precept or practice Balzac's dictum that " Le temps le mieux employé est celui qu'on perd." To be sure he was no judge, for he never did lose any.

The following refers to the Annual Meeting of the subscribers to the Corporation of Foreign Bondholders, a small but noisy section being opposed to the policy which the Council, with one exception, advocated.

YORK HOUSE, TWICKENHAM, MIDDLESEX,
March 26th, 1892.

MY DEAR LUBBOCK—You really must allow me to congratulate you on the way you managed those beasts at Ephesus yesterday. It was a most finished piece of art—quite classical in its perfection, I would not have missed it for a great deal. . . .

I am busy over my Geographical Address with which I am taking this year a great deal of pains.—Believe me, yours sincerely,   M. E. GRANT DUFF.

This is the meeting spoken of before, of which

his singularly successful and firm management evoked the astonished admiration and comment of his friend Mr. (now Sir Everard) Hambro.

At the end of April he attended the dinner of the Royal Academy and, not for the first time, returned thanks for Science.

His diary of May 4 records rather an amusing incident in the House. " I was sitting by Cunninghame Graham during the discussion of a Bill on the unearned increment, and Asquith was speaking, when I suggested that if this was just as regards land it applied equally to shares in companies. Cunninghame Graham said, 'Yes, you are right, the Bill is a swindle,' and jumped up saying something to the same effect very excitedly. The Speaker at once named him. I tried to pull him down but uselessly, and he was promptly suspended."

Under date May 17, 1892, is a letter from Sir Charles Tupper to Sir John, enclosing a copy of the resolution in favour of preferential trade between Great Britain and her Colonies which was passed by the House of Commons of Canada on April 26 of that year, together with some memoranda of the differential tariffs given by France and Spain to their Colonies. The letter concludes by expressing a hope " for a favourable response to the unanimous wish of the United Empire Trade League that you should accept the Presidency of the League for the coming year."

The Shop Hours Act Amendment Bill had passed through a Select Committee, but was in danger of perishing at the annual massacre of the innocents. The Government promised to help him through with it if the Opposition would agree, on which he wrote to Sir W. Harcourt who was then the Liberal Leader.

117 PICCADILLY, W.,
June 18, '92.

MY DEAR HARCOURT—I write to make an appeal to you about the Shop Hours Bill, the object of which in its present form is to enable local authorities to appoint Inspectors to carry out the provisions of the Shop Hours Act of 1886.

The Bill has passed through a select Committee by whom it was unanimously approved, and who took the somewhat unusual course of passing a special resolution urging the House to pass the Bill.

We had very strong, and I may say heartrending evidence as to the terribly long hours during which young people are being worked in shops, and the fatal effect on their health.

Stuart Wortley has informed me that the Government are willing to pass the Bill, if you will consent.

I write then urgently to beg you to allow me to say that this may be done.—Believe me, yours very sincerely,   JOHN LUBBOCK.

The Rt. Hon. Sir W. Harcourt, M.P.

To this Sir William Harcourt replied :

45 BROOK STREET, W.,
June 18*th*, 1892.

MY DEAR LUBBOCK—As long as I thought that the Government really meant to accelerate business with a view to an early dissolution, I did not feel myself justified in contributing to burden their list with additional measures, which might, or might not, give rise to discussion and delay. Now, however, that it is made apparent that they only desire pretexts to stave off the dissolution to the period which suits their own book, I feel I have no further responsibility in the matter, and have no reason either to assent or dissent to any course which they may think fit to take. I consider that in the spirit, if not in the letter, they have violated the understanding upon which I did all in my power to aid them in passing their bills. That being so, I consider I have no

longer any voice in the matter, and they are quite at
liberty to take what course they please. I need not
say that I have no disposition, except with a view to
expediting the close of the Parliament, to offer any
opposition to the shop-hours bill, but you must settle
that with the Government, who alone have now anything to say to the arrangement of business.—Yours
sincerely,   W. V. HARCOURT.

On June 21 Sir John is able to note " Provand
having left his Shop Hours Bill, I got it through
Committee and Third Reading."

On July 2 he writes: " This session I have
passed Public Libraries Consolidation Bill,
Ancient Monuments (Ireland) Amendments Bill,
London Water Bill and the London General
Powers and London Money Bills, besides doing
something to help the Shop Hours Act Amendment Bill."

At the General Election this year the Committee
of the University of London Liberal Association
did not oppose Sir John's re-election, but issued
the following protest : " We, the undersigned
members of the Convocation of the University
of London, while recognising that the distinguished public services and personal popularity
of the Right Hon. Sir John Lubbock make it
undesirable to contest his seat in Parliament
at the forthcoming election, nevertheless feel
it our duty to protest that on the question of
the government of Ireland he does not represent
our views, and to express with Mr. Gladstone a
real anxiety that the University of London
should do something ' to redeem the character
of our Universities from the charge of political
narrowness, which has unfortunately derived

colour from the uniformity of opposition offered
by their representatives in Parliament to what
we believe to be, in the great Irish question, the
cause alike of humanity, of justice, of reason,
and of union.' " The protest was signed by Sir
H. Roscoe, M.P. (President of the Association),
Mr. Picton, M.P. (Chairman of Committee), Dr.
E. Woakes (Treasurer), Dr. W. J. Collins (Hon.
Secretary), and thirteen others.

On June 28 he took the chair at the meeting
of the Chamber of Commerce of the Empire.
The Canadians moved a " Fair Trade " resolution,
which, however, was rejected.

On July 13 his diary notes : " With Alice and
the children and Daisy Norman to Switzerland."
They went first to Zurich, " then Stachelberg, to
the rockfall at Elm, up the Klonthal, then to
Wartenstein. Made an expedition to Vattis and
the head of the Kunchels Pass, the Gorge of the
Tamina, to Tamins to have a look at the Kunchels
from the other side." They returned home on
August 6. All the while, as in former Swiss
tours, he was collecting material for the book
which he brought out later on the Scenery of
Switzerland. " I have been working principally
at geology," he says, " and reading especially
Heim's excellent volume in the Swiss Geological
Survey, which seems a real masterpiece."

There had been some idea of their being with
the Tyndalls in Switzerland—joining forces for
a day or two, at least—but the Tyndalls do not
appear to have left England till later. Professor
Tyndall was much out of health at the time.
In August we find him writing from Switzer-

land to Sir John, who by that time was at home again.

The story of an amusing, though extremely natural, little mistake of Mrs. Gladstone's is noted in his diary on the 11th of this month. It was narrated of a dinner at the Sydney Buxtons' at which were Sir J. Grant, Mr. George Russell, and Sir Alfred Lyall : " Story of Mrs. Gladstone having sat next Lyall and saying afterwards she was so sorry she had not caught the name, she would so much have liked to ask him some questions about geology—taking him for Sir Charles Lyell."

On the 18th the appointment was announced of Mr. Sydney Buxton as Under-Secretary of the Colonies, which pleased Sir John greatly. His comment in his diary is, " I am sure he will do it very well."

Naturally he wrote to Mr. Buxton his congratulations, receiving the following from Mrs. Buxton in reply :

> 15 EATON PLACE, S.W.,
> 18 *Aug.* 1892.

MY DEAREST FATHER—Thank you so much for your kind letter of congratulation. We are delighted at Sydney's appointment. It is work he will like very much indeed, and he is particularly fond of Lord Ripon. Mr. Gladstone wrote a very nice letter (which came this morning) saying that he hoped Sydney would consider himself quite free to take part in Debate on the subjects he cared for outside his own Department.

Sydney looks forward very much to the work, and is very happy. But poor Edward Grey is rather blue, having just been told that he will get no holiday for some time, and never have his Sundays !

Our little gang of 5 has done well, hasn't it ? With two cabinet ministers, two Under Secretaries, and only

one member (Mr. Haldane) out of office. . . .—Your
loving daughter,   CON. B.

In October the *Beauties of Nature* came out.
It had a large sale and was translated into many
languages.   In Germany a cheap English edition
was printed, as an English reader for schools,
with a little dictionary of its own.

In this book he referred to the question
whether there had been any change in the moon
during historic times.   Some authorities thought
that there was in one case evidence of a slight
alteration.   He consulted Sir G. G. Stokes, who
replied :

LENSFIELD COTTAGE, CAMBRIDGE,
12th Dec. 1892.

MY DEAR LUBBOCK—When I wrote to you I had in
my mind a vague recollection of a discussion a great
many years ago in Section A of the British Association
relative to, I think, the spot called Linus, and my
recollection is that it was thought that there was no
solid ground for thinking there had been a change.   If
I rightly recollect, it was a suspicion of volcanic action
indicated by a slight red light when the spot was in
shade, as regards the sun.

On looking at the drawings of photographs to which
you referred me, I noticed at once, what doubtless you
too must have noticed, that the shadows lay opposite
ways, which is shown also by the difference of the dates
at which the photographs were taken—Aug. 15 and
Aug. 27.   Now imagine that you took two photographs
of a terrestrial range of mountains from a fixed point a
long way up, the photograph on one occasion being taken
when the sun was low in the east, and on the other low
in the west.   There would be a general correspondence
between the two of such a character that light in the one
would answer to dark in the other, and such there is
between the two drawings.   But we should not expect
all the details of light and shade to be just the reverse in
the one of what they are in the other ; for some parts of
the mountain would be in sun on both occasions, and

some in shade on both. Supposing therefore that there
were no change in Archimedes itself in the 12 days'
interval, I should not expect that the two photographs
would correspond like the positive and negative photographs of the same object taken on the same occasion.

I see Miss Shinn does not say a word as to these two
photographs affording any evidence of change. To
afford such evidence, pairs of photographs would have
to be compared which were taken as nearly as possible
at the same age of the moon for each pair.— Yours
sincerely,   G. G. STOKES.

Right Hon. Sir John Lubbock, Bart., M.P.

He received, from all quarters, very many
acknowledgments and reviews of the book, indicating how quickly all that he wrote found
appreciation even in the farthest distant corners
of the globe.

On August 14 he was at Birmingham, for an
Early Closing Meeting—" Stayed with J. Chamberlain who made an excellent speech and went
in for us thoroughly. It was a very large meeting." On the following day he was back in
London again at a Bank of England Meeting,
making what we may well suppose to be quite a
popular motion—" proposed to raise the salaries
of the Governor and Deputy Governor to £2000
and £1500." We may learn without surprise
that " it was carried unanimously."

So, all through October the diary shows its
usual record of happy and unceasing activity
both physical and mental. He was here, there,
and everywhere, " to Bristol, to open the new
Science Buildings at the Grammar School—the
great hall in the school is a beautiful room," to
Early Closing Meetings, and so on, and then, on
November 3, this happy note is all changed by

the record of a tragic occurrence which affected Sir John very deeply—the sudden and wholly unexpected death of his daughter Constance, wife of Mr. Sydney Buxton. " All her life she was nothing but a comfort and a joy to me," he writes. " She was indeed full of sympathy and thought for every one." And again, five days later : " She was indeed a joy and blessing and comfort to me, and I ought to be thankful that she was spared so long to us. To talk to her was like sunshine and sea air, and she was so utterly unselfish. I can hardly realise that we have lost her."

It is a charming and touching eulogy. Nevertheless, deep as Sir John's grief was he did not allow it to suspend his activities. In response to a request from Dr. Welldon, the Headmaster of Harrow, he gave a lecture on Natural Science to the School on the Hill. At the opening of the Medical Session he distributed the prizes at St. Thomas', and gave an address of which the concluding portion is worthy of passing notice.

He said that " In recent years Medical Science had made marvellous strides. Sir George Humphrey in his address last year had pointed out that when he began life anaesthetics and antiseptics had not been dreamt of, there were no excisions of joints, no abdominal operations. It was an antideluvian period without temperature thermometers, without stethoscopes, aspirators, iodide of potassium, salicylic acid, or even cod liver oil. The treatment of wounds was something horrible. During that period the knowledge of the localisation of brain function had become more extended, more precise, and had resulted, in the hands of Ferrier, Worsley, M'Ewan, and others, in those great achievements of brain surgery which had already proved so successful. He wished to impress upon them very strongly the importance of cultivating habits of business. Sir J. Paget had given some very interesting statistics which showed that out of 1000 medical students whose career he had followed, rather more than 200 left the profession or died early, more than 600 attained fair, some of them considerable success, but of the whole number only 56 entirely failed. Of these 56, 15 never passed the examination, 10 failed through ill-health or accident, and 10 through dissipation or intemperance. They might rest assured that if they had done their best they would have the happiness of feeling when old age came that they had led useful lives, that they had brought comfort and consolation into many a home ; had not only relieved the ailments of the body, but the still keener sufferings of the mind, and had enabled many, if not to realise, at any rate somewhat more to appreciate the inestimable gift of life and the interest and beauty of the world in which they lived."

In the autumn, shortly after Mrs. Buxton's death, he went to North Devon with Lady Lubbock and their daughter Ursula. Minehead was their headquarters. He writes that on Sunday they went for a " beautiful walk along the shore Westward, and back over the hill. In one place found well-marked ripple marks on the sandstones, which are highly inclined." On the following day he says, " Dear little Ursula much interested in the shore." This note is worth attention, for it is the first hint of an interest which he was at much pains to develop to the mutual pleasure of father and daughter. Of all his children none was a more zealous assistant in his later scientific pursuits.

Mr. Thomas Hughes (Tom Brown) was at him again this year to enlist his aid in the preservation of that equine specimen in chalk, which he loved so dearly, the old White Horse.

Abington House, Abington, N.B.,
1.9.92.

Dear Lubbock—I get letters from the Vale of White Horse, Berks, bewailing the condition of that " ancient monument " and crying out for something to be done before it disappears. The last letter says, that an " *Inspector* " as they call him came down lately, and, after examining, went to Lord Craven at Ashdown Park (close by), the owner of the freehold, who forbade him from doing anything. This is only gossip so far as I know, but I really should be glad if something can be done. I can't get at the statutes here, but my impression is that the White Horse and Wayland Smith's cave (a cromlech) were scheduled to the Ancient Monuments Act. If this is so, and you can do anything to put the Act in motion, you will much oblige me and all native West Berks men. Much as I distrust and dislike the Government, I am very glad of Acland's promotion, and hope it may augur some good for the W. M. College, which deserves to be put on a sound financial basis.

We have been enjoying our holiday in Scotland whence I go back now to work at Chester.—Ever yours very truly,   Thos. Hughes.

This is the first year, as it is also nearly the last, in which we may find him who had so ardent a faith in the " Duty of Happiness " concluding his annual summary on a note other than that of joyful thanksgiving.

" Another year gone : it has been a sad one. Poor Van's death was a great shock, and Conny's a terrible blow." And actually we find him admitting, " I have been feeling a good deal over-worked. The L.C.C. was a great strain and the Council of Foreign Bondholders has been very responsible."

END OF VOL. I

Printed by R. & R. CLARK, LIMITED. *Edinburgh.*

WORKS BY LORD AVEBURY

ON PEACE AND HAPPINESS. Third Impression. Globe 8vo. 3s. 6d. (Macmillan and Co., Ltd.)

ON MUNICIPAL AND NATIONAL TRADING. Third Impression. 8vo. Limp Cloth, 2s. 6d. (Macmillan and Co., Ltd.)

NOTES ON THE LIFE-HISTORY OF BRITISH FLOWER-ING PLANTS. 8vo. 15s. net. (Macmillan and Co., Ltd.)

FREE TRADE. Fourth Edition. 8vo. 2s. 6d. net. (Macmillan and Co., Ltd.)

ESSAYS AND ADDRESSES, 1900–1903. 8vo. 7s. 6d. net. (Macmillan and Co., Ltd.)

THE SCENERY OF ENGLAND, and the Causes to which it is Due. Fifth Edition. Crown 8vo. 6s. (Macmillan and Co., Ltd.)

THE SCENERY OF SWITZERLAND, and the Causes to which it is Due. Fifth Edition. Crown 8vo. 6s. (Macmillan and Co., Ltd.)

THE USE OF LIFE. One hundred and eighty-sixth Thousand. Globe 8vo. *Popular Edition*, 1s. 6d. ; sewed, 1s. *Library Edition*, 3s. 6d. 8vo, 1s. ; sewed 6d. *Pocket Edition*, Fcap. 8vo, Cloth, 2s. net ; Leather, 3s. net. (Macmillan and Co., Ltd.)

THE BEAUTIES OF NATURE. Eighty-seventh Thousand. Crown 8vo. 6s. New Edition, without Illustrations. Globe 8vo. Cloth, 1s. 6d. ; paper, 1s. Also 8vo, sewed, 6d. (Macmillan and Co., Ltd.)

THE PLEASURES OF LIFE. Part I. Two hundred and seventy-second Thousand. Globe 8vo. *Popular Edition*, 1s. 6d.; sewed, 1s. (Macmillan and Co., Ltd.)

THE PLEASURES OF LIFE. Part II. Two hundred and thirty-second Thousand. Globe 8vo. *Popular Edition*, 1s. 6d. ; sewed, 1s. (Macmillan and Co., Ltd.)

THE PLEASURES OF LIFE. (Two Parts in one Vol.) Globe 8vo. 2s. 6d. 8vo, sewed, 6d. *Pocket Edition*. Fcap. 8vo. Cloth, 2s. net ; Leather, 3s. net. (Macmillan and Co., Ltd.)

SCIENTIFIC LECTURES. Fourth Thousand. 8vo. 6s. net. (Macmillan and Co., Ltd.)

FIFTY YEARS OF SCIENCE. Being the Address delivered at York to the British Association, August 1881. Sixth Edition. 8vo. 2s. 6d. (Macmillan and Co., Ltd.)

WORKS BY LORD AVEBURY

BRITISH WILD FLOWERS CONSIDERED IN RELA-
TION TO INSECTS. With Illustrations. *Nature Series.*
Eleventh Thousand. Crown 8vo. 4s. 6d. (Macmillan and
Co., Ltd.)

FLOWERS, FRUITS, AND LEAVES. With Illustrations,
Nature Series. Ninth Thousand. Crown 8vo. 4s. 6d.
(Macmillan and Co., Ltd.)

THE ORIGIN AND METAMORPHOSES OF INSECTS.
With Illustrations. *Nature Series.* Eighth Thousand. Crown
8vo. 3s. 6d. (Macmillan and Co., Ltd.)

ON SEEDLINGS. With 690 Illustrations. Two Volumes.
8vo. 36s. (Kegan Paul, Trench and Co.)

ON SEEDLINGS. *Popular Edition.* With 282 Illustrations.
Second Edition. Crown 8vo. 5s. (Kegan Paul, Trench and Co.)

ANTS, BEES, AND WASPS. With Illustrations. *International
Scientific Series.* Seventeenth Edition. Crown 8vo. 5s.
(Kegan Paul, Trench and Co.)

ON THE SENSES, INSTINCTS, AND INTELLIGENCE
OF ANIMALS. With Special Reference to Insects. With
100 Illustrations. *International Scientific Series.* Fifth Edition.
Crown 8vo. 5s. (Kegan Paul, Trench and Co.)

CHAPTERS IN POPULAR NATURAL HISTORY. 12mo.
1s. 6d. (National Society.)

MONOGRAPH ON THE COLLEMBOLA AND THYSAN-
URA. 1871. (Ray Society.)

PREHISTORIC TIMES. As Illustrated by Ancient Remains
and the Manners and Customs of Modern Savages. Sixth Edition.
8vo. 18s. (Williams and Norgate.)

MARRIAGE, TOTEMISM, AND RELIGION. 8vo. (Longmans, 1911.)

THE ORIGIN OF CIVILISATION AND THE PRIMI-
TIVE CONDITION OF MAN. Sixth Edition. 8vo. 18s.
(Longmans, Green and Co.)

ON REPRESENTATION. Eighth Edition. Crown 8vo. 1s.
(Swan Sonnenschein and Co.)

ON BUDS AND STIPULES. *International Scientific Series.*
(Kegan Paul, Trench and Co.)

LA VIE DES PLANTES. 8vo. (J. B. Baillière et Fils.)

Printed in the United States
By Bookmasters